About Island Press

Island Press, a nonprofit organization, publishes, markets, and distributes the most advanced thinking on the conservation of our natural resources—books about soil, land, water, forests, wildlife, and hazardous and toxic wastes. These books are practical tools used by public officials, business and industry leaders, natural resource managers, and concerned citizens working to solve both local and global resource problems.

Founded in 1978, Island Press reorganized in 1984 to meet the increasing demand for substantive books on all resource-related issues. Island Press publishes and distributes under its own imprint and offers these services to other nonprofit organizations.

Support for Island Press is provided by Apple Computer, Inc., Mary Reynolds Babcock Foundation, Geraldine R. Dodge Foundation, The Energy Foundation, The Charles Engelhard Foundation, The Ford Foundation, Glen Eagles Foundation, The George Gund Foundation, William and Flora Hewlett Foundation, The Joyce Foundation, The John D. and Catherine T. MacArthur Foundation, The Andrew W. Mellon Foundation, The Joyce Mertz-Gilmore Foundation, The New-Land Foundation, The J. N. Pew, Jr., Charitable Trust, Alida Rockefeller, The Rockefeller Brothers Fund, The Florence and John Schumann Foundation, The Tides Foundation, and individual donors.

DEATH
in the
MARSH

Tom Harris

DEATH
in the
MARSH

ISLAND PRESS
Washington, D.C. ∎ *Covelo, California*

The author expresses gratitude for permission to reprint material from the series "Selenium: Conspiracy of Silence," which appeared in the *Sacramento Bee* in September 1985.

Library of Congress Cataloging-in-Publication Data
Harris, Tom (Tom H.)
    Death in the marsh / Tom Harris.
      p.   cm.
    Includes bibliographical references and index.
    ISBN 1-55963-070-1 (alk. paper). —
    ISBN 1-55963-069-8 (pbk. : alk. paper)
    1. Selenium—Environmental aspects—California—Kesterson
National Wildlife Refuge.
    2. Selenium—Toxicology—California—Kesterson National Wildlife
Refuge.   3. Selenium—Environmental aspects—West (U.S.)
    4. Selenium—Toxicology—West (U.S.)   5. Soils—West (U.S.)—
Selenium content.   6. Kesterson National Wildlife Refuge (Calif.).
I. Title.
QH545.S45H37   1991
574.5'26325—dc20   91-22602
                                          CIP

To Red . . .

the light and spice of my life,
may you never have to spot
another Astragalus bisulcatus

Contents

Preface

Every reporter dreams of being at the very edge of some riveting new issue, there at the very beginning to discover, interpret, and record a cascade of events so fresh and startling, so important and unique, that they become a watershed to an emerging national crisis and, hopefully, correction. We fantasize not just about writing the first, exclusive accounts but of riding the crest of the subsequent wave of events to their conclusion.

We don't go around looking for telephone booths in which to change from Clark Kent look-alikes into caped crusaders. But most of us do prefer exposing problems that provoke urgent meetings rather than covering the meetings themselves. That kind of investigative journalism usually involves skulking around hallways and dark corners, lubricating sources in coffee houses or bars, obtaining revealing memos and incriminating documents. For nearly a quarter of a century, my skulkings have more often than not taken me to some fairly glorious surroundings: primeval redwood parks, rugged coastlines, wild rivers, and raucous marshes. As a full-time environment writer for two aggressive regional newspapers in California in that time, I have had the kind of job most newsroom junkies dream about. To be sure, there were meetings and workshops and press conferences and sometimes the "great outdoors" was a sewer plant, hazardous dump site, or oil spill. But tracing the evolution of modern-day environmental concerns over parts of four decades has had more than its share of rewards.

One of those, the preeminent one of those, has been tracking down a silent killer: selenium, a unique, if not bizarre, natural soil element that now is laying waste to birds and fish and crickets and frogs in dozens of western marshes. I was not the first, or even second, reporter to uncover its lethal impact on Kesterson National Wildlife Refuge, in the prolific farm fields of California's San Joaquin Valley. Deborah Blum, then with the *Fresno Bee*, and Lloyd Carter, then with United Press International wire service, can claim that distinction. But a transfer in 1984 to the *Sacramento Bee*, the flagship of McClatchy Newspapers, put me closer to the Kesterson scene and to the remarkable U.S. Fish and Wildlife researchers and biologists charting selenium's grisly toll there.

My first brush with this lethal trace element was not the stuff of high drama. After my speech to a group of aspiring environmental journalists at the University of California, in Berkeley, a Sacramento-based reporter asked if I had heard about "something called selenium" and some bird deaths at a place called Kesterson. I had not. And it bothered me enough that when I got back to my San Jose office, I asked the paper's library staff to do a story search on the subject. That prompted my first bit of selenium research.

"How do you spell it?" the library assistant asked. Hmmm, good question, I thought. "Just a minute. Let me look it up in the dictionary and I'll get right back to you." But I didn't get right back. For even the spelling of this element presented a major challenge.

Well, I thought, there would be time enough later for all the hows and whys and so forth. Now, I could at least spell it for the librarian and see what happens from there. And a lot did happen after that. Not immediately. It took a dozen phone calls, or so, to track down whose refuge it was, state or federal, and who had been doing research there.

There were more blanks than live rounds, but, finally, I wound up talking to U.S. Fish and Wildlife Service research biologist Harry Ohlendorf.

And the start of what would be an eight-year-long search and research process with this natural element came over the phone line, into my computer, and onto the pages of my paper then, the *San Jose Mercury*, complete with a strip of full-color photos of the most gruesomely misshapen hatchlings you could imagine.

What follows in these pages is a roughly chronological summation of how it felt to be carried along on the very crest of discovery, swept from revelation to chilling revelation by the principal researchers. Others have likened this effort to tell the story of "the Kesterson effect" through the central characters involved to "a mystery . . . an environmental murder mystery, in the marsh." Murder is, perhaps, too strong a word, for it implies knowing, willful, merciless calculation. What happened at Kesterson, and at dozens of other places just like it in nearly every state west of the 100th meridian, a line running due south from about the middle of North Dakota, was terrible and unfortunate and a lot of other things. But it wasn't purposeful. At best, it was a cruel trick of nature. At worst, it was the predictable price of arrogance, greed, and tunnel bureaucractic vision.

What lifts this story above most others of its kind is the resolve of certain gutsy editors to go beyond hard-hitting investigative journalism, beyond the normal secondhand account of environmental tragedies, onto the frontline of discovery. The search for selenium was driven by the commitment, and integrity, of government employees and citizens who believed more in their mission and responsibility than in professional advancement.

While this is not a story about a story, little of what follows would have been possible without the courage and vision of the *Sacramento Bee* to do what the U.S. government was afraid to do. And while much of the focus is necessarily on marshes turned into silent graves, the book ranges much further afield—from the agonizing failures of mystified ranchers to the scarred careers of researchers who put service above self and committal to truth above fear of reprisal.

It was nearly sixty years ago that researchers first proved selenium was the toxic agent responsible for widespread livestock poisoning. Then it was tracked to specialized plants that could not grow without it but which were the source of agonizing illness and death to cattle, horses, sheep, pigs, and even poultry. In the late 1950s, its role as an essential micronutrient to humans and certain animals was proved. It was not until June 1983, on an eerily still marsh in California's midsection, that its impact on waterfowl and other aquatic marsh life was discovered by federal research biologists. Ironically, in those decades between recognition of selenium's essentiality and its toxicity, it was widely promoted as the cure for everything from cancer and heart disease to sexual dysfunction and baldness. Even today, without any long-range study of its implications for public health, selenium pills are being ingested daily by millions of Americans. Selenium supplements are being added, without government supervision, to most of the nation's beef and dairy cattle, swine, and poultry. And its fumes and particles are being belched from the country's fossil-fuel-powered electrical generating plants and emitted as a by-product from the exhaust fumes of motor vehicles.

The element is so much like sulfur that it often slips into vital amino-acid formation processes in place of it, wreaking havoc instead of good health. Selenium *is* essential to healthy growth, but in amounts so tiny it would take a powerful microscope to see the proper dose. It becomes highly poisonous, five to ten times more potent than arsenic, in just tiny increments more. Experts who have studied the toxicity of heavy metals and trace elements say selenium has the narrowest range between safety and danger of any of them. Yet, selenium has a remarkably low environmental profile in this "hazardous-waste-of-the-week" society of ours. Selenium remains one of the least understood, least regulated, of all toxic elements . . . a persistent trend that only now is beginning to change.

DEATH IN THE MARSH

Chapter 1 | NIGHTMARE at KESTERSON

Barrel-chested Felix Smith pushed the canoe away from the reedy shoreline, settling into the stern seat with a grace that belied his bulk. The craft glided into the heart of the marsh as his slender paddler at the bow set the pace toward a fluttering, fluorescent patch in the cattails that ringed the far shore. Harry Ohlendorf paused to study the map across his knees, checking numbered squares against a chart of code names that looked more like an algebraic formula than a list of bird nest sites.

Smith was doing his own cross-checking as he drove the canoe along with steady, powerful strokes, noting discrepancies almost subconsciously. His mind was on automatic now, whirring through one well-ordered bank of memory after another, sorting, characterizing, evaluating each new incoming observation. Things were falling into place quickly in that well-ordered world, however seemingly disconnected the input. Each bug and each wing stroke, every noise and pattern, was subliminally recorded for comparison with the master tape from a lifetime of such experiences.

The harmony between remembered and observed experience was the magnet that kept pulling the burly biologist back to places like this, a recognition that here, at least, nature was resisting society's frantic pace of change. There was something peacefully reassuring about a place where patterns, colors, and sounds did not change at the whim of man: something pure and dependable. It was enough just to feel a resonance with the thrum of the wind through the wall of cattails, to be stirred by the staccato chatter of thousands of feeding ducks and the metallic honking of big northern geese.

But something was out of tune today: some small dissonance in the rhythm of the place, some tiny glitch that disturbed the natural order of things. It had been like that since the two men had raced daybreak to the marsh to watch the creeping warmth of the sun gently uncover its fog-shrouded beauty, a wake-up call for the refuge's slumbering residents.

"This makes it all worthwhile," Smith had murmured, afraid that even a whisper would be an unwarranted intrusion. "Nothing compares to a marsh at daybreak."

Their early arrival had as much to do with pragmatism as with the poetry of nature. Even as early in the year as June, California's great Central Valley can feel like an oven by noon. Most years, the flanking Sierra foothills and low-slung Coast Range are scorched a barren, straw-colored hue by early June.

But the magic of the marsh at dawn seemed subtly tarnished this day in 1983.

The dusty road from the office of the Kesterson National Wildlife Refuge to the backside of the marsh had been just too virgin. It is one thing to put the first footprints of the day onto any trail. It can be curiously disquieting to feel like they are the first in time. The soft earth that framed the gravelled levee road should have been an intricate, lined tapestry from the daily traffic of marsh inhabitants. The tiny, matched chevrons of valley quail, the wavering trails of snakes, and the hippity gait of bush bunnies should all have been recorded there. So, too, should the telltale tracks of herons, egrets, and dozens of other crea-tures, great and small.

But they weren't.

The launching of the canoe should have been accompanied by a cho-rus of complaining blackbirds, bullfrogs, crickets, and other common marsh residents. It wasn't.

It should have sent streams of ducks and coots rocketing out of the cattails, flapping furiously to get airborne. It didn't.

The discrepancies began to mount.

Biologists don't like things out of place and they don't like mysteries, especially not in naturally harmonious if somewhat raucous places like marshes.

"Man, the silence around here is deafening," Smith boomed, his deep bass voice an exclamation point to the eerie stillness. He was not one to suffer in silence.

Ohlendorf, a reserved counterpoint to the gregarious Smith, looked up from his charts and swiveled around. "Yeah, it does give you a funny feeling," he countered before bending back to his maps and his work. He had his own demons to wrestle and they were every bit as real as Smith's perceptions.

He and other wildlife agency biologists were growing increasingly concerned about the experiment. As the $3.5 billion complex of the Central Valley Project and the $2.5 billion State Water Project's dams and canals siphoned more water from the valley's seven major rivers for thirsty farmlands, the rich, meandering wetlands there grew drier . . . and smaller. Riverbeds once laced with oxbows and sloughs framed by dense riparian forests are now bermed and cemented into sterile, man-made aqueducts; adjacent marshes have been obliterated.

Before the bureaucratic plumbers moved in, there were more than 4 million acres of such habitat along the 400-mile-plus valley trough formed by its two main sculptors, the Sacramento and San Joaquin riv-ers. Vast pockets of freshwater marsh once dotted the valley from Bakersfield, in the south, nearly all the way to Redding in the north. Framed by canopies of broadleaf oak, cottonwood, and other deciduous trees, the thirteen main tributaries to those major arteries carry moisture and nutrients down from the great Sierra Nevada, bookended by the 14,000-foot-plus peaks of Mt. Shasta, on the north, and Mt. Whitney to the south. Together, the vast mosaic of wetlands once harbored so many ducks, geese, swans, and cranes—an estimated 15 million migratory waterfowl in all—that their arrivals and departures darkened the skies. Today, the birds number fewer than 3 million and barely 150,000 acres of that waterfowl haven remain. The water that once nourished widgeon grass, cattails, and wild rice now sustains row-crops, cotton fields, rice paddies, and orchards. The Central Valley, though dramatically degraded from its historic condition, continues to support 60 percent of the waterfowl that use the Pacific Flyway, one of the nation's three major migrational corridors.

The rectangular, mirrored surface of the man-made ponds across which the two U.S. Fish and Wildlife Service biologists cruised came from subsurface field drainage from 8,000 acres of northwestern Fresno County farmland,[1] more than 30 miles away. Ohlendorf and Smith had seen the dull, concrete sumps in the lowest corners of the fields on earlier trips through the valley and they knew all about the drainage ditches that carried the surplus irrigation seepage away from the fields to the concrete drainage canal. What they couldn't see, but knew about all too well, were the buried, perforated pipes 10 feet below the lush crops. More water was applied to the fields than the crops could use or that could percolate down through the San Joaquin Valley's underground layer of hardpan clay. But for the subsurface pipes that carried the excess seepage from the fields into the main San Luis Drain, and thence to Kesterson, the root zone of crops would be completely saturated and the plants drowned.

Laced with dissolved salts and minerals, the tainted drainage was a lethal brew. Too saline to leave in the fields, it was being dumped into Kesterson as part of an experiment to convert pollution into providence. Ultimately, federal plans were to extend the San Luis Drain 72 miles further north so that it discharged into the sprawling Sacramento–San Joaquin Delta, just upstream of San Francisco Bay. In 1983, Kesterson was simply the interim terminus for the 84-mile-long cement-lined drain, a place where the saline drainage could temporarily be managed by reducing its volume through evaporation and percolation through unlined pond bottoms. But before the U.S. Bureau of Reclamation could complete the plumbing and discharge those flows to the delta, it needed a discharge permit from California's State Water Resources Control Board. And that agency had ordered a full round of water quality testing to look for adverse biological impacts from agricultural drainwater.

The bureau managers argued there would be benefit to all and adverse impact to none by using the tainted but nutrient-laden drainage to supply water for depleted marshes. It was a policy being implemented not just in California but throughout the semiarid West. Most of the irrigated farmlands there are carved out of beds of ancient lakes and inland seas and their fine-grained, nutrient-rich, clay sediments are also laced with salts left over from evaporation. Flows from the buried drains became a brew that all parties would live to regret.

"The day we agreed to take their drainage for our water was the day we made a bargain with the devil," said Smith of the federal Reclamation Bureau's maneuver. Biologists and environmentalists feared the drainage would be contaminated with herbicides, pesticides, and fertilizers. Only a year before Smith and Ohlendorf glided peacefully across one of those "managed wetlands," they had learned that the drainage also had leached from the soil such poisonous natural elements as arsenic, boron, chromium, and something few had ever heard of: selenium, a sulfurlike element that is almost a metal but officially classed as a metalloid.

Substituting tainted drainwater for natural snowmelt and rain was instinctively repugnant to biologists who studied or managed wildlife in the valley and most of their colleagues. But it didn't change the fact that the bureau and its farmer-clients needed a place to put the waste and possessed the clout to override all objections. Nor did it alter the need of the Fish and Wildlife Service to offset dwindling supplies of clean water for its national wildlife refuge marshes.

Kesterson was ground zero for that experiment.[2]

Tabletop flat and sloping only a degree or two northward, the San Joaquin Valley forms the growing fields for nearly half the nation's supply of fresh fruits, nuts, and vegetables . . . and a good share of its cotton. Once covered with marshes and home to birds, grizzly bears, and tule elk, it now is checkerboarded with huge "factory farms" owned by rich corporations and smaller but still substantial family holdings.

Drainage from only a fraction of the 2 million–plus acres of farmland had been eddying slowly through the constructed ponds of Kesterson for only three years, waiting for the rest of the master drain to be linked to the confluence of the Sacramento and San Joaquin rivers. The vast river systems mingle and spread into a fertile 750,000-acre crescent after draining opposite ends of a tublike valley so large that it would reach from Boston to Norfolk if it were on the eastern seaboard.

The rich estuarine waters of San Francisco Bay provide critical corridors to upstream spawning grounds for tens of thousands of salmon, steelhead, sturgeon, striped bass, and shad. They remain a crucial nursery to what is left of the migratory offspring and the spawn of crabs, shrimp, and other ocean species that seek out the shallow, protected waters to reproduce. Like the waterfowl populations, the numbers of migratory fish have declined dramatically in the last three decades—in the receding wake, that is, of the giant water project diversions. Spawning runs have been wiped out altogether on some rivers and declined 50 to 95 percent on others. Key stretches of the north-flowing San Joaquin River have dried up, while the south-flowing Sacramento has been converted to the unnatural and persistently high flows of a huge aqueduct.

About 60 miles south of where these two great river systems converge, Kesterson is an artifice of rectangulation. Its twelve machine-gouged basins were designed to let drainwater percolate from the bottom and evaporate from the top until the San Luis Drain could be completed and the drainage dumped into the meandering river delta. It was a mechanism of waste disposal by design and a wildlife refuge only by coincidence.

When environmentalists finally succeeded in blocking the last leg of the drain to the delta in the mid-1970s, because of its excessive salinity, the reclamation agency was desperate for some place to put the farm wastes. To gain time for political maneuvering, the Interior Department—and Congress—authorized Kesterson as a temporary terminus for the drain. To mute environmentalist opposition, the evaporation ponds were called "managed wetlands" where the aim was to prove that not only nature can create symbiotic relationships. Agribusiness would take the clean, untapped river water in one pipe and discharge a reliable yield of nutrient-laden but saline drainwater to the marshes in another. It was an arrangement they optimistically hoped would be the best of both worlds.

Instead, for Ohlendorf, Smith, and many, many others, Kesterson became the birthplace of a bizarre odyssey.

The experiment to swap drainage for clean water, and the federal Bureau of Reclamation's ultimate plan to discharge drainage directly into the Sacramento–San Joaquin Delta, called for detailed biological monitoring. That kind of sampling, to detect changes in the water quality of the marsh and the health of its aquatic-based food chain, was ordered by the State Water Resources Control Board before it would grant a delta discharge permit. It was that monitoring which brought the gregarious Smith and reserved Ohlendorf together at Kesterson. They checked nests and counted eggs, always on the lookout for anything abnormal that might need to be checked more closely back at Ohlendorf's cramped lab on the University of California campus at Davis, more than 100 miles north. It was slow, tedious work: paddling, pausing, collecting samples of eggs and nestlings, making chart entries. Lead research biologist with the Patuxent Wildlife Research Center's Pacific Field Station, Ohlendorf had a sense of what might be in store because of earlier analysis of tiny mosquito-eating fish called gambusia. Agency fishery biologist Mike Saiki had collected the finger-sized fish a year earlier, in 1982, when there was no sign of bigger game like bass and catfish reported to be thriving in the newly created 1,280-acre pond system. Since the ponds contained frightfully high levels of selenium and no other species were present, Ohlendorf had an ominous expectation that waterfowl reproduction might be similarly afflicted.

Saiki's curiosity about the fate of the bigger fish had begun growing weeks before, when he spread his own test results out on his desk in Davis. The gambusia contained what were then the highest levels of the trace element selenium ever recorded in living tissue, concentrations reaching a maximum of 380 parts per million (ppm).[3] To this day, no one knows why they lived at all, but their survival triggered an intense search for clues to the unusual soil element's source, makeup, distribution, and toxicity. Ohlendorf had found some of the answers just weeks before his latest Kesterson sampling run. His office computer gave instant access to a detailed, if somewhat obscure, bibliography on selenium revealing a wide range of early scientific papers and test results, some more than fifty years old.

The third report of the series was scrolling up on the computer when the words, and their implication, literally jumped off the screen. Given too much selenium supplement in their feed, commercial hens either failed to produce progeny at all or, worse, gave birth to monstrosities.[4] Ohlendorf painstakingly reviewed everything he could find on the subject before punching his own careful, straightforward evaluations into the computer about the potential for a similar fate for nesting waterfowl at Kesterson. Respected as much for understatement as for fine science, Ohlendorf's reports began circulating through the service early in 1983. Near the end of June, the day before he and Smith began sampling at Kesterson, the preliminary findings and fears came up in a meeting of the drainage and marsh study task force in Fresno, about 90 miles south of Kesterson. Ohlendorf was not at the meeting but Smith was and said that the warnings that selenium-tainted drainage was a threat to valley wildlife were aggressively challenged by representatives of the Reclamation Bureau and the Westlands Water District, from whose fields the drainage was coming.

As reactions to those preliminary reports and warnings grew more defensive, Smith became more curious. And the more he thought about the potential impacts, the more worried he became. What sleep he got the night before the Kesterson canoe trip was fitful at best. Breakfast, the standard by which his days are judged, was little better. A robust eater, he complained of a "nervous stomach" and only picked at his food. The disquieting experiences with trackless dusty trails and the eerie hush of the marsh did nothing to improve it.

Ohlendorf interrupted his musings, pointing out the first of the flagged nesting sites that had to be checked for eggs or chicks. The two biologists thought they could cover more of a cluster of nearby nests by each wading to separate ones rather than checking them one at a time by boat.

Smith reached over to test the depth with his paddle before stepping out of the canoe. At first, he was surprised. It had appeared only 2 or 3 feet deep, but was nearer 5 feet. The clear water had magnified the view of the bottom. Then one of those vague impressions that had shadow-boxed with his mind most of the morning clicked into place.

"Damn!" he shouted. "That's it! It's the water. Look how clear it is. We can see right to the bottom." No observation could be more uncommon about marsh water, whose pea-soup thickness is legendary. Choked by algae, duckweed, and floating mats of widgeon grass, clouded by wind-whipped, decaying organic matter and suspended silt, it usually has all the clarity of a dirty boot.

"It had an almost jet-black quality to it because you could see all that organic ooze on the bottom so clearly," Smith told me later. It was just another disjointed, however unsettling, observation: one more discrepancy. There would be others as the survey progressed.

The pair did not see a single crayfish scuttle out of their way. Smith wondered about a discernible lack of bluebottles, the marsh's dominant species of dragonfly, darting among the lush stand of cattails. There were no torpedo-like wakes from big carp startled from shallow grazing flats into thrashing escape. And there were no bewhiskered catfish, feeling their way through what should have been murky pond waters.

Each unfilled niche, each missing voice in what should have been the marsh's raucous chorus, increased the sense of unease for both biologists. Each knew enough to suspect that something was wrong, seriously wrong.

Just after noon, at one of the last nests they checked that day, what had been merely disquieting became chilling. Most of the nests they checked had some eggs, but in many of them the growth switch of the tiny embryos inside seemed to have been inexplicably flipped off and their development arrested.

They had paddled or waded from one fluorescent flag to the next, noting the identification number of the nest, whether it held any eggs, and, if so, the approximate stage of development. They had labored like that into the early afternoon, painstakingly noting and recording each nest, whether it was for gadwalls, mallards, teal, or other species of ducks, including the ugly duckling of the marsh, the American coot, better known to hunters as mud hens or, because of their ungainly take-off, splatter asses. Wading and shorebirds were checked too, including black-necked stilts, avocets, and killdeer.

Then, at nest C-66 on Ohlendorf's marsh map, Smith's voice boomed through the wall of cattails.

"Hey, Harry. You better come and see this. We've got one over here . . . but it just doesn't look right."

Indeed.

One tiny hatchling was dead, floating in the water beside the nest. Another, one of four in the nest and the one that riveted Smith's attention, was still alive, but only partially clear of its shell. Ohlendorf cradled it gently as he waded to shore for a closer look.

Mistakes happen in nature, too. But seldom on the scale he was about to discover.

He turned the limp head over and grimaced. "No eyes," he muttered, "just a face full of feathers. And look at the beak. The lower half is missing." When he removed the chick from the eggshell he found that its feet also were missing.

Ohlendorf still grimaces when he recalls the grotesque experience. "You get used to the odd deformity in the wild. It happens," he said. "But many of the deformities we found were really stunning."

Most of the chicks were without eyes, their beaks either crossed, corkscrewed, or missing altogether. There were only stumps where wings should have been and many had no legs at all. "When we began the study, I did expect some reproductive problems to surface," Ohlendorf said. "But when it came right down to the fieldwork, the intensity and the severity of the deformities were surprising. I had never seen anything like that before, and I'm still not aware of any other place where it has been as great."

The nightmarish reality of his discovery left him shocked. Ohlendorf looked up at his companion. "Well, here's the evidence," he sighed, the proof he had feared in hand. "They can't deny it exists, now." Smith, still cuddling the misshapen hatchling in his thick hands, added, "I don't think our lives will ever be the same."

Egg counting and sample collecting continued an hour longer, but nothing dispelled Ohlendorf's growing unease. Months later, after tedious calculations, the truth would emerge: Kesterson would go down in the annals of science as one of the worst episodes of birth deformity ever recorded among wildlife in this or, perhaps, any country. And it would send political shock waves across the West.

For Ohlendorf, it was more than just another telling piece of detective work in a career of steady progress. It was a startling discovery that would set him on a collision course with powerful forces. His science was questioned, his commitment and courage sorely tested. Ultimately, even his government career was threatened.

No more deformed hatchlings were found that day, but they took back many eggs from nest C-66 and others. Ohlendorf listened, sometimes only absently during the 90-mile drive home, as Smith gave voice to the kinds of fears he himself was only beginning to confront in his own mind. The timbre of his partner's voice merged with the steady whine of the tires eating up the flat, boring miles of Interstate 5 on the way back to the lab. Ohlendorf's thoughts kept racing ahead to what he might find there in the days and weeks ahead.

They were tired and exchanged only perfunctory goodbyes at Davis that night. But the next day, Ohlendorf was back in the lab he shared with three others, tucked away in a remote corner of the University of California campus at Davis, about 15 miles west of Sacramento. Now there was time, space, and the proper tools for a thorough examination of the previous day's samples. There were no gasps or startled exclamations as he gently peeled away the shell from one egg after the other, weighing, measuring, examining with the precision for which he was so highly regarded in the research ranks. But he grew more numb with each succeeding discovery.

Some embryos had quit growing at only the halfway point of development, their cell growth mysteriously shut down. Others seemed completely normal, though Ohlendorf wondered what subtle, hidden defects they might carry from such a tainted creation. Some nests yielded a bizarre mix of each, probably a function of the gradual accumulation of selenium by the hen. There was a distressing number of more deformed embryos or hatchlings.

Ohlendorf, true to his science, kept amassing the evidence, visiting the marsh each week, testing, cross-checking, retesting. His report carried staggering numbers. More than 40 percent of the nests checked contained at least one dead embryo. Some 20 percent yielded at least one embryo or chick with multiple deformities. Coots and eared grebes were hardest hit: a 64 percent rate of embryo death or deformity. Ohlendorf's unvarnished report was mailed to regional headquarters in Portland, Oregon, where it triggered a nervous in-house review. But it was what he did next that sent the issue beyond the isolated labs and outside the bureaucratic chain of command.

Rumors about the death and deformity had reached the press. When

I telephoned Ohlendorf, he was candid, though restrained, in his answers and agreed to my request for the loan of his graphic color slides. A panel of the pictures of Kesterson's misshapen victims was stripped across the top of the Science section in the October 25, 1983, edition of the *San Jose Mercury*. The most graphic was the grotesque little nestling cupped tenderly in Smith's thick hands, the one from nest C-66. Within hours, the story and pictures were picked up by other newspapers, magazines, and, of course, television stations. The sight of bulging—or missing—brains or eyes, wingless or legless creatures with "figure-eight" beaks, external stomachs, or other malformed organs outraged the public.

Chapter 2 | COVER-UP

As the storm over the drainage and its effects burst into public debate, Ohlendorf kept shuttling back and forth between Kesterson and his laboratory. One day he was collecting more eggs or twisted hatchlings to send to the agency's wildlife research lab in Columbia, Missouri, for detailed chemical analysis. The next would find him hunched over his desk completing charts and graphs for the report on the biological impacts of using irrigation drainage to replenish marshes.

There was no more stark a contrast of the costs and benefits of that effort than Kesterson and Volta National Wildlife Refuge, just 6 miles southwest. Since Volta received clean river water instead of selenium-tainted drainage, it was selected as a control site so that biologists had an unpolluted system for comparison. At Volta there were no trackless, dusty trails. The cattails were alive with blackbirds and coots and ducks and shorebirds of every description. The full quacking, cheeping, whistling chorus of Volta's winged residents mingled with the metallic chirp of crickets and the throaty profundos of bullfrogs. Dragonflies flitted back and forth above the naturally turbid water and decaying algal mats.

But Ohlendorf, a meticulous researcher, had more on his mind than his understated reports and how sharply their findings differed from those of Volta. His reports on Kesterson were as lean on opinion and speculation as they were on hyperbole . . . and therefore hard to contest. But they touched sensitive nerves at headquarters, nonetheless, and triggered an escalating debate which Ohlendorf struggled to avoid. Superiors conducted endless reviews of his comparisons between contaminated Kesterson and untainted Volta. And although they suggested strongly worded changes, Ohlendorf resisted. At Kesterson, his data showed that up to 41 percent of all the nesting birds he checked suffered some form of reproductive failure. The rate varied from species to species, but everything from mallards to coots, from avocets to stilts, suffered either infertile eggs, deformed hatchlings, or both. For others, there were no eggs period. At Volta, nesting success was normal. Not a single deformity was discovered.[1]

The case against using irrigation drainage for managed marshes started growing the day Ohlendorf's report began circulating within the service and beyond. Dave Lenhart, the wildlife agency's regional contaminant specialist in Portland, was reading the memos—and blunt appraisals of their implications by Felix Smith, the region's environmental assessment specialist in Sacramento—and he passed them up the line. Lenhart was getting worried, too.

"One week he was being assured by the Bureau of Reclamation that, essentially, there was no selenium in the valley," said Smith, "and the next week he was looking at Saiki's data on the mosquito fish and some of the old reports that Harry dug up on selenium." The bureau's negative report on valley soils was based on what its officials said was a "comprehensive soil study of the San Luis Unit." That part of the massive federal water diversion project is on the western side of the San Joaquin Valley and includes the 8,000 acres from which the subsurface drainage began flowing into Kesterson in 1979.

Instead of sparking open discussion between agencies or being released for public comment, the reports were held up by administrators, especially during the fall of 1983. Though initially the details were withheld from the press and the public, the general thrust of what was happening began to leak out. When the first formal report was withheld from even the normal round of interagency review, Smith, Ohlendorf, and others worked on a "White Paper" to set the record straight. But that report, too, was heavily censored and not released for publication. Unwittingly, Ohlendorf's work had spawned a cover-up that would rock the Department of Interior.

The early fish research by Mike Saiki had shown alarming concentrations of selenium in the mosquito fish—averaging 247 parts per million (ppm). Ohlendorf's work proved that selenium had invaded the waterfowl's domain, too. Yet the Reclamation Bureau's initial reports were confusing. Their soil classification studies reported valley soil with a hundred times *less* selenium than levels thought capable of causing the kind of toxicity seen in the marsh. But the bureau's water quality tests from 1981 to 1982 (though their significance was not recognized then) showed selenium counts of several hundred parts per billion in drainwater at Kesterson and in the San Luis Drain.

Blocked by the more bureaucratically powerful reclamation agency and challenged about the accuracy of their own analytical work, Wildlife Service researchers sought out independent help from chemists and geologists in the U.S. Geological Survey, their sister agency in the Interior Department.

In September 1983, one of the USGS's highest-ranking scientists, noted geochemist Ivan Barnes, and analytical chemist Theresa Presser loaded their sampling equipment into Barnes's custom-built mobile laboratory, dubbed "The Rhino" by his cohorts because of its quarter-inch-thick steel plating, and left their Menlo Park headquarters. More tank than truck, the customized camper lumbered along Highway 152 and over Pacheco Pass of the Diablo and Coast ranges that separate the Central Valley from the teeming San Francisco metropolis. It was night-time as "The Rhino" cruised past the shores of San Luis Reservoir and down into the fertile San Joaquin Valley. When they met their Wildlife Service counterparts in a Los Baños motel just after 10:30 that night in the heart of California's Central Valley, Barnes and Presser got a reception neither would ever forget.

"The door was wide open. It was real dark inside, and very quiet," said Presser. "Then we saw these horrid pictures projected on the wall. They were showing the deformed birds. I will never forget it. They were a bunch of real serious people right then. Nobody was talking. It was deathly quiet."

It was, indeed, a riveting experience for the small, pleasant chemist, whose delicate stature, complexion, and bookish appearance stood out sharply against the beards, weather-beaten faces, and rough demeanor of the room full of biologists and refuge workers. She reflected on the sudden shift in her own situation the next morning as the miniature caravan of Wildlife Service cars, and Barnes's ponderous portable lab, made its way over the bumpy, tule-lined, levee roads. "One week I was a water analyst for the Environmental Protection Agency in Ohio," recalled Presser in a later interview, "and then I got a job with this legendary geochemist in a customized lab on a beautiful campus setting near San Francisco Bay. The next thing I know, I am bouncing across a levee in the middle of some flat, forsaken valley in a rattly old lab truck painted a screaming 'safety orange.' "

"The Rhino" became an oven in the sweltering midday 105-degree heat that eighth of August 1983 as the pair sorted and worked on the samples. Pressurized nitrogen gas forced the turbid marsh water from the Kesterson ponds through compact filters—a long, slow process to cleanse them of sediment, suspended organic matter, and even bacteria. As they waited, Barnes, an avid bird-watcher, walked along the levee road, introducing her to the winged residents of Kesterson. With his flaming-red, soft-brimmed hat turned down in front, Barnes seemed impervious to the heat. He was still wearing his fishing vest, pockets stuffed front and back with the trinkets of field geology. The

sample water, once sterilized by passage through the microscopic pores
of the filter, was put into small bottles that went into "The Rhino's"
small refrigerator right next to Barnes's ever-present bottles of Anchor
Steam Beer from the specialty brewery in San Francisco.

It was the first of three field trips the two USGS scientists would make
to Kesterson, methodically combing the surrounding hills, creeks, and
network of sumps and drainage canals to find out where the selenium
was coming from and how it cycled through the environment. On the
second trip, October 12, Barnes brought his lumbering laboratory to a
shuddering halt on one of the narrow roads twisting up into the foothills from the valley floor. He leaped out and pointed to a series of snow-
white patches on the barren slopes of the overgrazed hillsides. It still
was summer in a part of California where hilltops are seldom graced
with snow even in the coldest winters. "Look," said Barnes. "They're all
over. That evaporative salt crust is where we'll find the selenium if it's
here." They started at the top and worked their way down, crawling
over steep banks and scrambling down dried-up washes to sample saline seeps and collect sediment and water from small, shrinking pools
in the beds of seasonal streams. At the toe of the slope, where the erosional cut of the canyons opened into the V-shaped alluvial fans spreading out onto the vast, mineral-rich farmlands of the San Joaquin Valley,
they finished their work, concentrating on the background selenium
levels in the water and soil there.

Their third trip to the valley, on December 1, was made more eventful by aggravating roadside repairs to "The Rhino's" balky starter. Ultimately, the pair collected hundreds of samples of rock, salt crust, and
tepid water. Their last collection run concentrated on the drainage itself—from the fields and sumps of the Westlands Water District,
through the San Luis Drain, to the Kesterson ponds where Barnes also
scooped up a sample of slimy, green algae.

Before their geological uplift millions of years before, the modestly
elevated hills—it would be stretching topography to call them mountains—formed the bed of what first was part of a gigantic arm of the Pa-

cific Ocean and, next, a huge landlocked sea. The upthrust seabed, whose structure and content reflect its marine origin, now separates California's massive Central Valley from its crowded coastal terraces, forming a wall along the west side of the rich farmland. Its thick layers of mud have since been compressed into shale formations by time and pressure exerted by centuries of accumulated erosion. They are highly saline and laced with toxic trace elements like selenium, boron, arsenic, uranium, and molybdenum. Extensive volcanic eruptions during Cretaceous times, Barnes said, are thought to be the primary source of selenium.

The last trip ended just the same as the others: at the USGS's sprawling Western headquarters complex in the San Francisco suburb of Menlo Park, late at night. In the days that followed, Presser prepared the samples for chemical analysis. Barnes went back to his real passion— proving that carbon dioxide gas, not explosive, superheated steam, was the driving force behind volcanic eruptions, a theory his contemporaries could not readily accept. Barnes spent more time trying to persuade scientific journals to publish his detailed if unconventional papers than pursuing the selenium riddle.

Preparing, analyzing, checking, and cross-checking the samples took weeks. Presser, still uncertain of the implications and feeling no pressure to move more quickly, slotted the selenium work in between dozens of other analytical projects already crowding the laboratory shelves and cabinets. "I never realized how critical all of it would become," said Presser. "It just seemed like another of Ivan's unique projects. He was always into something and our lab was backed up with work."

But as the disparity between the selenium measurements by the wildlife and reclamation agencies became more obvious, Barnes and others in the Water Resources Division of USGS quickly became more interested. A selenium symposium had been scheduled for February 1984, and the Bureau of Reclamation was still pushing the results of its outside laboratory in Sacramento showing virtually no selenium present in the basin or its drainage. Desperate for confirmation, the Fish and Wildlife Service researchers urged Barnes and Presser to complete their analyses and report in time for presentation to the conference at the Davis campus of the University of California.

When the first round of results came out with much lower numbers than expected, the pace grew frantic. Barnes and Presser refined the analytical process and the tests were repeated. The numbers came out much higher the second time, so a third round was done for added clarification. "By then, it was the day before the Davis meeting and the Wildlife Service was really banking on our numbers to back them up," said Presser. "Just to make sure we were right, we ran some extra quality control tests, and they proved out." She was up almost to midnight and then back in the lab about 6:30 the next morning, firming up and recording the data in a format the agency called a "letter report." They had found enough selenium to poison ten Kestersons.

One water sample, from a sump that routed field drainage into the concrete San Luis Drain for shipment to Kesterson, became a standard for selenium contamination, albeit a very brief one. It contained 1,400 parts per billion (ppb)—so much selenium that it constituted a hazardous waste that could legally be disposed of only in a Class I dump site reserved for the most toxic of society's poisonous trash. Such a facility has to be lined with two layers of impervious plastic over a tightly compacted layer of clay and then fitted with caps and leak-detection monitors to make sure what goes into the dump stayed there. But instead of being safely contained in any of only three such sites still in operation in California, the waste was flowing into a national wildlife refuge . . . and exacting a deadly toll at nearly every link in its food chain. Barnes and Presser winced as they went down the list of test results. A water sample taken from a sump beside a nondescript crossroad upstream from Kesterson, at Nees Avenue, contained 4,200 ppb, the highest water concentration of selenium ever recorded in California.

Barnes's passion for precision yielded another significant discovery.

His insistence on sampling not just the water but everything around it paid big dividends in Pond 11, second to last in the sequential Kesterson circulatory system. There was too little selenium in the water— only 14 ppb—to explain the extreme toxicity to fish and birds there. But the balled-up clump of algae that Barnes collected there contained 13 ppm, a biological buildup from the surrounding water column of more than a thousand times.

Later Wildlife Service work would show even more astonishing cases of bioaccumulation, the combined effect of absorbing such elements from the water and ingesting them from the food chain. Some organisms held hundreds of thousands times more selenium than the water around them.[2] Without knowing its cause, Smith and Ohlendorf had sensed the devastating potential of such compounding months earlier: on the unmarked dusty paths, in the muted chorus of wildlife, in the puzzling water clarity of the quiet marsh. Kesterson's water was devoid of the clouds of minute plant and animal organisms—phytoplankton and zooplankton—and larger strands of algae and suspended decaying organic matter that give marshes their turbid appearance. Instead, its water had a distilled and lifeless clarity.

Barnes and water quality specialist Marvin Fretwell looked at the test results over Presser's shoulder as she recorded the final round of confirmatory analyses. Later, after all of the tests had been recorded and typed into the report, Barnes leaned over and tapped the data tables with the stub of a well-worn pencil, going from one finding to the other. Drainwater flowing into the marsh averaged 290 ppb of selenium. That was more than eight times above the Environmental Protection Agency standard of 35 ppb to protect freshwater aquatic species. EPA would later scale that safety number back to only 5 ppb as it learned from the wildlife biologists just how dangerous selenium is: five times more poisonous than arsenic.

"That does it," said Barnes. "There is so much selenium out there that they'll never get the genie back in the bottle. No matter how hard they try to conceal the truth, it's in the public arena now," he added, flipping through other pages detailing the trace element's widespread presence in the foothills, farmland, sumps, canals, and ponds.

The next afternoon, Fretwell presented the report to the crowded conference. Until then Barnes had spent most of his thirty-year career with USGS in comparative academic isolation, acquiring an almost-legendary status for his meticulous science. Now, suddenly, his work had put him on the cutting edge of controversy. He was not an altogether unwilling victim. One of the most respected scientists in USGS ranks, he could be blunt and surprisingly acerbic at times. Possessor of the agency's highest civil service rating for nonadministrative scientists—GS 16—and with it the informal but coveted rank of "super-scientist" among his contemporaries, Barnes was no stranger to controversy.

Reporters soon learned to value both his widening grasp of selenium geochemistry and his uncommon candor. He never sought out the press. But if reporters called, and knew which questions to ask, he often unleashed a river of information, not all of it precisely geological in nature. Asked whether he, like others, had been told to avoid interviews and controversial statements, or whether he was gambling with his career, Barnes often defiantly responded: "Look, I know who I work for. If you want to know what I know, ask. I work for the public, not for some frightened bureaucrats in Washington."

That kind of temerity led to his downfall. Still trying to cope with the death of his first wife and the pending divorce from his second, Barnes was exhausted from weeks of parallel efforts. When he wasn't pushing his volcanic eruption work he was tracing the pathway of selenium from source rock to the irrigated fields below and from there into the concrete canals that led to Kesterson. Even on his best behavior, he was an unlikely candidate for a diplomatic career. During his worst moments, which were increasing in frequency because of relentless demands of the media and his colleagues and others curious about selenium, he could be testy and impatient. Some of his less disciplined

comments about the ability and integrity of Washington-based superiors wound up in print. In 1987, Barnes was reassigned—some would
say banished—to what essentially was a teaching post at the Oregon
Graduate Center in Beaverton, just south of Portland.

But in the scientifically tumultuous year that followed Ohlendorf's
1983 discovery of the Kesterson tragedy, it was Ivan Barnes, the legendary geochemist, perhaps more than any other person, who was responsible for recognizing how selenium moved and was concentrated in the
environment. Together with Presser, he also played a critical role in
learning how to detect and measure selenium with precision. Widely
respected for his knowledge of states of equilibrium between aqueous
solutions and minerals through in-field analysis and preservation techniques he perfected for unstable chemicals, Barnes's results gained immediate acceptance.

Buttressed by other Fish and Wildlife Service tests that showed selenium bioaccumulation through the marsh's food chain, the findings
of Barnes and Presser cast a cloud over the analytical abilities of the reclamation agency's contract laboratory. Others in Interior called for a
full audit of the outside firm by two of the top experts in USGS, Marvin
Fretwell and the chief of the Survey's central laboratory in Denver, Marvin Fishman.

Although he was not involved in the audit, Barnes closely studied the
January 31, 1984, results that rated "the overall operation . . . very
poor." Never one to mince words, Barnes himself gave the Reclamation
Bureau's lab a failing grade. "I'd give them an F," he said. "Their analytical methods were shoddy. Their quality control was poor. And their
handling of samples in the field was definitely substandard." The audit
found that tests done for the bureau routinely understated selenium
levels at Kesterson from 100 to 200 times.

It was no mathematical miscalculation. Presser discovered serious
errors in the preparation of bureau samples. The dominant form of selenium, oxidized into selenate, does not register on the sensitive atomic
absorption instrument used in the analytical process. Only when it is

reduced to a less oxidized form—selenite—will it register an accurate signal. Unless the selenate form is boiled in hydrochloric acid for precisely forty-six minutes, the recorded selenium levels are far below what is actually present. Conversely, if the sample is boiled longer than that, much of what is there is lost.[3]

From the start, the chemical nature of selenium and its various oxidation or conversion states under a variety of conditions had confounded researchers—which is hardly surprising, for the nonmetallic element comes in four forms. *Selenide,* the form with the least oxygen, is usually associated with sulfide ore bodies. *Elemental* selenium, the pure ore, is concentrated usually with metals like copper or sulfur in three forms: amorphous (both black and red), crystalline (red and gray), or insoluble (gray). *Selenite* is highly toxic when soluble but normally bound tightly to iron, aluminum, or other metals and hence not available as an active toxic compound. *Selenate,* which is very soluble (dissolves readily in water) and highly toxic, is easily leached from the soil in this form in an alkaline environment and is readily taken up by roots of many plants.

Once the elemental form is extracted from copper ores it is refined into pure selenium for a variety of industrial uses. It can be found in such electrical components as rectifiers, in some kinds of copying machines, in photoelectric cells—like ones that turn street lights on and off automatically—and in dyes, ink pigments, plating solutions, paper processing, antifungicides, and even antidandruff preparations. It is widely used as a therapeutic agent by veterinarians to remedy eczema and fungal infections and to treat everything from white muscle disease in livestock to exudative diathesis, a similar ailment, in chicks. Properly used it does everything from tinting glass to vulcanizing rubber, from bluing gun barrels to shampooing dry scalps. Improperly used, it can poison livestock, poultry, and people. Those commercial sources and industrial emissions from burning of fossil fuels for energy generation are estimated to contribute more than 2 million pounds of selenium a year to the environment. There is some evidence that selenium fallout from airborne pollution may be one of the key toxic agents in acid rain.

Laboratory chemists working for the Bureau of Reclamation had poor success in separating all these forms in their testing process. In the same Nees Avenue sump where Presser identified 4,200 ppb selenium,[4] the bureau's chemists found only 20 ppb, an error factor of 210 times. The same chemists also reported that drainage entering Kesterson was "below detectable levels" of "1 or 2 ppb." Presser and Barnes, however, reported an average inflow concentration of 280 ppb.[5] The USGS results were confirmed by other Wildlife Service labs, all of them highly respected in analytical circles.

Instead of resolving scientific conflict, the USGS's efforts to referee the growing interagency dispute only dragged it deeper into the controversy. "That's when all hell broke loose," Felix Smith said of the swift effort to realign bureaucratic responsibilities and replace the Reclamation Bureau as lead agency in the widening government investigation. Reclamation managers did more than misstate the geology of the San Joaquin Valley soil and the chemistry of its water. From the start—according to many of those privy to the hushed debates that characterized the bureau's initial activity—they disdained and discouraged the work of the Wildlife Service.

It started during one of the first informal meetings convened on the subject, in Fresno, in June 1983. But it became more pervasive by September when the bureau's representatives gathered to discuss Ohlendorf's unsettling discoveries. "That was a pretty good meeting, except for the bad-mouthing by the bureau," Smith said. "The technical people were very open and receptive, especially from DWR (California's Department of Water Resources, which operates the huge State Water Project). We told them that the data were still preliminary but that we had done our homework. All the lab and field work wasn't finished then, of course, but the evidence was mounting and it was clear that selenium was doing the damage."

That version didn't sit well with regional bureau managers in Sacramento, the agency's largest western office, nor with their superiors in the nation's capital, who became more involved with each new development. There were phone calls and memos in November, and again in December, ordering Smith to end his press contacts, especially with wire service and network television reporters. "It was simple and direct: to button up, period," said Smith, claiming that the bureau's new regional director, David Houston, "was screaming to our bosses that 'Your people in Sacramento are totally out of control. Rein them in.'"

Felix Smith was getting a higher profile than was healthy, even though his job was to assess the combined impacts of such water projects on wildlife and their habitat. His name was on one long, blunt assessment report after another: reports that warned of wider and wider circles of damage and cost and urged more intensive defense of wildlife. The courier was as unhappily received as his message. Smith's star in the bureaucratic firmament dimmed rapidly after he took the lead in organizing the UC Davis conference at which the Barnes-Presser data were unveiled, in February 1984, even though Smith was a career civil servant with major awards for work highly respected in the wildlife community. He helped arrange a wider audience than Reclamation Bureau and even Wildlife Service administrators had in mind. Inviting experts from as many scientific disciplines as possible meant more talk and more people involved, many of them well outside the bureau's range of influence . . . or control.

As the waves of impact energized environmental groups into a new round of opposition to federal initiatives on drainage disposal, more aggressive agency managers were brought in from Washington, D.C. Among those transferred in were the new regional director, David Houston, and the new agency lawyer, David Lindgren. The bureau's chief western public relations officer, Jerry King, was fired after an attempt to laugh off the seriousness of the Kesterson discoveries backfired on network television. King was replaced with Douglas Baldwin, whose talents as a damage control officer had tempered the controversial leadership of Interior Secretary James G. Watt. The Wildlife Service, too, shuffled administrators, replacing regional leaders in Portland with others more attuned to the political realities of Washington, D.C.

"They started complaining about my activities just for trying to gather more information on selenium," said Smith. "Most of us still were pretty much in the dark about the element then." His involvement, as well as his profile, continued to escalate after that first meeting in Fresno, in June 1983, and had begun doing so through the summer and fall as he worked with the Department of Conservation and Natural Resources on the University of California's Berkeley campus to stage a scientific symposium on the subject on December 3. That session prompted a broad exchange of views between scientists from academia and representatives of environmental groups, sports and commercial fishery interests, waterfowl enthusiasts, and the general public, as well as the press.

Within a week, the Reclamation Bureau had scheduled its own December seminar in the seclusion of a private hotel room in Sacramento. The initial guest list, before Smith learned of this clandestine exclusive critique of the Berkeley seminar, excluded the press, the public, environmentalists, and the roster included far fewer academics. Environmentalists said the exclusivity was meant to stifle open debate and understanding. If so, it didn't attain either objective. The day before the closed-door session was to be convened, Smith alerted Tom Graff and Dr. Terry Young, senior counsel and senior scientist of the West Coast office of the Environmental Defense Fund, who pressured Houston, the bureau's new regional manager, to open up the meeting. Not only was the venue changed to a larger conference room in the hotel, but the list of invitees was expanded to include the press and environmental representatives.

"Two particular statements we made at that December conference were picked up on by the press," said Smith. "One was that some of us felt that as much as 500,000 acres of valley farmland might have enough selenium in it to cause wildlife problems. The other was that continued bird die-offs caused by the drainage, and even continued operation of Kesterson, could be violating the international Migratory Bird Treaty Act (MBTA). We were told to sharply scale down our size estimates and to be quiet about the MBTA," he added.

But it was too late. By then, Smith had been swept inexorably into the heart of the Kesterson controversy by the demands of an increasingly voracious press, sometimes to the exclusion of other water-related environmental issues whose wildlife implications it was his duty to assess. "It got very difficult then," he said. "Even my friends in the department were afraid to be seen talking to me. Others would call on the phone, but if I wasn't in they would hang up when asked to leave a return call message."

Smith's problems worsened as the interagency battles proliferated. In late 1985 and early 1986, his Portland superiors threatened him with suspension, transfer, and, finally, outright dismissal. With the help of U.S. Congressman George Miller (D–Calif.), then chairman of a key Interior oversight subcommittee, Smith filed for, and received, protection under the Civil Service Reform Act of 1978. This act's "whistle-blower" provisions shield from retaliation any civil servant who brings to light government fraud, waste, corruption, or mismanagement. Attorneys with the Washington-based Government Accountability Project (GAP) successfully blocked the Fish and Wildlife Service's disciplinary actions. Their representation, along with Miller's congressional intervention as chairman of the House Interior Committee's water and power subcommittee, had a chilling effect on the reprisals. But one strategy Smith followed may have had an even greater effect. "I kept this big three-ring binder with copies of all the letters and memos and reports on phone calls," he said. "I think they laid off because they were afraid that what I was saying publicly about the dangers to wildlife and the duty of the service to come to their rescue was the truth."

Felix Smith was not the only one disciplined by Washington superiors. Punishment eventually reached even those at the top of the regional bureaucratic ladder in Portland. In 1988, western regional director Rolf Wallenstrom was demoted, reassigned, suspended, and, finally, fired for his part in trying to protect the independence of service scientists. His staunch defense of his staff's independence was linked not only to the emerging selenium issue but also to equally controversial hearings about proposed water diversions from the tributaries that feed San Francisco Bay. But the issue over which Wallenstrom took the most heat was the release of a preliminary report about harmful environmental effects from further oil exploration and development along the California coast, especially northern California. The report played into the hands of environmental groups fighting to block more offshore oil exploration along the coast and angered White House aides for whom more offshore drilling was a prime tenet.

When the disciplinary actions against his scientists continued, Wallenstrom accused his boss, Wildlife Service chief Frank Dunkel, of harrassment and retaliation. Much to the chagrin of the apolitical Wallenstrom, the political backlash occurred in the closing months of the 1988 presidential campaign. The deposed regional chief later won reinstatement, with full pay and legal fees, and Dunkel was removed from his position. "In retrospect," Felix Smith muses, "I don't think any of that would have happened if the politically sensitive agency administrators had just concentrated on the issues at hand and not been afraid to speak the truth." What happened, however, was that the full details of Kesterson and the attempted cover-up became public.

The long-suppressed "White Paper" that Ohlendorf, Smith, and other service scientists had prepared was lost for months in a maze of upper-level review and policy rewrites. "It just totally disappeared from view," charges Smith. Angry and concerned that censorship would kill the selenium search, Smith released a copy of the document to the press early in 1984. He says he responded to a legitimate formal request from one of the most persistent of the valley reporters, Deborah Blum, then the environment writer for the *Fresno Bee*.

For the very first time, the press had official government reports, frank opinions, and scientific numbers to quantify just how badly things had gone wrong at Kesterson. The media had a field day, but none more so than the United Press International wire service team of Lloyd Carter and Gregory Gordon. Their five-part series in August 1984 was the most detailed press account of events leading up to Kesterson and its early impacts. Powerful statewide papers like the *Los Angeles Times*, the *San Francisco Chronicle*, and the *Sacramento Bee* ran full-length articles on both the evolving ecological crisis and the increasing political intrigue that shadowed it. Television stations showed prime-time clips of deformed waterfowl and aired interviews with outraged bird lovers and Reclamation Bureau spokesmen.

The pace of bureaucratic response to the growing problems quick-ened. In September 1984, the Wildlife Service began round-the-clock hazing efforts to drive birds from the Kesterson ponds, using auto-mated miniature cannons, airboats, and noisy three-wheeled, off-road vehicles. Kesterson was silent no more. There had been growing con-cern, too, about the potential threat to people who might shoot and eat any of the tainted waterfowl. Most of the waterfowl examined con-tained so much selenium that just a single meal could provide un-healthy amounts of the element. Toxicologists from the state Depart-ment of Health Services advised the Department of Fish and Game to post public health warnings in both Vietnamese and English. Most of the concern centered on families of Hmong immigrants, the South Viet-namese hill people whose customary hunting and foraging habits often took them to wildlife refuges to collect a wide assortment of animals to supplement their diets. Duck hunters too were warned to be cautious about their intake of Kesterson waterfowl. Women of childbearing age and children under the age of fifteen were advised to avoid eating *any* ducks shot there. Healthy adults were advised to limit their consump-tion to 8 ounces a month.[6]

Although it would be years before the full truth of such threats es-caped the bureaucratic walls being erected by politically attuned Inte-rior administrators, the essential meaning of Kesterson and its sele-nium woes was moving steadily into a very public arena.

Chapter 3 | LEGACY of POISON

The curiosity of USGS geochemist Ivan Barnes about just where the selenium riddle would end may have been distracted by his passionate interest in the source of volcanic eruptions, but he kept coming back to it. Time and again Theresa Presser saw him pawing through the stacks of the USGS library. It was there, among thousands of technical volumes, that he discovered the pioneer work of the noted University of Wyoming research chemist Orville Beath. Barnes discovered, to his astonishment, that botanists, agricultural and soil researchers, chemists, and plant physiologists had solved many of the selenium riddles decades ago. In fact, some of the references that turned up in his historical literature search dated back to the prior century. In two classic texts by Beath, now deceased, and his colleagues, Barnes found long tables of laboratory results showing selenium levels in hillside seeps, farm crops, soil samples, streams, and even livestock tissue.

Beath's work revealed a lifetime of dedication to the subject. Barnes found books with pictures taken by Beath of his wife, seated in their classic chrome-trimmed Packard sedan, parked in the middle of a field of blooming woody asters or next to an outcropping of telltale marine shale. There were pictures of unique and highly seleniferous regions all over the West, pictures of deformed and dying livestock, the victims of a distinctive genus of selenium-loving weeds, and pictures, sketches, and diagrams of the plants themselves by the score.[1]

Even more insistent in his day than Barnes, Orville A. Beath literally combed the West, often on his own time and at his own expense. He found evidence that selenium was the cause of unexplained deaths to cattle and sheep, sometimes to herds of 15,000 at a time, in rangeland from the Dakotas to New Mexico.[2] Beath became an expert on the botany of selenium, discovering and classifying the distinctive plants he called "primary selenium accumulators," almost all of them members of the botanical genus *Astragalus* but which grow only in soil with elevated levels of selenium.

But where Beath's considerable grasp of the botanical signposts of selenium's subterranean presence limited him to aboveground sightings, Barnes, the geologist, used his maps to pinpoint the formations of host rock. Huge, multicolored plots with complex legends, they traced the makeup and age of the earth's crustal block across the face of the continent. To the expert eye, at least, they offered a broad, comprehensive view of just how far and wide the selenium search would stretch. The kelly-green splotches described by Barnes covered large parts of the West, denoting the marine shale formations in which selenium is most often found at levels high enough to give rise to poisonous plants. Maps prepared by Beath and Hubert Lakin, one of the earliest USGS researchers to study selenium, showed the presence of selenium-bearing plants and soil across the thousands of square miles of the West to which another federal geologist, J. David Love, had referred. Much of that distribution pattern covered substantial parts of the Plains States' grain belt.[3] In some places the distribution of plants or source-rock outcroppings was uniformly widespread. In others, they appeared like twisting ribbons along the outlines of low-lying ridges and foothills.

As one historic find led to another in late 1983 and the early months of 1984, Barnes turned to the electronic magic of computerized libraries. "You wouldn't believe it," he told me. "I did this literature search, punching in selenium as the key word, and out rolled nearly a hundred source citations. Wham! It was unbelievable. Some of that stuff was nearly a hundred years old."

Barnes and other scientists involved in the search for more information about the behavior of the unusual trace element continued their work in the laboratories and libraries. The regulators, too, were busy, preparing reports and holding hearings into the spreading pollution problems. News of Kesterson flashed into public view almost daily, turning an unsettling environmental story into a prime-time political bombshell. Some of the most dramatic episodes came in a rush in the early months of 1985. The first was on February 5. After months of hearings marked by conflicting testimony and increasingly pointed legal threats from landowners adjacent to Kesterson, the State Water Resources Control Board designated the drainage flowing into Kesterson a hazardous waste and the refuge itself a public nuisance. The Reclamation Bureau was ordered to plug the drainage canal and clean up the refuge.

These key decisions had been precipitated by rancher Robert James Claus, whose 900-acre holding next to the refuge was managed for livestock grazing in spring and summer and private duck hunting on the flooded pastures in fall and winter. Claus, squarely on the side of livestock and wildlife, had gone to the Central Valley Regional Water Quality Control Board nearly a year before, in March 1984, demanding that the drainage be ruled in violation of state water quality laws. The Central Valley board was one of nine such regional bodies in the state's water quality control system, and several of its directors were tied directly to agriculture. The board took no immediate action. Impatient at best, and contentious at his worst, Claus waited only two months before carrying the dispute to the next higher level. He filed a formal petition of appeal in May 1984 with the state water board, urging it to take jurisdiction. The parent body, however, moved even more cautiously, taking until October to hold its first hearing. Caught in the eye of a growing political storm over how much leeway to give the San Joaquin Valley farmers, the appointed five-member state board held a second hearing in December—setting the stage for its February ruling which designated Kesterson a public nuisance and ordered its cleanup.

Under normal circumstances, that might have seemed like an aggressive enough response to the problem. But ducks and other waterfowl continued to perish at Kesterson. An entire nesting year of one of the state's few remaining flocks of tricolor blackbirds, a candidate for protection as an endangered species, was wiped out by the continuing selenium threat there. And rising groundwater, heavily contaminated with selenium and other dissolved elements, was endangering, if not damaging, both of Claus's ventures. Damage mounted, too, on the adjacent Freitas Ranch, where livestock were dying and the family's health was deteriorating. When the state board gave the Reclamation Bureau five months to come up with a cleanup plan and another three years to actually implement it, Claus was livid. Before he stomped out of the Sacramento hearing room, carrying his customary load of government reports, restricted memos, and sometimes even legal depositions from retired federal workers involved in the issues, he vowed that the grace period would not stand.

Three days later, he made good his threat. Still chafing at the board's inability to act swiftly on Kesterson, Claus appealed to the courts. He sought—and won—an order from Merced County Superior Court Judge Donald R. Fretz that required the state board to shut down Kesterson immediately or appear before him on March 15 to argue the merits of the case.

The momentum of one Kesterson initiative often overtook the inertia of another. Judge Fretz's order was one such example. Claus's determination quickly provided another. Neither his lawsuit to force the state water board to act more quickly nor the continual hazing to discourage waterfowl from using the tainted marsh stopped the death toll there. Not only were birds continuing to die at Kesterson but Claus had seen reports by federal wildlife biologists that operation of the refuge might be a violation of the international bird treaty between the United States, Mexico, Japan, Russia, and Great Britain, the original signatory for Canada when that country was still a dependent dominion rather than an independent sovereign entity.* Early in March, Claus notified Interior officials, by letter, that he would sue them for violating the treaty provisions if they didn't take prompt action to abate the problem.

The political turmoil over Kesterson sparked heated debate between congressional representatives from different parts of the state, too. Valley legislators sought protection for their farming constituents while those from the urban Bay Area, from San Francisco to San Jose, from Oakland to Marin County, urged strict enforcement of environmental rules to protect the estuary. In January 1985, before either the state board's order or the court's subsequent override, Congressman Miller, a Democrat from the Bay Area and chairman of the House Interior subcommittee on water and power, scheduled a day-long field hearing for March 15 in the pastoral farming town of Los Baños, not far from the tainted marshes. The stated objective was to seek expert testimony on the problem. But those close to Miller said its main purpose was to build a record for congressional action to force Interior to correct the drainage problems.

Several months earlier, in October 1984, San Francisco's public television station, KQED, had aired its documentary on Kesterson, "Down the Drain," and attracted the attention of CBS's powerful "60 Minutes" program in New York. Kesterson was about to become a network event. And Felix Smith, the Wildlife Service whistleblower who was being besieged with media requests for information, played a key role in orchestrating the timing.

The "60 Minutes" program aired on Sunday, March 10, and included key footage from "Down the Drain." One scene showed wildlife researcher Harry Ohlendorf up to his thighs in one of the ponds, scooping up a dead nestling and saying, "It's hard to tell the species at this point. It could be a mallard. It has normal feet. It's hard to tell but the eyes seem to be normal in size. There isn't anything obviously wrong with it . . . except that it's dead." A later scene showed pictures of refuge personnel, clad in masks and protective clothing, operating noisemakers and driving loud three-wheelers around the ponds while the voice-over commentary explained, "The Fish and Wildlife Service has instituted what it calls a hazing program to scare birds away from the wildlife refuge. While the government insists that the refuge is not a hazard to public health, workers must wear masks and protective clothing while maintaining the noisemakers on a 24-hour basis."

Yet another part of the film interviewed Janette Freitas, whose ranch home was only yards away—and downslope—from Kesterson's most tainted ponds. Said Freitas, "In the past I've always been able to plant flowers in my yard and they would grow and bloom and be healthy looking. But in the last couple of years everything I plant starts to grow and then dies before it ever gets any bloom on it." Near the end of the clip, Ohlendorf is shown again, hands on hips, looking out over the marsh as the commentator asks: "This place is incredibly silent for a marsh. . . . Is that normal . . . at this time of year?" The taciturn Ohlendorf pauses, reflects, and without any outward show of emotion replies: "It is rather silent."[5]

The closing scene of the episode brought the media storm to a crescendo. Co-anchor Ed Bradley was standing near the edge of one of Kesterson's more contaminated ponds, angrily demanding to know "Who is responsible for this?" from the Reclamation Bureau's stammering public relations officer Jerry King. While King recounted the bureau's claims that there had been a lot of speculation and exaggeration but very little proof of selenium poisoning, pictures of Ohlendorf's twisted waterfowl chicks were superimposed on the screen.

For the Reclamation Bureau, it was a public relations disaster. The program mentioned the fears of wildlife researchers that terms of the international bird treaty were being violated and cited Claus's threats that he might take legal action to enforce the multilateral pact. Just days before Congressman Miller's scheduled hearing in Los Baños, Interior Secretary Donald Hodel summoned his top aides to a rare weekend meeting in Washington, D.C., to discuss the ramifications of the rapidly worsening developments at Kesterson and to consider launching a preemptive bureaucratic strike.

Those who heard partial accounts of the weekend session claim that Frank Richardson, the department's in-house counsel at the time, told Hodel that he and other Interior officials conceivably could go to jail if the operation of Kesterson were found to constitute an "illegal taking" under the international agreement. Only hunters, or wildlife researchers, could legally take or kill birds protected by the treaty and only then in accordance with sports hunting regulations or by special permit. Felix Smith, environmental assessment specialist and nemesis of the bureau, prepared a detailed report on the legal ramifications of a treaty violation, and his superiors sent it to Hodel's in-house attorneys for review. The document cited chapter, verse, and legal precedent for such rulings, including particulars of how operators of oil waste ponds in several parts of the country had been prosecuted for causing similar bird deaths years earlier.

Hodel acted swiftly. First he advised Houston, director of the Reclamation Bureau's regional office in Sacramento, to get his own private counsel. Then he ordered preparation of an order to shut down Kesterson at once and plug all of the farm connections to the San Luis Drain that carried selenium to the refuge. The announcement was transmitted to Hodel's special western regional assistant, Carol Hallett, just minutes before the congressional hearing was convened in the multipurpose room of the Merced County Fairgrounds in Los Baños.

Marc Sylvester, of the USGS Water Resources Division staff in Menlo Park, was one of the Interior staff people ordered to testify at the hearing. "People were milling around in the hallway, just outside the hearing room," recalls Sylvester, "and all of the Interior people were sitting together. Then someone whispered something to Houston and he left to take a telephone call in the lobby. I could see him through the crowd.

He listened for a long time, had a short conversation, and then came to tell us everything had changed—that we would not have to testify but just sit there while Hallett read a statement from Hodel."

There were more than a hundred people in the audience, most of them farmers worried about rumors of lawsuits, drain closures, and the impending threat of bureaucratic action from both the federal and state agencies. "There was a real undercurrent of tension, of anger," says Sylvester. "You could feel it." Within minutes, he and others found out why.

The crowded hearing room quieted when Carol Hallett stood up to read Hodel's statement. Most people there, including the congressmen, expected nothing more than a perfunctory statement of concern and a call for more time and congressional funds to solve the problem. Instead, Hallett conveyed Hodel's astonishing decision. The San Luis Drain would be plugged and all federal water supplies would be cut off to those fields from which the contaminated drainage was flowing.

Chaos reigned. Miller, his committee, and staff people all appeared stunned. The farmers were outraged. They had been betrayed by the reclamation agency not once, but twice, they shouted. One instance of duplicity, they said, was the bureau's failed promise to complete the San Luis Drain all the way to the Sacramento–San Joaquin Delta. The second deception, they yelled, was the unexpected loss of both irrigation flows and drainage facilities. Many shouted that they were being driven out of business. Others said the livelihood and well-being of their families were being threatened. Miller kept trying to restore order, pounding his gavel. While he voiced irritation with Hodel's unexpected announcement a uniformed California highway patrolman entered the hearing room, hurried up to Houston, and whispered in his ear. Marc Sylvester was about to experience an armed escort for the first time in his life.

"Houston turned and told everyone from the agency to file out behind the officer. Now!" says Sylvester. "We were led outside. Everyone was angry and there was a lot of shouting. Then we were told by the CHP that they had received telephoned death threats against us and were escorting all of us to the airport, where Houston, his assistant Lawrence Hancock, and Mrs. Hallett could enplane for Sacramento. The rest of us left immediately and drove directly from the airport to our various offices."

Arguments raged for weeks. How could the drainage be regulated so that economic ruin would not be forced upon one of the state's major industries nor environmental havoc wreaked against valley waterfowl habitat and the important San Francisco Bay system? When the state water board indicated it would give the federal government even more time to experiment with lower-cost cleanup strategies, Hodel, threatened by a Westlands Water District lawsuit to block the water and drainage cutoff, relaxed his order. Instead, he gave farmers until June 30, 1986, to phase out their drainage discharges.

The reprieve was only temporary. Farmers said that without drainage, they could squeeze no more than five or six more years of production out of their fields before the rising water table invaded the root zone and drowned the crops. Even that grace period, they said, depended on their being allowed to construct smaller and better-designed ponds on their own property and reducing drainage volume by sharply reducing the amount of water applied to the fields in the first place. They insisted that careful design and management would prevent the creation of several dozen new miniature Kestersons. For instance, pond banks would be contoured steeply enough to discourage shorebird use and sprayed with herbicides to eliminate vegetation that would provide nesting cover. The ponds, too, could be made too deep and steep for either wading birds or dabbling ducks to reach juicy invertebrates on the bottom. (Dabbling ducks are the ones you always see with their back ends pointed skyward as they probe the shallow, muddy bottoms.) It would take more active management to keep surface feeders off the ponds, though, including hazing, netting, or even dyeing the pond water an unattractive color.

Ultimately, however, the smaller ponds would fill with salt and have to be abandoned and replaced by others, leaving tons of toxic saline waste to an uncertain future. Environmentalists warned that wind-blown, selenium-laden dust from the ponds would be a threat to public health and a danger to wildlife every time they were rewatered by rainfall.[5]

As the farmers, state water regulators, and environmentalists sought more permanent solutions, the USGS grew more involved in defining the scope and source of the problem. Many from the agency attended a special selenium symposium staged jointly by the University of California's conservation and resource studies division and the environmentalist Bay Institute of San Francisco in March 1985. The large amphitheater in Berkeley's Dwinelle Hall was jammed with tier after tier of academics, bureaucrats, environmentalists, journalists, valley farmers, and engineering firm consultants. Just after lunch break, Ivan Barnes traced the geological history and mechanisms of selenium distribution. Sometimes the discussion roamed far beyond the limits of the audience. By the time he got into the complex geochemical processes involved, Barnes had galloped beyond their grasp and on to his own high terrain, furiously scribbling chemical formulas, one after the other, on the room-wide chalkboard. Each set of equations traced the succession of host-rock mineral forms through which selenium leached and was concentrated. The listeners, many of them scientists well regarded in their own fields, were rapt . . . but overmatched.

"I think that the chemistry of these weathering reactions is fairly well known," Barnes told the sea of doubting expressions. "There is an accumulation of selenium in the salt crusts, mainly in the mineral mirabilite, a sodium sulfate with 10 waters," he explained, warming to the task. "The salt crusts also contain the minerals konyaite, bloedite, hexahydrite, and halite," he continued, referring to the white patches left in the wake of evaporation on the sides of the Coast Range. "The first two minerals are double salts of sodium sulfate and magnesium sulfate, with 5 waters for the konyaite and 4 waters for bloedite," he added, now speeding from one reaction formula to the next, "and hexahydrite is a magnesium sulfate with 6 waters."

If Barnes knew he had his listeners gasping for intellectual air, he didn't let on. He lived for these moments of tracing the complex mineral/water reactions. Geochemistry was his field, and his contemporaries say he was one of the very best in the world at it. From there it was a veritable blizzard of geochemical shorthand: "[MgNa$_2$(SO$_4$) 2.4H$_2$O]" and "[MgNa$_2$(SO$_4$)2.5H$_2$O]" and on and on until all but Barnes were totally bewildered.[6] Whatever puzzlement he sowed about the genealogy of selenium or doubt he left behind about the exactitude of the patterns and processes involved, Barnes left nothing to the imagination about its geographic implications when it came to question and answer time.

There was a long, awkward silence in response to the moderator's call for questions. Finally, they started coming. One questioner asked whether there was any public health threat from the gaseous forms to which selenium was converted by bacteria in the pond environment. Replied Barnes: "The answer is, we're not sure. We were asked those questions by people at the Bureau of Reclamation, who thought the answer would be easy to figure out. T. S. Presser said no, it may be very dangerous. They asked me. I stated that I work in actively erupting volcanoes and I wouldn't go in [the Kesterson ponds]. I just don't know. You can get the wrong conditions at the wrong time of year and all of a sudden all the selenium is reduced to selenium hydride . . . you can kill yourself." There was Ivan Barnes at his controversial best again.

Others in the audience wanted to know how much selenium there was, both in the flanking foothills and in the farmland below, and how long it might take to flush it out with intensive cultivation and irrigation. Answered Barnes: "The hills are Cretaceous in age. They have been at the present elevation for about 400,000 years. We'll run out of people before we run out of selenium. To remove it from the Coast Ranges, you're talking about millions of years."

Most of the discussion before an audience of about 200 scientists, bureaucrats, environmentalists, and journalists that day focused on the west side of the San Joaquin Valley, in California's midsection. The Saturday session concluded with a series of panel discussions and warnings about decades of slow but steady inflows of low concentrations of selenium from tributary waters into San Francisco Bay. Scientists warned that ultimately such "base loading" could trigger biological accumulation throughout the entire food chain of the world-class estuary. That contamination would start with microscopic plant and animal plankton and work its way up through bottom-feeding invertebrates to larger fish and migrating waterfowl and, ultimately, to the humans who ate them. In fact, it already had tainted waterfowl in both the Suisun and South Bay reaches of the main San Francisco Bay complex and had contaminated highly prized Dungeness crab in the central and northern reaches of the bay.

William T. Davoren, executive director of the sponsoring Bay Institute, who served in the Fish and Wildlife Service for nineteen years (eight as a special regional coordinator for the Interior Secretary), gave the day's last presentation. He traced the pattern of increasingly high levels of selenium found in striped bass, common ocean ducks called scoters, and crabs. He also reported on the pattern of selenium being dumped into the bay by oil refineries and community sewage treatment plants. Selenium is a natural constituent of oil, particularly in high-sulfur crude from [the San Joaquin Valley], and is used in the manufacture of a variety of glass, rubber, photoelectric, and semiconductor products from industries which discharge their wastes into the treatment plants.

Citing the continual low-level introduction of selenium to the estuary from San Joaquin River flows, Davoren concluded: "The law of gravity controls agricultural water use in California. As long as this is true, the bay will be the receiving waters provided by nature for agricultural wastes produced in the western San Joaquin Valley. A master drain, planned someday to extend all the way from Bakersfield to the bay, would double the bay's jeopardy from agricultural wastes. The threat of selenium poisoning to the life forms dependent on the health of San Francisco Bay's waters, perhaps including humans, is real and present. The danger is great enough and already sufficiently advanced to justify immediate actions by responsible agencies."[7]

Chapter 4 | **The**
SEARCH

It was not Bill Davoren's call for action at the selenium symposium that was headlined in the March 16 *Sacramento Bee*. I had stumbled onto a much bigger story. A late Friday afternoon telephone talk with Ivan Barnes, the day before the conference, provided a stunning assessment of selenium's presence elsewhere and yielded predictions with historic ramifications.

I had been chasing the unfolding story for nearly two years and still was unsure of its geological roots and environmental cycling patterns, subjects I knew Barnes understood. In preparation for the Berkeley conference, I had called him for some badly needed scientific underpinning. Besides, I knew of his penchant for blackboard formulas. I got a lot more than I bargained for.

It was another of those remarkable telephone interviews that defined much of my professional relationship with the crusty geochemist. Barnes never saw himself as disloyal to the government that employed him—nor to the taxpayers who provided the money for his salary— and he was again waxing eloquently candid about the evolving issues.

As always, in these mostly cryptic exchanges, my comprehension was lagging far behind his explanation, mostly because of his maddening devotion to the vocabulary of the expert, with "epochs" this and "Cretaceous" that. It was somewhere between the third "uhhh, would you try that, again?" and the fourth "what does that mean?" that his patience finally gave out.

"What the hell is the matter with you? Don't you understand anything I've been saying?" shouted Barnes. "Thousands of square miles of the West are involved. Selenium will be found in parts of virtually every state west of the Mississippi. Damnation, man, look at the maps. Look for the Cretaceous marine shale formations. They're all over the place . . . and most of them will be highly seleniferous. If they have irrigation projects and poor drainage, there will be other Kestersons. Don't you get it?"

Of course I got it . . . then. "I just love understatement," I countered defensively. "Why didn't you say so in the first place?"

The story appeared at the top of the front page the next day: "Selenium Threatens the West; Other Kestersons Predicted." Yes, I understood, finally . . . and so did the readers. And so did Barnes's colleagues in USGS and his contemporaries in the Fish and Wildlife Service. What they didn't get from the story they got from Barnes in a series of telephone calls and meetings. It hadn't come as a complete surprise to other scientists involved in the issue. They had read some of the historical literature now flowing from the research effort. But the Barnes "exposé" brought the issue to a sudden head.

Within a month, six Interior Department experts had sequestered themselves in Denver for three grueling days to map out plans for a precise search and discovery mission across the most threatening parts of those "thousands of square miles" of selenium-contaminated range and farmland in the semiarid West. Marc Sylvester was one of them and there were two others from USGS, two from the Bureau of Reclamation, and one from the Fish and Wildlife Service. Long into the night they mapped, plotted, and debated, looking for sites that matched the Kesterson model of geological deposits and intensive irrigation. And they found scores of them with drainage collector systems listed in the bureau's bulky "Project Data Book" that details more than 470 different federally funded water projects in the West. Most of them empty into wildlife refuges or habitat areas from North Dakota to New Mexico, from western Nebraska to Nevada, much as Barnes had predicted.[1]

Until Sylvester's return from Denver, I never realized how much career damage Barnes had suffered. Both Sylvester and Felix Smith told similar versions of how Barnes had been severely reprimanded by Washington superiors after the Berkeley conference for his overly candid assessments of selenium's widespread distribution and danger. Though Barnes never complained to me about the career pain my story had caused, Smith said that he heard all about it. "Ivan told me it got pretty heated. He was strongly reprimanded and he didn't take it kindly. There was a lot of shouting back and forth. And he was transferred out of Menlo Park soon afterward."

Sylvester said it was the combination of the "60 Minutes" program and stories about Barnes's predictions of thousands of square miles being at risk to selenium contamination in the West that precipitated the Denver meeting. "We got a call from headquarters and were told to put together a work plan to determine where else we should look for selenium problems," said Sylvester. "We drafted the plan and sent it up the line," he added. "It was massaged at headquarters and sent back to us. There were three or four iterations of it before it was finally approved by the chief hydrologist of USGS and forwarded to a five-member review committee at Interior headquarters. Finally, the document was approved and sent along to David Broadbent, Assistant Secretary for Water, Science, and Power, and from there to Interior Secretary Hodel."

It was in the office of Assistant Secretary Broadbent that the plan apparently died. On April 22, Broadbent asked the agency's in-house lawyer, the Solicitor's Office, for a legal opinion about undertaking what was described as "a broad water quality assessment" of the bureau's project drainage problems. Whatever else Broadbent might have told the Solicitor's Office is unknown. "That's when the plan disappeared," said Smith. "They killed it—apparently because the solicitor said it would raise serious questions about legal liabilities wherever it [selenium] was found."

Before his promotion to top Interior echelons, Broadbent was chief of the Reclamation Bureau when many of those same water projects were proposed by the bureau and approved and funded by Congress. He has never explained why the selenium search proposal died. The Solicitor's Office decision was never divulged either, and Broadbent's office declined repeated requests for interviews.

Interior Department spokesman Mitchell Snow said only that the plan for the comprehensive testing program—it would have been the largest water quality study of agricultural drainage ever undertaken—had not been killed but was merely "under review." In the interim, he said, Interior had completed a "broad reconnaissance" of some of the recommended sites as an alternative. Claiming that bureau and wildlife experts had conducted the screening, Snow said that "nothing was found that you would define as a Kesterson-like situation. They found only some minor problems on which we must remain vigilant. But there was no direct evidence of wildlife impact."[2]

There was doubt, however, whether even that "broad reconnaissance" was done. The bureau's largest division, the Mid-Pacific Region headquartered in Sacramento, neither conducted nor participated in any such effort. Asked whether that directive had been received or complied with, Lawrence Hancock, assistant regional director of the bureau, replied: "No. We haven't looked for that in other states or even in other parts of California."

Whatever the reason for the rejection of the field team's proposed work plan for a western study, whether to save the bureau more embarrassment or another round of legal and budget liabilities, it had a completely opposite effect. During this time I had been briefing increasingly curious editors at *The Bee* about the lack of progress on the proposed selenium search and the growing suspicions of many that a major cover-up was under way. There was talk about the possibility of a major investigative effort. In the space of three months, interest in a West-wide probe of our own into the "Kesterson Effect" was galvanized by the series of developments that started with the state's cleanup order, Hodel's action (subsequently softened to allow plugging of the drains to be phased in over fifteen months), and Barnes's riveting disclosures and predictions. Other concerns surfaced, too.

The economic liabilities for the federal government—and for the farmers with tainted soil and contaminated drainage—were as obvious as they were enormous. The Reclamation Bureau's preliminary estimates on what it might cost to clean up just the twelve-pond refuge at Kesterson bounced wildly between $30 million and $195 million. The least costly estimate was for merely closing the refuge down, draining the marsh, and maintaining a moderate monitoring presence for an indefinite period. At the other end of the cost scale was the prospect that the state's classification would force Interior to treat Kesterson like a Superfund site. That would involve digging up and trucking away for burial in a Class I hazardous waste disposal site nearly 1 million cubic yards of contaminated mud, organic ooze, and vegetation.

More than just legal and financial liabilities were involved. Fish and Wildlife Service biologists were convinced that, at best, the health and reproduction of locally nesting birds throughout the West would be severely depressed where selenium was elevated. At worst, they feared that the internationally migrating waterfowl would carry their acquired selenium burdens back to the breeding grounds of Canada, the Arctic, and as far away as the USSR. Western migratory waterfowl numbers already had plummeted in the 1980s, ravaged by drought, and perhaps other effects, at both ends of the breeding and wintering corridors.

Talk about the investigative project at *The Bee* grew more earnest. Still struggling to grasp the geology, chemistry, and toxicity of selenium, I motored to Menlo Park to seek help from Barnes, Sylvester, and Presser. Where, when, what, and how should we sample? That was in early May. I explained our frustration over not knowing how to scientifically screen the list of suspect sites to narrow it from several hundred to several dozen or less. Barnes handed me a thick packet of oversized geological maps showing all of the crustal rock formations of the continental United States. Presser gave me some valuable pointers on what and how to sample. Sylvester offered suggestions on water sampling and promising regions based on the work plan drafted in Denver. We exchanged personal experiences, mused about the ominous political implications and apparent bureaucratic disinterest, and commiserated about the career damage done to Smith, Ohlendorf, Barnes, and others by the interagency conflict.

Finally, just as I was about to head back to Sacramento, I asked Sylvester about the work plan he had mentioned. How detailed was it? There was an awkward silence before he replied. "Are you asking to see it?" he queried. "Yes," I replied, "as long as it isn't officially confidential. If it's confidential, then I demand to see it," I said in jest. He thought about that for a few moments. "Hmmm. There isn't any official department policy on the release of such documents and it hasn't been classified one way or the other." With that, he led the way to his office, leafed through a stack of documents on his desk, and handed over a modest twenty-page report. I thanked him, shook hands, said my goodbyes, and headed for home.

I didn't read the Denver-hatched work plan until the next morning. But when I did, the outline for our own investigation quickly took shape. Interior Secretary Donald Hodel had ordered the expanded search for Kesterson-like problems on other federal water projects on March 28, 1985. Initially, the Denver planners had identified 250 federal irrigation project areas, which drained into wildlife refuges or into rivers, lakes, or reservoirs used for drinking water, irrigation, or recreation. Later the list was expanded to 470 areas, ranging in size from a few thousand acres to hundreds of thousands in states from Oregon to Kansas, Montana to Texas, and California to Colorado.

The Denver plan called for a quick screening of sites by qualified experts to find out which areas needed extensive attention. The Geological Survey would select sites for detailed investigation and be responsible for collection, measurement, and analysis of samples, though the work would be done by teams drawn from both agencies. The Geological Survey, with Bureau of Reclamation cooperation, also would write the final reports. The conclusions about the threat involved would be based on samples of surface and subsurface water as well as sediments and biota on farms, in drains, in and around wetlands and refuges, and in rivers or lakes used for drinking water and recreation. The USGS, which had long maintained its scientific independence on such issues, insisted that all data be made public. The study targets would be identified by April 19, 1985, individual work plans completed by May 6, and the actual fieldwork started no later than May 13—a fast track for any bureaucratic undertaking. At least that is the way it was supposed to have been done.

Far more than selenium would be looked at. My copy of the plan showed an extensive catalog of contaminants usually associated with farm drainwater. It listed thirty-five different constituents, including heavy metals like mercury, lead, cadmium, and chromium, toxic trace elements like selenium, arsenic, and boron, dissolved salts like calcium, sodium, and chloride, and nutrients like phosphorus, ammonia, and nitrogen. Although this survey was far more sweeping than what *The Bee* had in mind, I could now see the strategy the Interior scientists had recommended and was able to map out the most likely target sites.

The next three days were filled with editorial conferences, discussions with outside sources and others about the implications of the now dead plan, and more research about selenium itself. Soft fluorescent light bathed the cavernous second-floor newsroom of *The Bee*, one of the West's most aggressive papers when it comes to investigative reporting. Where there had been frantic activity to meet the nightly deadlines just hours before, it was now quiet, almost deserted. Except for a page makeup editor who was shepherding the early editions of the next morning's paper to press, the rest of the staff had gone home. Near the back of the room, at a special project desk set up to file the growing mountain of selenium information, I tried to make sense out of the huge, multicolored geological maps of the western United States that Barnes had given me.

They covered—and overlapped—the desk, and little wonder. There were three of them: one for the eastern states, where there is only thinly scattered evidence of selenium's presence; another for the West, which historical reports already had indicated was liberally splotched with selenium; and one just to accommodate the complex legend for both sheets. Each map was 31 inches wide and 51 inches long. Across the top of the legend, six columns correlated the major geological units of the West: stratified (mainly marine), continental, engeosynclinal, plutonic, volcanic, and metamorphic. The left side of the legend was divided into the four major eras of geological time—Cenozoic, Mesozoic, Paleozoic, and Precambrian—and subdivided into eleven different groups of rock systems. Within each subdivision were tiny colored squares, 164 of them ranging sequentially through graduated hues of gray, yellow, green, blue, and red. Each box carried alphabetical keys corresponding to a bewildering kaleidoscope of colored blotches, whorls, and bands splashed across the map, each indicating a different formation or time period.

Barnes had told me to follow the marine shales, the ones colored kelly green. It was a perplexing task. There were thirty-four different combinations of colors and alphabetical keys to units and formations, tracing geological distribution and deposition during the Cretaceous period of the Mesozoic era, about 65 million to 145 million years ago. Barnes predicted, and a number of geological reports confirmed, that these rock types would hold the highest levels of selenium. The poisons were concentrated in eroding sediments that settled out on the bottom of ancient lakes and inland seas. Over millions of years, these muds also accumulated rich loads of decayed organic matter. When the seas dried up (or geological uplifting brought these deposits to the surface), farmers found them fertile ground for planting.

I swiveled back and forth from the maps to the reclamation agency's huge "Project Data" volume, thumbing through its 1,465 pages of maps, text, and descriptions to find federally funded water projects in zones where the color marking predominated for the ones Barnes said were Cretaceous shale formations. The bureau's sourcebook listed 198 dam and water diversion projects, most of them with multiple units, that might be affected. The total number of potential sites: 427.

Terry Hennessy, my project editor, was spending a lot of time figuring out how to set up the search so it wouldn't break the entire news budget for the year but would still be comprehensive enough to be valid. Both he and metropolitan editor George Baker, who pushed the project hard with executive editor Gregory Favre, frowned when they heard the number of potentially suspect sites.

"Can you narrow that down to something we can live with financially?" sputtered Baker.

"Sure," I said. "We can narrow the field and improve our prospects for success by choosing only the sites that match the Kesterson model. We'd look in places where annual rainfall was low enough that high rates of evaporation and plant transpiration would concentrate the selenium rather than flushing it out. Usually, that means less than 12 inches a year of precipitation."

Another question was whether the soil contained enough tightly compacted clay to impede natural drainage to the point that perforated drainpipes had to be buried 10 or 12 feet underground to prevent the rising water table from drowning the root zone of crops. If this was the case, then lethal drainage would be brought to the surface somewhere nearby. The likelihood of impact would be greater if the drainage was dumped into dead-end ponds or lakes where evaporation would further concentrate the toxic brew. Kesterson was a refuge in name only— a series of constructed ponds whose sole purpose was to collect agricultural drainage and serve as a terminal evaporative and leaky repository. The question was: how many other national wildlife refuges or wildlife habitat were being contaminated?

Most important, however, was whether the source rock itself was present. Did the kelly-green map markings for selenium-bearing Cretaceous marine shale match up when the geological charts were superimposed on the geography? Selenium is widely present in many soil types, but usually in concentrations too minute to pose a threat. But in the ancient sea and lake bottoms of the West, levels are high enough to be a serious risk, especially after those lands have been tectonically uplifted to create low-lying foothills and valleys. When the soil is tilled and weathered, the selenium is oxidized to a water-soluble form that can easily be dissolved in the excess irrigation water and brought to the surface by the collection system of tile or perforated drains.

There were other factors, too. Was there any record of inexplicable wildlife or livestock deaths in the region? Was the water there more alkaline? In this case, selenium would be more readily mobilized in the water column and able to damage the food chain. With each set of correlations, I swung around to the softly glowing computer terminal to add another potential search site to the growing project outline being drafted for the editor's approval. As the cursor blinked rapidly across the lines, I typed out the final paragraphs of the scientific part of the project.

Although *The Bee*'s editors were strongly supportive, they paled when the word "budget" came up. Not only would the tests cost at least $50 apiece but multiple samples would have to be collected from each of the twenty-four sites proposed in the final project outline. Accustomed to expense accounts of a few thousand dollars for airfare, lodging, and meals for a few days, they blanched at the combined costs of sending two reporters out to criss-cross the West for a month to collect, package, and air-express dozens of samples back home for costly analysis. All of the groundwork increased our chances of success, of course, but it still was rank exploration with all its attendant risks. At least the selection process and homework, we hoped, had cut down the odds of failure.

Favre, the executive editor, gave the final approval, touching off weeks of final preparation. Sources of information were cultivated and then tapped . . . often in places far from my California base where I had built up trusted relationships over seventeen years of environmental writing. Sites had to be picked, most of them in places I had never seen. Laboratories had to be contacted and screened, sampling protocols approved, and agreement reached on the right kind of analytical techniques. Whatever the outcome of the search, its results would be subjected to compulsive scrutiny. The Reclamation Bureau's contract laboratory already had suffered an embarrassing failure with selenium sampling, having underestimated its actual presence by 100 to 200 times. The California Department of Agriculture, too, had experienced similar controversy from its efforts to pinpoint selenium concentrations in food crops raised in seleniferous soil near Kesterson.

Barnes and Presser helped *The Bee* avoid a similar fate. They forwarded a copy of the report from their exhaustive search for the source of selenium in Kesterson. The carefully detailed section on laboratory methods and equipment was given to the West Sacramento laboratory the newspaper hired to do the chemical analysis. (The selection of the laboratory itself was discussed with those who certified them for the Environmental Protection Agency and California's Department of Health Services.) Finally, the trip itinerary was drafted and the last of the textbooks and technical reports were read . . . and reread. Our selenium search and discovery mission was ready to be launched.

As there was too much area for one reporter to cover in a month, one of *The Bee*'s best general assignment reporters, Jim Morris, was added to the team. He had worked well with me on the paper's nationwide exposé of hazardous waste problems at military bases the year before, a series that won the prestigious George Polk Award and made it to the finals of the Pulitzer Prize judging for 1984. Morris, now an environment writer for the *Houston Chronicle,* was assigned the tier of southern states and I took the northern route. Each of us was equipped with a liberal supply of sample bottles, waterproof pens and labels, briefcases full of notes, maps, charts, and field contacts . . . and a cooler well stocked with dry ice. We would sample all of the assigned sites on our routes, interview contacts, and make as many useful observations as possible before returning home.

My last night was spent packing notebooks, maps, charts, textbooks, phone numbers of sources, and, of course, the sampling supplies. They went on one side of the trunk and the usual supply of clothing and personal items on the other. My wife, Glenda, had chosen to keep me company on the marathon journey. (Actually, "chosen" doesn't quite capture the full flavor of the decision. It was either that or come home to an empty house. But such a trip without her, four or five weeks on the road, thousands of miles through parts of the West she had never seen, was unthinkable. Anyway, her bags were always packed for any pretext to travel.) The journey began early the next morning, May 20, under brilliantly clear skies. The probe for Kesterson clones was officially under way.

Crossing the High Sierra and circling Lake Tahoe's south rim was a breathtaking beginning. Snow still crowned the peaks framing the striking alpine lake, one of the clearest and deepest on earth and so uniquely situated, near the crest of one of the continent's steepest mountain scarps, that John Muir called it his "sea in the clouds." Beyond the Sierra, eastward to the Wasatch Front Range in Utah, stretched the Great Basin and its majestic, if barren, Basin and Range country, where steep north-to-south-trending mountain ranges were separated by long, narrow, flat valleys, one after the other.

The eastern side of the Sierra Nevada tapered abruptly down through spring-greened slopes to Nevada's Carson City and its flashing neon casino lights and from there into the sagebrush monotony of the desert. Only the fringes of the Carson River, and irrigated agriculture around Lahontan Reservoir, broke the otherwise barren landscape. About 40 miles east of Carson City, in a swale formed by gently sloping hills, is where the Bureau of Reclamation's effort to water the West started in 1902. In fact, the federally funded Newlands Irrigation Project was the first "reclamation" effort in the nation. But in trapping the "surplus" runoff of both the Carson and Truckee rivers to create a new alfalfa industry and a limited acreage of row crops, the system of diversion dams and distribution canals dramatically altered the natural waterscape.

Our first stop was 20 miles further east, just beyond the bustling farming, ranching, mining, and gambling hub of Fallon. There a merged national wildlife refuge and state waterfowl management area called the Stillwater Wildlife Management Area nestled in the shadow of the mountain range of the same name. Inside his modest little office beside Fallon's even more modest airport, refuge manager Morris LeFever offered a warm welcome and remarkable curiosity about the sampling project. "I was stationed at Kesterson once and have followed what is happening there very closely," he said.

For good reason. The whole midsection of Nevada had once been covered by ancient Lake Lahontan. Even after the massive inland sea disappeared in the wake of the continent's last great ice age, the sprawling desert depression at the foot of the Stillwaters became a vast and fertile marsh. There is rich archaeological evidence that Indians thrived around the ancient marsh for at least 5,000 years, feasting on its clouds of waterfowl, its rich fishery, and a variety of big game animals and marsh mammals.

But the steady intrusion of irrigated agriculture in this century has altered the marsh dramatically. As the river flows were diverted to irrigate the desert, Stillwater slowly retreated, shrinking from its historic size of nearly 100,000 acres to barely a fifth of that size. Instead of being rejuvenated each spring by the freshets tumbling down the Carson and Truckee rivers, the marsh was shriveling into a salt-crusted sink, fed almost solely by leftover farm drainage. Maps in some of the historical reports showed signs that selenium would turn up in both soil outcroppings and plants. As at Kesterson, the drainage canals that fed Stillwater were almost certain to be loading it also with dissolved selenium and other toxic trace elements leached from the salty, mineralized desert soil and scattered volcanic outcroppings known to serve as host rock for the element. Maps in hand, Glenda and I headed out to tour the refuge, starting with two of the main drainage canals that served as the area's water supply. I stuffed handfuls of algae and smelly organic ooze into the sample bottles.

Soft, spring winds spilled down the Lahontan Valley from tne snow-crested scarp of the Sierra to the west, rustling cattails and bulrushes around the sprawling oasis of Nevada's otherwise arid heartland. But even in such a sylvan setting there were disconcerting signs of trouble. The lakes and ponds of the refuge, swollen to overflowing by extremely wet winters three years before, had now shrunk to less than half their former size. Whatever materials had been brought to them by excess flows from the eastward-flowing Truckee and Carson and the southwest-draining Humboldt River were being rapidly concentrated. Bathtub rings of death circled Cattail, Alkali, Foxtail, Lead, and Dry lakes. Thousands of rotting fish carcasses lined their shores, a putrid belt of carp and smaller tui chub. They were the victims of either increasing levels of hazardous compounds, salinity, or both. Dead muskrats hung from debris-draped skeletons of long-inundated salt cedar and other shoreline brush.

But the circuitous banks of T. J. Canal, which drains the saline Paiute–Shoshone Indian Reservation land, yielded an even more unsettling discovery. There we found the decomposed remains of eighteen white pelicans dotting the gray-green carpet of sage and grasslands like clumps of snow. Others were scattered in the desert brush around nearby Carson Sink. The stately birds make a daily 40-mile round trip from their island nesting colonies on Pyramid Lake to feed in the shallow, chub-rich waters of Stillwater. The long-distance feeding increased as upstream diversions from the Truckee River caused Pyramid's water level to drop precipitously, wiping out both the shallow feeding flats and the once abundant but now endangered supply of qui-oui, a small, chublike fish that was the pelicans' main menu item. The shallow flats where small fish congregate are vital to the birds because, unlike the oceangoing brown pelicans, they don't dive-bomb but merely dunk for their prey.

Stillwater has changed dramatically, too. Centuries before, the swelling marsh harbored a rich and diverse wildlife population, springing to life just where the Carson and Truckee rivers were ending theirs, in the sinks of the Nevada desert, about 60 miles east of the present-day gambling mecca of Reno. Geese, ducks, cranes, swans, rails, and migratory waterfowl and shorebirds of every imaginable description had once blackened the skies over thousands of acres of marsh, meadow, and shimmering desert playas, dried-up lakebeds. Beaver, otter, lynx, and muskrats had foraged in and around ponds thick with protein-rich duckweed and algae mats, where large schools of fish fed voraciously on the rich storehouse of invertebrates and swarms of brine flies and shrimp. But that was a long time ago.

Generations of Shoshone and Paiute Indians also flourished around the banks of the mighty marsh then, as scores of burial mounds along its reedy shoreline attest. Uncovered by the cycle of droughts that parched this land in the mid-to-late 1980s, these shallow entombments and the artifacts, middens, and shell mounds that surround them show that Stillwater Marsh was once home to abundantly more—and more varied—wildlife than now.

We finished an extensive driving and walking tour of the marsh and wound up back at the refuge office just in time to catch LeFever and his chief wildlife biologist, Steve Thompson, before they left for the day. They were shocked that we had found so many dead pelicans just by casual observation in so short a time. Death on a refuge is no stranger. But lately, they said, it was occurring in epidemic proportions and with increasing frequency at Stillwater. The trend had become so discouraging that Thompson often sardonically called the place "Deadwater."

"There is something terribly wrong with this place," said LeFever. "Death seems to be stalking us all the time. It's just one thing after another." Thompson, who had come back into the cramped office from another "death patrol" of the marsh, was feeling more like a mortician than a biologist. "I got into this business because of my love for wildlife and places that could be a true refuge for them. Here I spend more time taggin' and baggin' wildlife than I do looking after them. It is really depressing," he said. (Shortly after LeFever's comments were published in *The Bee,* he was scolded sharply by superiors for speaking too candidly about the marsh's problems and transferred to another refuge in northern Oregon. Thompson, also verbally disciplined, lasted longer but eventually was transferred to Texas.)

As our interview drew to a close, LeFever eased up out of his squeaky chair and opened one of the drawers in the filing cabinet against which I was leaning. Glenda had returned to the privacy of the car, never one to intrude on the business parts of our many trips together. As LeFever riffled through the files, he stopped here and there to thumb through anecdotal accounts of repeated cycles of fish kills and botulism outbreaks that had piled up year after year. One sheaf of papers carried body counts from the botulism epidemics, and others had reports of rapidly declining productivity among redhead ducks. Stillwater was besieged. "We had to stack the carcasses from the botulism outbreak into big piles and set them ablaze like a bonfire. The smell was revolting," said LeFever. But no one had ever mounted a serious search for the cause.

Both LeFever and Thompson were aware that the initial diagnosis of a 15,683-bird die-off at Kesterson had been ascribed to "avian cholera" by deputy regional Fish and Wildlife Service director Joe Blum in Portland in January 1985. They knew, too, that Harry Ohlendorf had written to Blum, reminding him that the service's own Wildlife Health Center in Madison, Wisconsin, had diagnosed selenium toxicosis as the cause of death in thirteen of fifteen birds and strongly suspected it in all five other birds Ohlendorf sent in for inspection. (The Bureau of Reclamation was chided two years later for repeating the avian cholera misdiagnosis of another 103 birds collected from Kesterson, also victims of selenium poisoning.)[3] "We don't know what to make of these increasing botulism outbreaks," said LeFever. "Is it really botulism or is it caused directly or, perhaps, even indirectly by selenium? We don't know. But someone had better start finding out soon, while we still have the chance."

That was not the kind of dialogue for a good night's sleep. But in a morbid kind of way, it boosted the prospect of finding selenium's impact at our very first stop. We resumed our selenium circuit the next morning under crisp desert skies. From the outskirts of Fallon and its rich hay meadows—the last irrigated vegetation for hundreds of miles—the shimmering path of pavement led past a lonely brothel and the nearby Fallon Air Station, with its jet fighter bombing and gunnery range. The road twisted around the toe of the Stillwaters, just beyond the last "Beware: Low-Flying Aircraft" sign. I wondered what kind of evasive action a motorist was expected to take if confronted with the chilling sight of a fully armed jet fighter streaking right at him only 50 feet off the deck of that barren stretch of salt flats. It never happened to me, but ranchers from nearby Dixie Valley swear they have been blown right off their tractors by the wind shear accompanying the wake of even subsonic overflights that close to the ground. The cracked plaster of their walls and broken windows of their modest ranch homes attest to the impacts of sound-barrier-cracking flight when speeds go sonic. But by midday, all of that was far behind us and the boring, almost hypnotic, miles of Highway 50—the "Loneliest Road in America"—began to take their toll. The geologically fascinating Basin and Range country can rivet attention for only so long, even for a rockhound like me.

Conversations with my wife were more than a diversion. We loved to drive the back roads reminiscing about the past and dreaming of the future. But those lively discussions finally petered out. To fight the boredom, I tried estimating how far it was from the top of one pass, down through the valley, and up to the next one. But the monotony turned my mind to mush. More often than not, I forgot to check the odometer until we were halfway through the next Basin and Range combination. Some people fight the tedium by counting the number of road-kill jackrabbits or, at night, the real live thing, when the light-blinded hares careen wildly along, rather than across, the pavement. But the mid-1980s must have been the bottom of the bunny cycle, for we saw few of the former and none of the latter. The number of other vehicles we encountered, in either direction, could be counted with the fingers on one hand. Any distraction, however trivial, was welcomed.

What seemed like hours of silence later, my copilot suddenly leaned forward, peering intently ahead. "What's that . . . there . . . on the right shoulder?" she asked. "A coyote?" My eyes strained the mile or so up the road. Too far. Finally, the dark object lunching on a road kill took shape. A huge golden eagle, wings spread protectively over the kill, turned, eyed our approaching vehicle, and hopped off to one side as we passed. That generated another burst of talk until the repetitious pattern of Basin and Range, Basin and Range, numbed our senses again.

My mind drifted back over the last few months of activity. Here I was, streaking across the plains toward South Dakota and a bunch of watering holes I had never seen, attempting a project no other journalist in his right mind would consider. One of the keys to success hinged on my winning over a sometimes recalcitrant retired surgeon in Rapid City. His home state would be the halfway point of our looping journey through Nevada, Utah, Wyoming, South Dakota, Montana, Idaho, Oregon, and then back home. The doctor had done this kind of thing before. He'd know what to look for, and where and how. Moreover, he claimed to have voluminous files on the subject, with names, places, and dates . . . and, best of all, lots of test results from other sampling programs, some of them done half a century ago.

Why him? Maybe it was because he had followed Ivan Barnes to the podium on that March 1985 program of the Berkeley symposium and had seemed so straight-spoken. Too, he had just the right touch of belligerence that captivates journalists. Or maybe it was just his stance, that banty-rooster cockiness, and the thick glasses, which gave his deep-set eyes a rather owlish look. But there was a current of electricity when he spoke, an anticipation in the audience that something interesting was about to happen. His name, Dr. Arthur W. Kilness, certainly had been making the rounds among the biologists studying the Kesterson syndrome. For months, Felix Smith had hardly been able to finish a selenium conversation (the only kind he was having) without qualifying it with, "Well, Doc Kilness says that . . ."

Kilness looked anything but imposing when he settled himself behind the lectern that day, nervously setting and resetting eyeglasses that kept sliding down the high, thin bridge of his nose. He was small and wiry, about 5 feet 7 inches tall and no more than 150 pounds. He looked the crowd over carefully and spoke straight out in a quavery, high-pitched voice: "I haven't been hired by anybody . . . so I can't be fired by anybody. I can say just about what I want to, and I am not promoting anyone's special interest."

The symposium had been a long, hard day of deeply technical presentations, some of them more boring than interesting to the several hundred scientists, academics, environmentalists, and journalists. Then this strutting little doctor from Rapid City pulled the plug on all the tension among the sometimes stuffy scholars and scientists. The burst of laughter was heartier than the remark deserved, but it came against a backdrop of charges that Wildlife Service biologists still were being muzzled by superiors. Some were not allowed to present reports, the charges ran, or had had their papers heavily censored for "policy implications." Several references to such politicized manipulation had peppered the earlier parts of the one-day conference.[*] Rumors had been circulating that representatives of the powerful agricultural industry would attempt to filibuster the proceedings, as they had the previous selenium conference in Davis in February 1984. The setting may have been collegial, but there was tension in the room.

This general practitioner from the country lectured a roomful of hydrologists, geochemists, wildlife biologists, and Ph.D.-holding researchers about the chemistry, botany, and toxicology of this rediscovered element. It was an unlikely matchup of speaker and audience. But Kilness turned out to be far more than some precocious and presumptuous country doctor. He had forsaken a comfortable general practice to become a board-certified surgeon and still served as a member of the surgical staff at the University of South Dakota School of Medicine in Vermillion. Instead of retiring after severe arthritis forced him to undergo double hip replacement, Kilness became a clinical researcher, devoting himself almost full-time to selenium issues he had been following in his native state—and sometimes far afield—for nearly forty years.

Kilness seemed a natural and valuable source: someone who could cover the history, botany, geology, toxicity, and medical health implications of this bewildering compound undaunted by an audience of so many single-discipline specialists. He was one of the country's few medical doctors who understood—and conceded—selenium's dual role as not only an essential micronutrient for humans and most animals but also a toxic trace element five times more potent than arsenic. And he was the only doctor in the nation with a caseload of patients diagnosed and treated for selenium poisoning.

But there was another side to this Dakota bantam that gave me pause for reflection. During a break in the afternoon session of the conference, I went up and introduced myself. Although we had spoken over the phone a few times, this was our first encounter. The exchange was more crisp than cordial, more guarded than garrulous. There was a streak of suspicion in Doc, a defensiveness that hadn't seemed so evident before. Still, Smith, Ohlendorf, and others swore by his grasp of the subject and his independence and frankness. Reproach seemed a small price to pay for a frank, knowledgeable, and independent source, someone able to chart passages through rough terrain. So my efforts to enlist his aid continued. Slowly, stubbornly, the reticence melted. An interview back in Rapid City was promised . . . and quickly arranged before he changed his mind. But assistance was conditional. There surfaced, in that exchange and countless others, almost to his death nearly four years later, a perplexing point and counterpoint of promise and withdrawal, munificence and manipulation. Offers were hinted, not quite spelled out, then quickly qualified or just withdrawn.

"I have, perhaps, the greatest single collection of research material on selenium in the world," he said one minute, implying access and open interviews. But, always, the conditional shadow-boxing followed. "But I have never opened it to anyone," he added. "There are a lot of people who would love to get their hands on it for their own purposes. Just what do you plan to do with all of this information?" he asked, without hesitation or subtlety. "What do you intend to write about this?"

Two could play that game, I thought. "The truth," I parried, "if I can find it. No one tells me what to write, though they often presume to tell me how," I added, in a snide reference to editors. "Only the facts dictate or constrain what I write," I added shamelessly. "All I have to do is find them."

There was not so much chemistry in the exchange as contention. Maybe the reply was just presumptuous or irreverent enough to pique his own curiosity. In any case, it had worked. Weeks later, as my planning drew to a nervous close, the phone on the cluttered project desk back in Sacramento had rung at a surprisingly early hour. That was another of the country doctor's traits soon to be discovered: early rising. He picked up the conversation as if there had been but a moment's passing since our brief exchange in Berkeley. "Well," he barked, "when are you coming out here to start finding out the truth?"

It had not been the beginning of one of those long and wonderful friendships you sometimes hear about. It was more a relationship than a friendship, certainly at the start. But it was interesting and it was eventful. In fact, there were times when it seemed it would not last the hour, much less the days, weeks, or months ahead. But at the start, our sparring relationship played a key role indeed in getting the project launched.

The miles and hours of Nevada's stretch of Highway 50 dragged endlessly on, through the Basin and Range country, climbing steadily over New Pass Summit, elevation 6,348 feet, down through another valley and then twisting back up the Toiyabe Range, past the worn-out little mining town of Austin. It was like that for hours, our passage marked seemingly by only the summit signs: Hickison and Pinto summits that flanked the town of Eureka, then Pancake, Little Antelope, Robinson summits, and, in the dark, way ahead, the lights of Ely. The next day offered more of the same: Confusion Range, then basin; Spring Range, then basin; Thomas Range, then basin; all trending from northwest to southeast. Finally, we nudged into the western fringe of Mormon heartland. You knew by the place-names. "Entering Deseret," read the road sign, then "Hinckley," then "Delta," and on up to "Nephi." Interstate 15 took us through Spanish Fork, through Provo and its famed Brigham Young University, and on to Salt Lake City.

Phone interviews the next day brought the first disappointment of the trip. Successive winters of major snowfall had sent the Great Salt Lake spilling over thousands of surrounding acres of desert plain, flooding most of the Bear River National Wildlife Refuge. The Bear River drainage basin was another of those reported to contain signs of selenium source rock. Other nearby points where random sampling was expected to yield fruit were similarly flooded. One was Lake Utah, west of Orem and Provo. Lake Utah is fed by the Provo River, and the canyon through which it flows is thickly layered with some of the West's most seleniferous shale formations. In fact, the nation's highest single selenium concentration in such shales was found in Provo Canyon in a sample with 96 ppm.[5] Another promising alternative was the complex of slag ponds at the huge Kennicott copper mine and smelter, just across the interstate from the southeastern corner of Great Salt Lake. Sierra Club members had told me of recent large die-offs of California gulls there. But access to those, too, was cut off by floodwaters. (The commercial production of selenium is a by-product of copper smelting, as copper ore is one of the many sulfide ore bodies in which the element is routinely found.)

Detoured by nature, our mission took us into the semiarid desert of south central Utah, where geological maps had indicated selenium in the region's prolific surface coal deposits. I had heard reports of highly saline seeps in the valley below the coal-studded cliffs, some with dissolved salt levels twice those of seawater. Our sampling target, Desert Lake Waterfowl Management Area, was south of Price and just northeast of the tiny farming hamlet of Cleveland. Most of the farming there, as near Kesterson, was on the rich alluvial fans that spread east out of the mountain canyons. And as at Kesterson, there was a federal irrigation project, widespread strata of semipermeable clay, and buried drainpipes that fed a series of oblong evaporation ponds which had been converted into a wildlife refuge. Desert Lake did have one variation from the Kesterson mold. It was not wholly a dead-end terminal. In spring, when the freshet is strong, an outlet at the south end of a series of five ponds allowed overflow to a small creek that is tributary to the Green River.

I arose at the crack of dawn, dressed quietly, and headed south, while Glenda luxuriated in the surprisingly elegant inn in the nearby mining city of Price. It was a warm spring day. The sky was full of fleecy white clouds. Only a slight breeze rippled the water of the marsh.

There were no body bags or blazing bonfires at Desert Lake. But there was something almost as unsettling. The same eerie silence that spooked Smith and Ohlendorf at Kesterson pervaded the isolated Desert Lake. It was a stark and unnerving contrast to the pulsating marsh chorus of croaking frogs, chirping crickets, and other harbingers of the birth and death of day. A wall of round-stem bulrush formed an impenetrable palisade around the ponds. It should have been alive with the raucous cacophony of blackbirds, the wheeling, screeching presence of grackles and other bird life. Instead I heard only the steady thrum of the wind and the sandpapery scrubbing of the rushes against each other, punctuating the silence of the high desert. The only sign of bird life at all was the family of locally nesting Canada geese across the pond: a white-cheeked drake and hen proudly convoying a solitary gosling.

For hours I lunged through the thick rushes, slogging through knee-deep and smelly black muck of the pond bottoms, in search of birds or at least their nests. Occasionally I paused to scoop up samples. But I found neither birds nor nests nor eggs. Nothing. Criss-crossing the adjacent meadow and hay field, I circled back. Again, nothing. Not a single nest from which egg samples could be collected. I did see, however, clumps of woody aster and prince's plume scattered around the edge of the isolated marsh. They are the same species of telltale accumulator plants that University of Wyoming research chemist Orville Beath used to trace the path of selenium across the West.

Glenda and I spent most of the rest of the trip northeast, to Doc's house, sightseeing. Between Price and Rapid City, we made only one other sampling stop: at another Kesterson-like region in Utah's far northeastern corner. One of the geological maps showing distribution of selenium source rock had assigned a big kelly-green splotch to the encircling crescent of low-lying hills around Vernal, not far from the Dinosaur National Monument. But although I sampled creeks and drainage canals downslope of the shale-laden foothills, I could find no obvious organisms to check for the possibility of biomagnification of selenium up the food chain. That shortcoming was solved by a pair of young boys hiking back from Stewart Lake Waterfowl Management Area, just south of nearby Jensen. One carried a string of catfish. They were one small, ugly, bewhiskered fish lighter and ten dollars richer after our chance meeting . . . and, no doubt, confirmed believers of all the tales they would ever hear about "crazy Californians."

There was still time, that day, for a side trip to the Dinosaur National History State Museum in Vernal and then a trip out to the actual dinosaur quarry, where we watched paleontologists unearth the relics of another era. The brief wait at the visitors center for the bus to the quarry yielded another bonus. There, among colorful pictures of the wildlife, vegetation, and geological specimens of the low-lying shale bluffs, was a photograph of a desert prince's plume, one of the unique selenium indicator plants. Underneath was an explanation that the plume was a common sight in the area, as the subsequent bus ride proved. There were hundreds of them sprouting on selenium-rich soil just uphill from the intensively irrigated fields around Stewart Lake.

Back in the car we swung north again, along Highway 191, through Wyoming's Flaming Gorge National Recreation Area, along the Green River to Rock Springs and Interstate 80. It was the West at its best, long, straight stretches of uncrowded highway, splitting the green-splashed spring of Sweetwater County's high-mountain plateau country and over the Medicine Bow Range to Laramie and, then, Cheyenne. Almost always present on this drive through the high desert country were the buff-colored outcroppings of marine shale. Barnes's dramatic estimates of "thousands of square miles" of source-rock formations were beginning to seem less and less exaggerated.

But the science was deferred. The rich scenery was more captivating. Each dip and turn in the road, it seemed, was marked with discovery: a herd of antelope grazing in a draw, bands of elk browsing among the leafing alders of a bubbling mountain creek, even the startling sight of a wolverine, loping in its familiar hump-backed gait across an isolated ridge.

We turned north again, at Cheyenne, and drove through the historic Chugwater country of western badlands days and then along the North Platte River to Bridger's Crossing and Douglas. It was hard to keep focused on poisonous trace elements and deformed ducklings when every road sign or place-name reeked of western lore. Mile after breathless mile of the Thunder Basin National Grassland was polka-dotted with the white rumps of antelope, hundreds of them, grazing peacefully on the remnant of native short-grass prairie. But for the absence of bison, and the presence of an occasional barbed-wire fence, much of it looked like it must have centuries ago.

We turned hard right, and east again, at Gillette and took Highway 14 to and over the Black Hills, the signs once more evoking great history: Sundance, Beulah, Spearfish, Lead, Sturgis, and Deadwood, the now-resurrected gambling town where Wild Bill Hickok cashed in his final chips at Saloon No. 10. Finally, our dust-covered sedan was weaving around most of the chuckholes along quaint Chapel Valley Road, in Rapid City, and to the quiet cul-de-sac where Doc lived.

Two months had passed since the barked invitation "to come out here . . . and start looking for the truth." But even after months of intensive study and planning, I felt more anxiety than eagerness. It is one thing to hit the road in search of secret reports and feisty minority opinions, invoking the Freedom of Information Act to obtain documents from secretive bureaucrats and playing off one side's experts against the other's. Investigative reporters do that all the time—mining one known vein of information to discover the next—but the process feeds ravenously on paper and dozens of diverse sources.

This was different. My search was for something that could neither be seen, smelled, nor touched, except only indirectly through the indicator plants. I had seen only a smattering of the explicit reports that chronicle so much of selenium's history of western impact. Throughout the trip I had struggled continuously to stifle morbid hopes that I would find nests full of dead or deformed ducklings or pastures littered with dead livestock, any visible evidence of selenium's toxic presence. Here, at last, was an expert source to tap, some files to read, some secrets to discover, some sites to visit, some victims to interview. Doc had promised that and more. He had promised to open the vault of a lifetime of research.

I mounted the cement steps to the front door and rang the bell. The door opened, Doc's owlish eyes peered out, flickered in recognition, and then were followed by the rest of his banty-rooster frame, bony hand thrust forward in welcome. The greeting was stiff and awkward, but quite tolerable compared to the discomfort of the interview that was to follow. Somehow the tables were turned. Instead of the journalist, it was the crusty country doctor who was doing all of the challenging, questioning not only my motive but my competence.

There was no guile in Doc. As I was to discover through the demanding days, weeks, and months ahead, he was as unpretentious as he was unambiguous. He could be curt and impersonal one minute, almost brusque, as he probed and plumbed your knowledge, interest, and commitment. But if your bruised ego and battered pride could survive his challenging, he could be warm and engagingly candid the next. There was no room for doubt: Doc was in charge. But if he felt your interest was sincere and your commitment clear, he could be absolutely unstinting in his help.

Those first demanding hours were rougher than expected. Make the mistake of interjecting when Doc was only out of breath, not observation, and your lines would be swept away in a torrent. But Kilness also was an absolute sucker for the truth and a little honest bewilderment. Roll the eyes helplessly, turn on a smile of surrender, and shake your head in unabashed puzzlement and he would show more patient explanation and insight than you could ever have expected.

The information trickled out at first. An anecdote here, a frayed and yellowed newspaper clipping there, and, always, the promise, just the scant promise, of access to the rich inventory held in the battered metal filing cabinets in the corner of the living room. A flurry of his pointed questions, many revealing my sweeping ignorance on the subject, unlocked the gate of suspicion and reserve. Doc had gestured, for hours, toward the filing cabinets. But not once had he moved any closer to them.

Then, without warning, he rose from the couch, crossed to the cabinets, eased open one of the drawers, and brought out a bundle of tabbed, bulging file folders. Each held a treasure of articles from newspapers, medical journals, dog-eared case files of his own patients, correspondence with other researchers, and government and private reports. And there were data sets on hundreds of samples analyzed for selenium in the blood of his patients, in the food they ate, the forage of their livestock, the soil of their gardens . . . the works. Some dated back more than sixty years. Doc doled them out slowly the first few days, explaining each with painstaking deliberation. Whether because his own patience ran out or his eagerness overcame restraint, Doc's caution and reserve melted away in a torrent of presentation. Out of those battered filing drawers came a lifetime of research, sometimes in a bewildering, overwhelming flood.

Xerox stock must have jumped that week in Rapid City. Copies coughed up by the score until I had enough in hand to prepare the foundation for *The Bee*'s special report. By the fourth day, even Doc had tired of the paper chase. The lecturing, the patient explanations, the promises of interviews with victims, ended. It was time to hit the road.

Chapter 5 | **TRAIL**
of
TRAGEDY

We didn't have far to go, Kilness and I, an unlikely duo of country-doctor-turned-researcher and journalist-cum-apprentice. As my wife preferred her own company and sightseeing to the world of high science, she took in the museums, galleries, and historical points of interest in Rapid City. On the outskirts of town, where a new shopping mall was being bulldozed out of the prairie sod, Kilness scrambled up a small hill with an agility that belied his two artificial hips. Suddenly he bent down, plucked some beautiful purple wildflowers from the yellowish dirt, and thrust them at me for inspection.

"Smell them!" he ordered. The pungent odor is neither pleasant nor soon forgotten. It was not unlike the distinctive bouquet remembered from my school days back in Canada, when a seatmate in English literature popped a garlic capsule and rolled it under the teacher's desk.

"Notice the shape of the blossoms and how they droop from the stem," said the surgeon-turned-botanist. "This is *Astragalus bisulcatus*. It grows only where there is a high concentration of selenium. It's like a flag for the stuff. Wherever you see it, there is selenium."

For both *bisulcatus* and its myriad selenium indicator relatives, that is true. But it isn't necessarily true in reverse. There are places where elevated selenium levels occur and neither *bisulcatus* nor *Astragalus pectinatus* . . . nor *Stanleya pinnata, Haplopappus fremontii, Oonopsis condensata,* nor any other of the unique selenium flags grow. But where the some twenty-seven species or varieties of the pealike milk vetch, mustard, prince's plume, goldenrod, or woody aster grow, high levels of selenium are invariably present.[1]

On that trip, and others later, Kilness spotted the telltale flags with amazing regularity . . . and in or near some unsettling places. The speed of the passing car didn't seem to inhibit his hawklike vision either. Once, on the sprawling southern outskirts of Denver, when we were looking for other problem areas in 1988, he pointed out a new subdivision springing up on the east side of I-25. "If those people eat too much garden produce," and many of the houses had large backyard gardens, "they could get more selenium than they bargained for . . . and never know where it came from or what it was that made them sick," he said, jamming his thumb into the passenger-side window as he gestured toward the location. "Five years ago, this whole area was alive with *Xylorrhiza* at this time of year."

Doc was like that. It was hard for him to abandon the vocabulary of the researcher. Out of the corner of his eye, appearing to look straight ahead, he watched the puzzled frown spread across my face. After an appropriately humbling pause, and with a sly grin creasing his weathered face, he added: "Oh, yeah. I keep forgetting. You haven't memorized the names yet. That would be woody aster. You know, the ones I showed you up on Mike Henry's spread in Edgemont, the ones with the white daisylike flowers."

The aster's common name may have slipped from memory, but not the details of the young South Dakota rancher and his costly selenium lesson in the Edgemont Valley. There, tucked away in the remote southwest corner of the state, almost surrounded by the Buffalo Gap National Grassland, a carpet of untamed native grasses stretched off to the horizon in every direction, broken only by the distant outline of the Black Hills to the north.

Mike Henry was the first patient Doc trusted me with during that summer selenium tour of 1985. He was almost the last, too. A third-generation rancher who doubled as a county road grader to make ends meet, Henry took us on a tour through his pastures, bringing his pickup to a shuddering stop at the top of a rise, near what looked like a pile of junk and old rags. It wasn't. As we walked up the sloping hill, the junk came into focus as piles of cow bones. The "old rags" were rotting carcasses, dozens of them, piled crazy-quilt atop one another. Henry had made the discovery of the old bone pile nearly five years before, just after escrow had closed on his new ranch and new stock had been turned out on the range.

He scuffed the debris around with the toe of a well-worn boot. "It hit me like a bolt out of the blue," said Henry. "There's an old well right here, nearly a hundred feet deep and three feet across . . . and it's chock full of carcasses. The prior owner used it for a bone hole, but I didn't know that then. I've got a couple of my own piles now, just over the rise," he added, pointing to the south. There, outlined against the lush spring green of the unbroken prairie and framed by the widest sky in the world, were the relics of the lethal, natural poison at work. Both the sight and smell were jarring: hundreds of dead livestock, worth tens of thousands of dollars, were rotting, bloated, or bleached white in the hot prairie sun and chilling winters. "It's not a pretty sight, not now and not when they are dying either," mumbled Henry. "It's more than just the money. A rancher loves his animals, loves to see them strong and healthy, grazing out here to their heart's content. You hate to see them suffer."

But suffer they do. Livestock have suffered painful death from selenium ever since the pioneers first started driving them into the then-virgin prairie. Only then the symptoms were called "alkali disease" or "the blind staggers." Hardly a cowboy movie was ever made without scenes of one or both maladies, shrinking water holes framed by carcasses and bone piles, often marked with the familiar cattle skull nailed to the nearest post or tree as a warning. Drovers thought the death potion was the alkali salt crust or some "poison" in the water.

They had it partly right. Selenium in those small ponds easily could have been concentrated to levels lethal to horses, cows, or even humans. Or it could have combined with arsenic to do the same thing. While arsenic counters the poisonous effects of selenium in an acidic environment, the elements actually magnify each other's toxic impact in a wet alkaline environment. And much of the semiarid plateau country of the West is decidedly alkaline. (On the logarithmic scale of chemical neutrality, the pH scale, 7 equals the midpoint. Each successive numerical increase, up or down, represents an effective gain of ten times. Hence, a reading of 8 is ten times more alkaline than 7, and a reading of 9 is a hundred times more so. The same ratios apply toward the lower part of the scale that measures acidity.)

In Mike Henry's case, as in countless hundreds or thousands of others across the western states, the animals died from what the ranchers called "the blind staggers," the malady brought on by chronic exposure to low levels of selenium in the grass and brush they ate. Selenium's more acute form of poisoning, known widely as "alkali disease," is believed to be caused by inorganic forms of selenium that the primary indicator plants assimilate and then convert into deadly organic forms. These protein compounds represent a dual risk. Not only are they more toxic, per gram, but because they have been rendered more soluble they are more easily picked up by the roots of virtually all other vegetation. "Only *Astragalus* plants and other indicator species can pick selenium up from the soil when it is in elemental or inorganic forms," explained Kilness. "But every time one of them dies, it lays down a death halo of selenium available to virtually all other kinds of vegetation."

To emphasize his point, Doc dug into his jacket pocket and produced a well-worn monograph on the subject that he had fished out of the filing cabinet the night before: "The Story of Selenium in Wyoming," by the late Orville A. Beath, selenium's premier researcher. Kilness turned to dog-eared page 17 and read aloud: "At the onset of acute poisoning (alkali disease), the movement of the animal becomes abnormal. The animal is likely to walk a short distance with an uncertain gait and then stop and assume a characteristic stance, with head lowered and ears drooped. Dark, watery diarrhea usually develops. The temperature is elevated. The pulse is rapid and weak, 90 to 300. Respiration is labored, with mucous rales, and there may be bloody froth from the air passages. Bloating is usually pronounced and is accompanied by abdominal pain. Urine excretion is greatly increased. The mucous membranes are pale or bluish in color. The pupils are dilated. Before death there is complete prostration and apparent unconsciousness. Death is due to respiratory failure."

We were still parked on a knoll of Henry's ranch, the light breeze bending the sea of prairie grass in a rhythmic, waving pulse as Doc turned the page. The signature of the chronic "blind staggers" turned out to be only slightly less gory. While the end result may be the same— death due to respiratory failure—the pathways to it differ. In the first stage, Doc droned on, "stricken animals exhibit a marked tendency to wander, frequently in circles. The animal disregards objects in its path; it stumbles over them or walks into them. It will attempt to walk through a fence or will bump a solid object, such as a post or wall. In this stage, the body temperature and respiration are normal. The animal shows little desire to eat or drink, and may suffer impaired vision. The third and final stage is paralysis and, usually, extreme emaciation."

Henry didn't know any of this when his father staked him to the 1,600-acre spread of grassland in 1980. But he nodded knowingly as Doc read on about the second stage and more aimless wandering: "Instead of turning to one side or backing up to avoid a solid obstruction, the animal insists on going forward. It tends to carry its weight on its hind legs and may rest its head or neck in a slumped position against the solid wall or other object it has encountered. Thereafter, the front legs weaken more [and] the animal slumps to the ground. Temperature and respiration are still normal but vision becomes greatly impaired and the animal shows no interest in eating or drinking. The third and final stage is one of paralysis. The tongue and the mechanism of swallowing become partially or totally paralyzed. The animal is nearly blind. Respiration becomes labored and accelerated. There is evidence of great abdominal pain, which may have been marked even in the second stage. The pain causes constant grating of the teeth and driveling. The body temperature is subnormal. The eyelids are swollen and inflamed, and the cornea is distinctly cloudy. The mucous membrane of the mouth is pale. In most cases, the third stage comes on suddenly and is followed by death within a few hours." Again, death is due to respiratory failure.

No one knows how many hundreds or thousands of animals owned by other western farmers and ranchers are, or have been, similarly afflicted. Nor is it known how many times such tainted properties change hands to owners as unsuspecting as Mike Henry. He had bought what he had been led to believe was a healthy ranch, trucked in some prime cattle, sheep, and horses from his dad's ranch, and started up his own outfit. By 1985, his accumulated losses had soared beyond $60,000 and the cattle or sheep that hadn't dropped dead were still in trouble.

"We're still trying to put weight back on some of the cows that nearly died that first year we came on the place," said Henry. "They just can't seem to get over it. They're still bone thin." It was more sudden than that for four cows and twelve calves that became selenium victims in the first four months, dying painful and agonizingly mysterious deaths. They were only bones, period, in the summer of 1985. But none of the losses was more sudden than one in the spring of that year when one of his prize remaining Herefords "ate just one of those damn weeds . . . it must have been the only one in the pasture," Henry recounted glumly. "Boom. She was down in thirty minutes," he went on. "Dead as a stone. We lost both her and the calf she was carrying."

Henry had heard about Kilness and his knowledge about similar problems throughout the region three years before. He was trying to control the selenium-accumulating *Astragalus* weeds, either chopping them down with a hoe or spraying them with herbicides. But that wouldn't do anything about the organic selenium still in the soil or the pasture grass, which routinely contains about 20 ppm of the element and sometimes as much as 90 ppm. (The U.S. Department of Agriculture guideline for toxicity recommends that livestock not consume vegetation with levels above 3 ppm.) But at least the physical removal of the plants stopped further conversion to the form that threatened sudden death. One plant I dug up in the lower pasture that day was later found to contain 252 ppm. That figure pales, however, against the 14,500 ppm selenium recorded in an *Astragalus* plant collected from the same pasture a few years earlier by Kilness. (Orville Beath, when he was the dean of selenium researchers at the University of Wyoming and author of two definitive volumes on the subject, wrote that the primary indicator or accumulator plants he collected routinely held from 1,000 to 10,000 ppm.)

The poisoned plants were not much kinder to Henry's sheep. "The conception rate of the ewes was just terrible," he related. "We got only 89 lambs when we should have had at least 120, and most of those were badly deformed." Indeed. "They had clubbed feet and legs turned almost inside out they were so crooked," recounted the rancher, ticking off other deformities like misshapen heads and eyes, not unlike those that biologists Smith and Ohlendorf found in the coots and ducks at Kesterson. Striding back to the pickup, Henry scuffed the dun-colored soil of the pasture. "This is our hottest pasture," he said. "Selenium levels here [in the pasture grass] are 19 to 90 ppm. The cattle can stand it for only three months in the fall, when the levels are lower, but only if you can keep them away from the accumulator weeds." Then, sweeping his arm in a wide arc to the west, he added: "This whole valley, clear into Wyoming, is like this."

Henry was left with few options and a dream he couldn't seem to keep alive. He kept trying to dilute the effect of the tainted grass, buying as much clean feed from out of the area as his modest wages with the county road crew allowed. Their wood-frame house was weather-beaten, the paint chipped and peeling. It was not the perfect ranch home, framed by manicured lawns, shade trees, and painted picket fence, that Henry and his wife, Bonita, had dreamed about when they started out.

Even their grocery bills grew higher than the budget allowed because they couldn't trust home-raised vegetables, milk, and home-cured meat. "We can't even have fresh eggs, for heaven's sake," said Bonita, in obvious frustration, one leg swinging back and forth as she sat on the back stoop. "We can't raise chickens out here. They are all deformed when anything does hatch. It really makes you feel cheated. It isn't like we dreamed it would be at all."

Veterinarians have been little help to Henry and others like him. Taught virtually nothing in school about the toxicity of selenium, they almost always diagnose the puzzlingly similar symptoms as a *deficiency* of the element. An essential micronutrient, selenium is indeed necessary for healthy development and growth—that is, a few millionths of a gram per day. Selenium deficiency can cause "white muscle disease," weight and hair loss, and a variety of other ailments. But in only slightly higher doses, it triggers many of the very same ailments that its deficiency creates.

"The vets just don't know anything about this," said Henry. "They keep saying it's selenium deficiency and prescribe more of it for the livestock—inject it right into them. Hell, we had our cattle tested by Doc here after a while and they were *loaded* with the stuff. . . and the vet still wanted to pump more into them."

The samples that Kilness drew were analyzed by a contract lab with years of experience in selenium analysis. They showed blood selenium levels of 5 ppm, hair at 12 ppm, and milk levels of 10 ppm, all elevated two to five times higher than the levels associated with animal toxicity.

"So what do you do about marketing the animals?" I asked Henry, wondering whether or how he could sell enough stock to eke out a living. Kilness went beet-red, angry that one of his friends and patients had been put on the spot like that, in front of him, by an interloper from California, a journalist yet. It was not the last time that the needs of one conflicted with the loyalties of the other. Henry broke the awkward silence by admitting that he shipped his cattle to market without any warning, even though he would not let his own family eat any of the meat. "I don't know whether that is right . . . whether one person will get enough selenium often enough to hurt them. But we *should* know," he said, looking to Doc for some help. "Someone has got to start asking those kinds of questions." Doc just stood there, rod stiff and silent as a stone, never once proffering his expert opinion on the risks, even though he had shared them, explicitly, while leafing through some of his reports in Rapid City.

The Henry family had health problems. Kilness strongly suspected selenium was the cause, especially since the symptoms almost disappeared when they followed his recommendation to quit eating home-produced food. The garden was fallowed. Bottled water was used for cooking and drinking. The beef and mutton were shipped to market and replacement groceries purchased at the nearest chain supermarket. The Henrys hoped that the mix from national blending would lower their exposure risk.

"What about your neighbors? Any of them have the same kind of experience?" I asked Henry. "Oh, the other ranchers won't talk to an outsider about it," he replied. "Hell, they'll hardly even discuss it with us. But they all know what is going on. They all have the same problem to one degree or another." The trip back to Rapid City started in utter silence. Then Kilness, hurt and embarrassed by the directness of my questioning, turned toward me and let loose an angry tirade. "I told you not to do that. These are friends of mine. They agreed to talk to you only because of me. They trust me and I won't have them embarrassed or degraded." Whatever his failings, disloyalty was not one of them.

An uneasy peace was made. Reporting is not always—nor even often—a friendly process, I told him. The search for truth is never painless. The probing would remain sensitive, I promised, but it would continue. He mused and brooded about it for miles, purposefully turned sideways in the passenger's seat with his back to the driver to show his disapproval. It was a stance with which I was to become all too familiar in the days and weeks ahead. Thankfully, those bouts never lasted long. After ten or fifteen minutes of strained silence, he shifted, casually assuming a more normal posture, cleared his throat a few times, and spoke.

"People still don't like to admit that the stuff kills animals and harms people, but I've seen it do both for a very long time." He paused, then added: "It's like trying to study the dark side of the moon. You just can't get any light on it. Hardly anybody knows about it . . . and those who do don't want to talk about it. It's a conspiracy of silence. The dirty herd syndrome. Nobody talks about it . . . even here."

The location was important. Because selenium, for all the mystery and ignorance about it elsewhere, was no stranger to central and southwestern South Dakota, where it had been studied for at least as long as anywhere else on earth and, quite likely, longer. Back in Rapid City, Doc's files revealed yellowed news clippings, pages torn from medical and scientific journals, personal correspondence with other doctors and researchers, and official reports on the subject. Many of them were about the element's presence and impact in South Dakota.

His own fascination, bordering on the compulsive, started when he was working his way through medical school, moonlighting as an assistant for Dr. Einar Leifson, head of biology at the South Dakota School of Medicine in 1940. One afternoon, in Leifson's laboratory, Kilness was told to mix a culture for placement in petri dishes that Leifson was using for a test to identify and count salmonella bacteria, one strain of which—*Salmonella typhi*—causes typhoid fever.

"Be careful with that powdery stuff when you mix it," the student was told. Kilness, ever curious, asked why. "Because it is very potent," Leifson replied. Only later did Kilness learn that "the stuff" was a powdery compound of sodium selenite, its reddish color naturally imbued from the elemental form of selenium. In fact, the mixture had been patented by Leifson four years earlier and is still in use in hospitals and clinics worldwide as an effective medium for culturing strains of salmonella bacteria.

Little wonder. Leifson had discovered that given a selenium-rich environment, populations of various strains of salmonella pathogens multiply a million times in twenty-four hours.

That revelation haunted Kilness for decades. In 1982–1983, one major outbreak of salmonella poisoning, from hamburgers, was traced by government scientists to South Dakota cattle. One year later, other researchers discovered the presence of salmonella organisms in 58 percent of feed mash and 92 percent of the bone meal being sold by commercial feed mills as a selenium-fortified poultry feed—even in areas where the native feed was already laced with potentially dangerous levels.[2]

After the U.S. Department of Agriculture, in February 1987, found that four of every ten chickens sold in the country were infected with salmonella, Kilness wrote his own heavily referenced report on the possible connections. A summary of it in the international medical newsweekly *Medical Tribune* warned about the increasing use of selenium fed as a supplement to nearly all beef and dairy cattle, hogs, and virtually all poultry raised in the United States. "One factor that should be considered," he wrote, "is the emergence of selenium as a component of feed supplements for animals [because] selenium is a component of many salmonella culture media used to isolate and grow the salmonella organism.

"The continuous intake of small dosages of selenium," Kilness continued, "has been shown to result in bioaccumulation of selenium in animals [which] can result in concentrations of selenium sufficient to act as a culturing agent for salmonella. Any chemical or feed additive that promotes the growth of salmonella warrants further study. Selenium belongs in this category and may prove to be a significant factor in the increase of salmonella in farm animals and the eventual transmission to humans." (The article, "Selenium and Salmonella, Clinical Perspective," appeared in Vol. 28, No. 1, of the international medical newsweekly on January 7, 1987, when Kilness was a consultant to the Department of Laboratory Medicine at the University of South Dakota School of Medicine in Vermillion.) So far the issue has not been addressed by the medical community, the Agriculture Department, or the Food and Drug Administration, even though at least one major California poultry firm reduced the amount of selenium supplement it used after finding elevated levels of selenium in its eggs.

Einar Leifson, under whom Kilness later studied and taught, was only the first to contribute to Doc's selenium files. Another early contributor was Dr. Raymond E. Lemley, who as both a private doctor and an army physician reported on human selenium poisoning cases as early as 1941. That was only eight years after selenium was first isolated and proved to be the toxic element responsible for the ranchers' dreaded "alkali disease" and "blind staggers."

In a 1941 article published in the British medical journal *Lancet*, Lemley reported on more than thirty rural residents from North and South Dakota, Montana, Wyoming, and Nebraska. Each, he claimed, had well-diagnosed symptoms of selenium poisoning, each had a diet that drew heavily on home-grown produce, and they all lived in areas known to have highly selenized soil. Both the food and the victims were tested and found to contain elevated selenium counts.

Lemley cited a variety of common ailments—excessive fatigue, slight but continual dizziness, depression, moderate emotional instability, indigestion, diarrhea, skin sores, and, in one case, cirrhosis of the liver. He conducted dozens of tests on farm animals which also had suffered classic signs of both chronic and acute selenium poisoning and which in fact contained sharply elevated selenium. "In view of our experience with humans and animals with selenium poisoning, it hardly seems possible that humans could show parallel concentration to animals which are severely sick and even dying, and not sustain material organic damage," wrote Lemley. He concluded: "We would like . . . to bring out some of the different symptom complexes that we have found to be due to selenium poisoning and to suggest that physicians throughout the known selenium areas suspect some of their chronic cases that have defied diagnosis or treatment to be selenium poisoning."[3]

Lemley's experiences were not confined to the western United States. He toured parts of South America in 1941, again reporting his findings in a *Lancet* article published two years later. Selenium-bearing marine shale formations, selenium indicator plants that were "everywhere evident," especially in Argentina, selenium toxicity symptoms in humans and livestock—all were found almost uniformly along the western slope of the Andes Mountains. Peru and Chile yielded similar findings, and there are historical accounts of severe human birth deformities among natives of Colombia who live in a valley with extremely seleniferous soil.

"A conclusion of the writer, after seeing selenium poisoning in its various phases throughout most of North and South America," stated Lemley in that report, "is that its economic importance is much greater than heretofore realized. The loss to the livestock industry lies not so much in the stock being killed by the poisoning but in the subclinical, chronic and low-grade poisoning so common and widespread. The total loss in weight and growth of cattle alone, produced by . . . subclinical poisoning must be of tremendous economic importance, hitherto unrecognized. It is the writer's opinion that human selenium poisoning is common, widespread, and in certain localities of importance to the general public health."[3]

Just how widespread is typified by history. The infamous "hoof rot" of Marco Polo's mounts as he crossed through Turkistan in 1295 is now widely believed to have been the dreaded "alkali disease" of western ranchers and the Argentine Pampas. One of its classic symptoms is the pronounced elongation of hoofs, which eventually rot and break off, and the lameness of both horses and cattle. Custer's cavalry, too, was nearly grounded by similar problems before the Battle of the Little Big Horn in 1876. The earliest written account of "alkali disease" came from the quill of U.S. Army surgeon T. C. Madison, describing how cavalry mounts at Fort Randall were afflicted on the banks of the Missouri River in what was then the westernmost part of Nebraska but now is in South Dakota. Madison listed all the classic symptoms of selenium toxicity: loss of the tail switch, coarse coat, loss of hooves, swelling of the throat, and a distemper-like nasal discharge. Many of the horses died, but not quickly. Death took months in some cases. Almost a century later, researchers probing the ruins of the Fort Randall chapel discovered that its walls were built of selenium-impregnated Niobrara limestone, levels running as high as 20 ppm.

Historical connections transcend the great American West. Even the mythical Don Quixote, the tragic figure in *Man of La Mancha*, had a selenium link. Searches through Doc's dusty piles of selenium reports unearthed—literally—a 1946 Spanish report that documents the presence and problems of selenium-bearing *Astragalus* plants "in the central part of La Mancha province." Several European researchers have linked the selenium-bearing plant to a disease called lathyrism, an illness with remarkably similar symptoms to amyotrophic lateral sclerosis (ALS), or Lou Gehrig's disease.[4]

There is nothing provincial about the distribution of selenium, however. Other published studies from Doc's files document the discovery of selenium-tainted grains from no fewer than seventeen countries. In addition to the United States, they are Canada, Mexico, Peru, Chile, Venezuela, Colombia, the Soviet Union, Spain, Bulgaria, Algeria, Morocco, Israel, Australia, New Zealand, China, and Ireland. There, in the land of the shamrock, in counties Limerick, Tipperary, and Meath, the soil contains up to 1,200 ppm selenium, tenfold that of the most seleniferous soils of the United States.

But nowhere are the ravaging effects of selenium more chilling than in Colombia. Lemley culled this numbing entry, made in the year 1560, from the journal of a traveling priest: "The corn, as well as other vegetables, grows well and healthy but in some regions it is so poisonous that whoever eats it, man or animal, loses his hair. Indian women gave birth to monstrous-looking babies who were abandoned by their parents. Some abnormal babies . . . were . . . covered with coarse or brittle hair. A number of travellers and priests have repeatedly commented on abandoned malformed Indian babies. Sometimes, whole villages were deserted."

A summary by South American researchers of similar citations also lists instances of farm animals losing their hair and hooves, being born with multiple malformations of the lips and legs, and suffering abortions and other reproductive damage. The latest report of such suffering in Colombia, in 1955, described "toxic corn . . . and streams that had no animal life" and stated that "men and animals using streams for drinking water showed loss of hair; horses suffered hoof damage and small mammals became sterile."[5]

In between the day-long file sessions at Doc's house, there were long nights of intensive reading and a few side trips to places like Hot Springs, Sturgis, and Buffalo Gap, each with a colorful Kilness story about some episode with a farmer or rancher with experiences like those of Mike Henry.

One of those trips was to the southwestern corner of South Dakota, just outside the once-bustling resort community of Hot Springs, to sample the Cheyenne River where it drained a basin known to be high in selenium-tainted shale. There another federal irrigation project— the Angostura—had pocked the fields with sumps to collect rising saline groundwater from waterlogged farmland. Once again, there were only surface indicators of the underlying trouble. *Astragalus* plants, rooted in the ubiquitous outcroppings of black marine shale, dotted the landscape. Was selenium there too in chemical forms and concentrations harmful to plants and wildlife or the humans who consume them? The answer would have to await the analyst's complex fingerprinting in the laboratory back in Sacramento. I scrambled down the sides of drainage canals to get the samples.

I said my goodbyes to Doc that night back in Rapid City. The ceremony was not nearly so stiff and awkward as the welcome several weeks earlier. He turned out to be a good and courageous person, a man who cared enough about others to devote his life to their well-being. He even grew to tolerate, if not to like, the reporter in me. The next day Glenda and I were back on the road, together, heading north for another of those irrigation projects in promising places. This one was the Belle Fourche Project, on South Dakota's western border, almost due north of the infamous town of Deadwood. There, too, underground drain-pipes had been installed to carry excess water away from the root zones of crops planted in soil with so much clay it was almost impermeable. And just like the others, it was selected because of historical sampling reports on soil and vegetation (and not a few of Doc's experiences with sickened cattle and ill farm families in the region).

The unbroken, rolling hills of the Belle Fourche region were covered with tiny pothole lakes and alkali-encrusted draws at almost every hand. Some of the old selenium searches, Beath's included, had sam-pled *Astragalus* plants in the area and recorded some with thousands of parts per million selenium. Kilness and Henry had said there were stories that almost every rancher had his own bone pile hidden away in some discrete corner of the land.

Bruner Rhineholdt turned out to be one of them. My search for a ma-jor drainage canal, just east of the town of Belle Fourche, was inter-rupted by the sight of a small draw, its sides crusted with alkali. Parking the car on the shoulder of the road, its California license plates perhaps a bit out of place, I took my camera with me out into the field. For a few hundred yards I followed the draw toward a canal whose banks were covered with what looked like the "turpentine gumweed" Kilness had pointed out days earlier while leading a similar field trip near Rapid City. There were pictures of the plant, too, in Beath's booklet, a copy of which was now tucked snugly in my own jacket pocket. The gumweed was ranked as "a secondary selenium accumulator," a plant that didn't need selenium to grow but could absorb it from the soil nevertheless. Up over a rise, across a gentle sidehill, down into a swale, the inspection continued. Suddenly, the search for plants ended. There, halfway up the slope, well hidden from the road, was a pile of rotting carcasses and bones, the remnants of dozens of dead cattle.

As I headed back toward the road, farmer Rhineholdt rolled up in his tractor. Alerted by a neighbor that "some tourist from California" was out in his field, taking pictures, the angular, quiet-spoken rancher had come to investigate. He dismounted and ambled over.

"Whatcha doin?" he asked, sounding friendly enough but hardly indirect.

Things get fuzzy fast at a time like that. You can't start telling some dairy farmer from Belle Fourche that you are in the middle of a controversial search for some exotic-sounding poison and that you've just stumbled on his hidden bone pile that proves the effect, if not the cause.

"Ah, well, I'm a reporter from California and . . . uhm, well." His eyes rolled heavenward.

The next try followed a less direct path. This time I mumbled something about being on a search for unusual weed specimens said to be fairly common in the area and having found some along the ditch bank that looked a lot like them. Sometimes, in situations like that, a good offense is the best defense. "Say, what's the matter with your cows over there? What happened to them?"

Rhineholdt, a dairy rancher on that piece of land for much of his life, turned out to be a classic example of those who don't like to talk much to outsiders about their problems.

"What cows?" he shot back. "How do you know anything's wrong with 'em, anyway?"

I shifted sideways, pointing back over the rise. "Those, over in the draw," I replied. "What's wrong with them is that about thirty of them appear to be dead."

The old dairyman winked and chuckled. "Oh, *those* cows. Well, the only people around here who haven't lost any cows are ones who don't have any."

Selenium was not part of his vocabulary, but he was no stranger to many of the symptoms of its dirty work in his own herd. He told of several cases in which he and his sons had had to prop up stricken animals to load them into a truck for transport to the nearest slaughterhouse. "If we can get 'em to market before they go down, we sell 'em," said Rhineholdt directly and with no sense of shame or deceit. "Once they get whatever it is they get, they just can't put no weight on, no matter how much feed we use. So there's no sense keeping 'em out here. The people who buy never test for anything. But if the animals are down, if they can't stand up on their own, they won't take 'em. Then it's a dead loss for us."

Anecdotes from dairy farmers like Rhineholdt and nearby ranchers helped locate drainage sumps and discharge points. But none of that was as explicit as the data point on page 16 of the USDA's Handbook No. 200 showing the results of a soil sample test decades earlier by department researcher A. L. Moxon. Collected "8.5 miles north of [the] Mobile Station at Belle Fourche, Butte County, S. Dak.," the sample, a composite of three separate soil borings, ranged from 16 to 21 ppm selenium and averaged 18 ppm. The test site was not far from Rhineholdt's dairy ranch.

Similar notations in the same book and other reference works showed elevated selenium levels on the high plains of Montana's northeastern corner, too, and pointed the way to the next sampling point: Bowdoin National Wildlife Refuge. After a pleasant Mormon Church service in Belle Fourche, we headed there the next afternoon. North and westward into Montana we drove, the windshield wipers swishing off rivulets from a steady rain, through Lame Deer and the Cheyenne Indian Reservation, well beyond the Little Big Horn River and the Custer Battlefield National Monument, up through Billings and Roundup and on to Lewiston and through the Charles M. Russell National Wildlife Range. The place-names reeked of pioneer history all the way to Malta.

The next morning started bright and cheery enough. After breakfast, we drove the 10 or 12 miles past undulating, bucolic fields. But when we dropped into the depression in which Bowdoin is nestled, it looked more like a hellhole than a wildlife refuge. Dust devils spiraled hundreds of feet into the air, sucking up towering columns of chalky-white dust from the vast bathtub ring around the remnant of 4,000-acre Lake Bowdoin, a preglacial oxbow of the Missouri River. Successive years of drought and years of serving as a sump for tainted agricultural drainage from the reclamation agency's Milk River Project had taken their toll here, too.

Bowdoin yielded yet another Kesterson transplant, refuge manager Gene Sipe, who knew all about the troubles at his former posting. Sipe kept abreast of the problems there by reading the occasional news clipping mailed to him by friends back in California. He also found some old technical reports that discussed the *Astragalus* plants and wondered whether selenium might be responsible for waterfowl reproduction problems at his own refuge. The number of waterfowl using the refuge had nose-dived in recent years, as had the number of successfully fledged nestlings. "I've seen the indicator plants right here on the refuge, so I know we have it," said Sipe as we walked out on a knoll overlooking the basin. Sipe didn't let his selenium curiosity go with a mere botanical observation and some research of historical reports. Instead, he used some unspent general research funds to hire Northern Montana College biology professor Everett Pitt to collect and analyze water samples from the refuge. Although Pitt acknowledged that his analytical methods did not meet USGS standards for sensitivity, the tests did reveal water levels up to 60 ppb—at least twelve times higher than concentrations known to harm aquatic organisms and waterfowl.

Sipe said that a brief period of excess moisture and intensive water management by refuge personnel in the 1970s interrupted a long downward spiral for Bowdoin. As at Stillwater and Kesterson, there had been a history of massive waterfowl losses to what had been diagnosed as botulism and cholera epidemics. "This used to be a real nasty sinkhole," said Sipe. It looked like it was getting that way again. Aware of his agency's errant administrative claims that the early Kesterson losses were due to avian cholera, he was worried whether similar misdiagnoses had occurred at Bowdoin.

And with good reason. Levels of dissolved salts and toxic trace soil elements increased dramatically in the 1980s while reproduction rates for many of the waterfowl species that nested there had plummeted. "There's no nesting to speak of going on this year," said Sipe in June 1985. "The birds are just hanging out, not even pairing up. They seem to sense when conditions for breeding are bad." At a time when the lake should have been dotted with goslings and ducklings, few could be found anywhere. And when thousands of birds should have been paired up for mating, we found only a few dozen mated pairs.

"We have good nesting success here as a rule," added Sipe. "But the past few years we just haven't seen the offspring from the ducks, geese, and pelicans at the later brood stages that we should. Somehow, we are losing them before they get that far."

The geese at Bowdoin are a case in point. One of the key roles of the refuge is to help build the population of the "Highline Flight" of Canada geese that have been coaxed with good feeding and breeding conditions to nest and reside in northern Montana rather than migrate to the tundra of Canada's far north. The resident nesting population at Bowdoin had peaked at 2,000 birds and normally produced some 400 to 500 young geese each year. "Last year, though," said Sipe, "we produced only 125 and it looks even grimmer this year. I don't know whether we will produce any to speak of this year."

They didn't . . . and little wonder. The salt buildup choked out the entire growth of cattails there that provide critical nesting habitat. It also cut in half the supply of hard-stemmed bulrush. Without either, waterfowl reproduction there is doomed. The worsening salt trend had already eliminated fish life at Bowdoin long before. "There used to be a big commercial carp fishery here in the winter," said Sipe. "Fishermen would net the carp under the ice. But there are no fish here now. It's too salty for them."

From Bowdoin, our sampling tour swung abruptly west and, finally, toward home. Our next stop was Benton Lake NWR, about 200 miles due west and just north of Great Falls, in the rolling prairies of the "Big

Sky" country of northern Montana. Two days of driving between there and the Freezeout Lake Game Management Area turned up numerous *Astragalus bisulcatus* and other indicator plants, obvious evidence of selenium's presence in the heavily farmed soil of the Reclamation Bureau's Sun River Project, near the Canadian border.

When I talked to Benton Lake's assistant refuge manager about any possible connections to the Kesterson effect, he acted like he thought I was crazier than even the Belle Fourche dairyman, Bruner Rhineholdt, suspected. Nevertheless, I wandered around the fringes of the system of ponds, braced against the omnipresent prairie wind, while Glenda caught up on her reading in the car. (She is a great fan of the classics.) Nothing looked more, or less, promising than anything else as I trudged along the pond banks. If selenium was leaching from anywhere in the gentle hills that flanked the refuge, I reasoned, it would most likely concentrate in the foul-smelling marsh mud at the bottom of the ponds. So I hiked to one nearest the inlet canal from Muddy Creek, which fed the system, thinking that the upper ponds would be a more likely selenium sink. Reaching beneath the small culvert that connected the first two ponds, I pulled up a handful of the black, dank ooze and scooped it into one of the few sample bottles I had left. Only after I had rinsed off the excess mud, from bottle and me, did I remember how much easier it was to record the time and location on the bottle's label *before* it got wet.

Later the stinking marsh mud would take on unsettling significance. The resident refuge manager, it seems, had used the nutrient-rich ooze to fertilize the family garden. What about the family's selenium intake from produce raised in the plots? Although there were no conclusive signs of ill health, later tests showed potentially harmful selenium counts in the garden soil and the practice of soil supplementing ended abruptly.

The potential for similar trace element mischief in other parts of the drainage basin showed up as we drove through the pastoral farming area. Glenda, whose *Astragalus* spotting abilities were beginning to rival

Doc's, motioned for me to pull over as we headed up a slight rise on the two-lane gravel road. "There, along that small ditch, on the side of the hill over there," she said, pointing to the left. "Aren't those *bisulcatus?*"

Indeed they were, dozens of big, bushy, bloom-laden plants the farmers there called "Canadian" or "purple" vetch. I dug out a few, crumpled them together, and sorted out a well-mixed sample small enough to cram into a plastic sandwich bag. We spotted similar patches of *Astragalus* in the fields around the nearby Freezeout refuge area, which is jointly owned by the state and federal government although management responsibility is vested solely with the Montana Department of Fish, Wildlife, and Parks. The water for six marsh units and Freezeout Lake was coming from saline seeps that were weeping from adjacent hillsides and from subsurface drainage flowing from nearby farms. Once through Freezeout, the leftover water moved on through Priest Butte Lakes and into the Teton River, a passage that occurred only during high water runoff. Otherwise, Priest Butte Lakes formed a drainage sink.

It was time for the final leg of the journey. We headed southwest, on State Route 200, down to Bowman's Corner and U.S. Highway 287, tracing the route of the Continental Divide southward through Wolf Creek along new U.S. 15 to Helena and the hard-rock mining country of Butte and Anaconda with their massive, lifeless tailings. Many of those piles were the metal-laden wastes of copper mining, a likely source of selenium I didn't discover until our sampling mission was over.

Similar mine waste sites in Idaho, and along its border with Oregon, were overlooked on our path across the southern end of Idaho's scenic panhandle to the state's semiarid southwestern corner. There, downslope from the spreading lava formations north of Boise, there would have been no lack of volcanic selenium emissions millions of years ago. But since the geology was markedly different, most of the selenium was still locked up in elemental form—either trapped in the volcanic host rock or, as Wyoming's Orville A. Beath discovered in his 1940s-era sampling there, in lethal concentrations in certain silver and gold ores. Beath recorded at least two species of selenium indicator plants in the Jordan and Owyhee valleys, south of the state's capital, Boise. Maps by the noted Western geologist David Love, and others, also reveal the presence of elevated soil selenium near Jordan and in the Boise Valley that forms the drainage basin for Lake Lowell, or All-American Reservoir, on which the Deer Flat National Wildlife Refuge is located.

We found a scattering of *bisulcatus* and prince's plume that late June morning on the sloping fields north of the lake and the Deer Flat refuge. We also found one other general (and not always accurate) selenium flag—a rough-coated, lame horse—in a pasture only a few yards from the southern lakeshore. While any of its multiple symptoms conceivably could have had a perfectly plausible explanation, the accumulation of misery made it seem unlikely. Not only was the horse lame but it had the telltale "overshoe" or elongated hooves. It had also lost most of its mane and tail switch. All are typical signs of "alkali disease."

We had to abandon the planned sampling program at Malheur National Wildlife Refuge across the border and southward into Oregon's arid southeastern corner. As at Utah's Bear River refuge, Malheur, too, was swollen and cut off by heavy spring flooding. Nevertheless, the drive through the lonely, rolling desert south of Burns, splitting the narrows between Malheur and Harney lakes to Frenchglen, was not without its blessings. Frenchglen was the end of the paved roads, for a while, but the gravel cutoff through Harney County took us through antelope-dotted grasslands and the spring-flooded playas of Bluejoint, Stone Corral, Mugwump, and Anderson lakes. The farther south we went, the wetter it got: into the bird-laden marshes around Hart, Crump, and Pelican lakes, on the very southern rim of Oregon. There were sandhill cranes, white pelicans, ducks of every description, and clouds of shorebirds and locally nesting geese almost everywhere we looked.

Soon it was over to Alturas in northern California and down the Three Flags Highway, U.S. 395, linking Canada, the United States, and Mexico. Our only other sampling effort on the drive southward, back home to Sacramento, came near Termo, about halfway between Alturas and Susanville. Here a patch of roadside *Astragalus*, species unknown, provided a good excuse for leg stretching and, finally, a real live nest to check. Perhaps the word "live" is overstated. The walk through the profuse wildflower garden turned up a small bird nest in the thick base of a mature *Astragalus*. The single remaining egg was filmed by dust and obviously abandoned. Nonetheless, it quickly became an unscheduled part of the sample collection. Four hours later, the spreading lightscape of sprawling Sacramento blinked its welcome. The search, at least my part of it, with the sampling and driving and wading and field trips, had ended. It had taken nearly six weeks and 5,000 miles.

The swing through the southern tier of sampling sites by reporter Jim Morris had been slightly more grueling than my trip, at least in the collection process. While I traversed the comparatively lush, pleasant climes of the north, Morris was working his way through some of the harshest, hottest, and driest climates in the country: from the southern tip of California and Arizona, through the dreary and equally arid midsection of New Mexico, to the riparian thickets of the Lower Rio Grande Valley in Texas.

The physical part of the search had ended. But the cerebral part was just getting started. We spent the first weeks of July deciphering bulging piles of steno notebooks filled with scores of interviews with ranchers, farmers, biologists, geologists, doctors, and bureaucrats. They had to be transcribed and fed into the computer's "special project" basket—newsroom jargon for that electronic receptacle, a holdover from the days when stories were turned in as paper copy, rather than electronic pulses, and dropped into a wire basket on the editor's desk. Entry by entry, the color, texture, and challenge of the state-by-state selenium search began to take shape.

Morris and I could not resist swapping war stories and reminiscing about our western odysseys, exchanging tales about hidden bone piles, herds of antelope, fields of *Astragalus* plants, and tense conflicts with the crusty Doc. Morris leaned back in his chair, propping the well-muscled legs of a dedicated runner up on the desk, and recalled some of the more memorable moments of his search.

"I'm not sure which part I remember most vividly," he chuckled. "Maybe it was the time near Yuma. There I was, out in the desert. It was over 100. I was sweating and the wind was blowing sand under my contact lenses. Oh, that was real adventure. The only thing I remember thinking was, 'What am I *doing* out here? Even if I find what I'm looking for, I won't know it.' Or maybe the high spot was slithering under the barbed-wire fence to reach a bog in the snake-infested Santa Ana NWR, on the Rio Grande River, near McAllen, Texas." At one point in his travels, Morris became so frustrated that he called me in Rapid City, desperately seeking more help with the kinds of indicators he should be looking for. "You know botany was never my strong suit. And you know I am invariably the last one to spot something from a moving car—and even then, someone has to point it out to me," he said.

Morris talked about how he happened to stumble onto an unexpected selenium source, a big pile of uranium mine tailings, while trying to spot *Astragalus* plants from the moving car in the northwest quadrant of New Mexico. Federal mine reclamation officials in Denver now worry that rainwater may be leaching lethal levels of selenium from those and hundreds of other tailings into underground water systems tapped by neighbors for domestic supplies. Morris had memorized many of the health effects known to be associated with selenium poisoning. He found it unnerving when residents of a housing development near the New Mexico tailings pile complained to him about sudden and profuse hair loss and extreme fatigue.

But show-and-tell time was over. Our editors, just George Baker and Terry Hennessy at that point, wanted to know what we had found out. No matter how subtly such questioning is conducted, the pressure mounts. They had approved huge expenditures and invested something of their own reputations in urging approval of the demanding project. Their anticipation, and expectations, were obvious.

"Well, did you find it? Did we nail it? Are there any more Kestersons out there? What do we have? What do we know? What can we say?" Their questions came out in a burst.

Morris and I were a bit guarded with our responses. Classic journalism training emphasizes the importance of distancing oneself from conclusions, from feelings of personal involvement in stories being investigated and reported. But that kind of objectivity is more easily managed when reporting on the failures or successes of others. The process is a lot more challenging in the new brand of "project journalism" practiced by investigatively oriented newspapers—of which *The Bee* was certainly an aggressive example—because the reporter often is so actively involved. So much for the old newspaper credo that "We report news, not make it."

I replied first. "It isn't quite time for headline writing, yet," I said, easing into the tricky business of trying to sum up something that was not yet confirmed by any test results. "Nothing will be certain until the numbers come in from the lab." Even then, however, proving that "thousands of square miles" of the West are tainted with harmful levels of a natural trace soil element would not be easy.

Loose investigative ends had to be tied up. I made frequent visits to the laboratory to collaborate with the technicians, carefully matching the precisely sequenced sample identification numbers with the field-scribbled numbers and mileage locations for future reference. Morris and I fed the interview notes into the computer and started looking for gaps in our reporting. Since we both had missed key people on our tour, we started contacting them by telephone to set up interviews. Throughout the month of July I read, and re-read, most of the voluminous documentation I had brought back from the copying sessions with Doc. Many of them were scientific papers and the technical language didn't seem nearly as clear as when he had explained it in Rapid City. As always, there was the paintstaking business of checking and cross-checking contradictory or confusing points. At last, we had done everything we could. We would just have to wait for the lab results.

Collecting environmental samples and analyzing them correctly is difficult enough when you're dealing with well-known compounds and standard methods of laboratory analysis. Unfortunately for us, neither selenium nor the accepted analytical protocols were well understood at the time. We were still near the beginning of a learning curve that was bending sharply upward. Most private laboratories in the country had done little or no selenium analysis or were still using methods like those that led the outside lab of the Reclamation Bureau astray on the initial Kesterson test results.

I had asked the lab chemist to let us know the minute they had even the first preliminary results. And he did. But it was not at all what I wanted to hear. I was expecting selenium concentrations in the low parts per million or, at least, hundreds of parts per billion range. What I heard was nowhere near that. Many of the samples were yielding less than 100 ppb selenium and some had nothing detectable at all.

This just couldn't be happening, I thought. I had done more research for that trip than in the rest of my career combined. I had selected sampling sites only after checking to make sure they coincided with the selenium source-rock maps and, where possible, with other sampling sites selected from historical reports. It was the one result I had tried most vigorously to avoid: no news; nothing out there. There was no sense mounting a search unless we were pretty sure there was something to find, some legitimate problem to uncover. It had to be there. We looked where it should have been. We looked where others far more expert had found it before. Where was the selenium now? Had it vanished? Had it weathered away somehow?

I broke out of my private pondering and directed my misgivings at the chemist: "Something must have gone wrong. It just couldn't have disappeared. Did you have any trouble with the samples?"

It was not the most subtle set of questions I ever asked. Both the thrust and the rush with which they came caught the chemist off guard. He was more accustomed to that kind of outburst when the tests showed high concentrations of some hazardous material and his clients faced the expensive prospect of regulatory action to clean it up. Now, he must surely have felt that the courier was going to be shot no matter what kind of news he brought. He ended a long, awkward pause and gave a hesitant explanation.

"Uhm . . . we encountered some interference problems, probably high levels of heavy metals in the samples," he said. "We could do some broad-scale heavy metals analyses to see what is causing it. You want to try that?"

Heavy metals? Now I was off guard. Neither Barnes nor Presser had mentioned anything about heavy metals clouding the ability to detect and measure the selenium. "How much would it cost to screen for the heavy metals?" I asked, not really wanting to hear the answer.

"About $450 for each sample," said the chemist. "It's a pretty complicated process because we'd have to look for all of them."

Something just didn't add up. I pushed for more details—about the sample preparation, the analytical work, everything I could think of as the possible source of trouble.

"Well, we were having some trouble with the graphite furnace a week or two ago. It was down for a while and we had to run some of the tests over again . . . at no charge to you, of course," he quickly added.

Wait a minute. What graphite furnace? "I don't remember anything about a graphite furnace being needed for this process. Aren't you following the Barnes and Presser protocols?" I demanded. "They don't call for any graphite furnace. You are supposed to be using the hydride generation method."

This was probably the exact kind of conversation the Geological Survey audit team had with the Bureau of Reclamation's contract lab after it botched the initial Kesterson samples, missing the selenium altogether. This was exactly what I had tried so hard to avoid. This was why I had obtained a copy of Barnes and Presser's report and given it to the lab vice-president when we ordered the work. I had specified the accepted USGS method just so the results couldn't be challenged because some different method was used. And he had agreed to do it that way.

The chemist stammered into his response. "Barnes and Presser? Protocols? USGS report? What are you talking about? What report?"

What report, indeed! "Why the USGS report, of course. Water Resources Investigation Report 84-4122, to be precise. The one your vice-president was given and agreed you would follow so the results would be less vulnerable to challenge."

Only in the subsequent exchange did it become clear that the vice-president had not in fact given the report to the technician doing the work. The chemist said he would get the document, follow the methods outlined in it, and get back to me as soon as possible with the results.

My blood pressure dropped back to something approximating normal. The harm could be corrected. So it would take another couple of weeks. What's a few more weeks in a project that already had taken nearly six months and a lot more money than the newspaper was accustomed to paying for its news, even by its bold investigative standards? Just a few more weeks of hell, that's all.

Baker and Hennessy grew less and less patient with every postponement, and Morris and I grew more and more tense. We couldn't start writing until the numbers were in hand. Without the data, all we had, really, was a lot of historical facts and a collection of anecdotes, though some were pretty unsettling. If we could do nothing to speed up the lab, there still was plenty to do, including lots more reading and telephone interviews.

Chapter 6 | **RESULTS**
and
REACTION

For nearly five months, in our search for selenium throughout the West, we had put almost the entire emphasis on mapping battle plans, researching likely sampling sites, cultivating networks of sources and prying loose confidential reports. We also had met with federal whistleblowers trying to prevent their bosses from bottling up what they considered one of the most important wildlife issues in decades, and, of course, had collected the samples.

It wasn't until the final set of verified, double-checked, quality-assured test results came in that the full enormity of the task struck home. In the summer of 1985, very little was known about what constituted a threshold limit for danger. To save on costs, we concentrated on sampling the marsh mud or algae, thinking that if there were elevated levels anywhere, they would be there. The search had been merely to find the selenium . . . to prove it was there. The crucial part of the process, trying to figure out what those levels meant and what they implied, proved a more daunting task.

This kind of work was uncomfortably far beyond investigative journalism, where the focus is on probing the work, malfeasance, and mischief of high-ranking others. I called what we were doing "discovery journalism." Others had different names for it, not the least offensive of which was pseudo- or voodoo-science. For weeks, we had been transcribing notes, filling in missed interviews, and closing some of the gaps in our initial reportage, waiting to find out what the laboratory chemists had found in our samples. By mid-August, everything else that could be done had been done. We had to have the test results.

I called the laboratory. The chemist told me they were finished with the actual analytical work but it still would be two weeks or so before they converted the raw data into a closely checked final report. I knew it was less than fully professional to transmit such technical information over the phone. I realized how easy it could be to miss, or add, a decimal point or put the selenium concentration numbers on the wrong line of the chart I had arranged on the computer screen. Nevertheless, deadlines were approaching. Time was running out.

"Look, I know that the final report is what we have to go by and I understand the importance of having the numbers down in black and white," I told the chemist. "But it would save us a lot of time if you just read them off to me now so we could start finding out from the biologists what they mean. You can be sure we will double-check them from the written report when we get it."

He didn't like that kind of informality. "We would prefer waiting for you to get the final report. There are fewer chances for errors that way," the chief chemist explained patiently.

"True," I replied. "But this is halfway through August and the project already is several weeks behind schedule."

I explained that even with the preliminary test results, it would take at least a week or two to write the stories that would be the project's centerpiece and several days more to edit, revise, and polish them before we were ready to publish. There would be plenty of time, I reassured him, to double-check everything from the final report, to make sure one site's numbers didn't get mislabeled as another's. "Just give us what you have and we'll be sure to verify it later," I insisted.

There was more tactful sidestepping. The chemist was worried about the interpretation we would put on the numbers, how they would be used, how the company's role would be portrayed. It was useful, necessary, and fully professional caution on his part.

"What we are going to say, how the numbers are going to be interpreted, or what spin we will put on the story is really beyond the contract requirements and nothing for you to worry about," I told him without rancor. "You were hired to do the analyses and that precise and limited role will be clearly pointed out. All we want from you are the numbers. As for the interpretation, we will get it from others who are experienced and qualified in that field."

Satisfied that the firm's integrity was not in jeopardy, the chemist read off the numbers. Slowly he fed me the data, taking care to repeat each lab and company identification number to ensure that it was assigned to the proper sampling site. I became increasingly tense. Objectivity is difficult enough to maintain at the best of times. It was agonizing in this circumstance. The chemist droned on:

"Stillwater . . . algae; level, less than 100 ppb.

"Stillwater . . . algae; level, 487 ppb.

"Stillwater . . . algae; level, 60 ppb."

It went on like that for site after site, nothing jumping off the screen as really striking. Only the soft clacking of the keyboard and my muttered "damns!" or "whats?" interrupted the flow. There were reports for samples that had no place-name, only numbers. Those would be the "blanks" we had given the lab to test the accuracy and reliability of their work. Spiked by other chemists with a known amount of selenium, they had been divided and (unknown to the contractor) the other half sent for analysis to another lab.

With each reported "less than 50 ppb," or even 200 ppb, my anxiety level increased exponentially. It was like that for all the results from Stillwater Stewart Lake, the first four stops on my sampling circuit. Not one of those samples exceeded a known toxicity threshold level. It was beginning to look uncomfortably like there might not be enough selenium to be concerned about, much less enough to reveal another Kesterson in the making.

Then came the Stewart Lake catfish.

"Seventyonefourteen," the chemist ran the numbers together.

"Uh. Could you try that again? How much did you say?"

"Seven thousand, one hundred and fourteen; seven, comma, one, one, four . . . ppb," repeated the chemist, sounding a lot less professionally detached himself.

That was something less than total vindication. It would take more than that to make Ivan Barnes or Harry Ohlendorf or Felix Smith blink. But it was a definite improvement over all those "less thans" or "non-detectables."

It was a struggle to keep things from falling into "good news" and "bad news" categories. From the start, the idea had been just to find out what was out there. What evidence of selenium could we find? But, however subtly, it had become less a question of testing the predictions of people like Barnes and Love and more a litmus test of our own abilities. For me, the conflicting roles dissolved in the hope that if there was, in fact, a real and spreading problem with selenium, my search would uncover it and lead to its correction. Nevertheless, my personal involvement and my authorial interest in the results, the feeling that my professional standing was riding on the outcome, would have been much better left out of the equation. It should have been a straightforward matter of just stating what happened, recording the results without fear, favor, or personal stake. But somewhere between that first prognostication by Ivan Barnes and the project approval from *The Bee*'s executive editor Gregory Favre, it had become personal. Journalism 101 hadn't covered this.

Objectivity was an easier case to make intellectually than practically. Tens of thousands of company dollars were at risk, a fact of life not lost on editors whose expectations had risen about as quickly as the budget. The newsroom is supposed to have its own set of checks and balances, just like the government. Editors are supposed to maintain just enough healthy skepticism to keep the enthusiasm of reporters in objective check. They are not supposed to buy your thesis, whole hog, at least not until your proof, documentation, and attribution overcome their professional unbelief. What began as a search for selenium was evolving, at least in some respects, into a search for personal vindication. Maintaining objectivity is tough enough when reporting the activities of others. It was an impossible ideal when applied to your own efforts . . . and results. All of that, and more, flashed through my mind as the chief lab chemist completed the readout.

If my expectations jumped a bit with the Stewart Lake catfish report, they absolutely soared with what followed. That modest, bewhiskered fish, all one pound of it, became the turning point. The next six sample results either met or greatly exceeded known toxicity thresholds, most of them well into the parts per million range for selenium concentration. By the time the whole data set had been recorded, fourteen of twenty-three sites sampled were solid selenium hits.

Barnes had been right after all. If that much could be found in such an unscientific search, one that barely scratched the list of place-names prominent in the historical literature as known selenium hot spots, then selenium really must cover and taint "thousands of square miles throughout the West." From the outset, we had discarded the notion that the selenium probe could be based solely on resurrected history. We needed fresh evidence. Besides, this was more a story about marshes and waterfowl and fish than cows, sheep, and horses. In the historical literature there had been virtually no mention of the element's presence in a wildlife or aquatic setting. That represented one substantial chance for our failure. Another was that we might not hit exactly the same precise sampling spots that our predecessors did and might thus become victims of selenium's sometimes quixotic distribution. A few miles this way or that and we might miss what we were looking for.

I finished typing up the lab results and next to them entered another column of numbers: concentrations that, biologists suspected, marked the spot at which selenium's toxic chain reaction began. After writing enough explanatory text to provide a fairly comprehensive progress report for the editors, I punched the "print" key on the computer enough times to spread copies around to all team members, reporters, editors, photographers, and illustrators. The column of selenium poisoning thresholds had taken hours to put together. I had compiled a master list from all of the written material I could find on the subject and from phone calls to wildlife biologists doing current research in the field. Slowly, but steadily, the researchers were learning that the Kesterson effect didn't spring forth, full bloom, only when the selenium concentrations reached the levels measured at the ravaged California marsh. The toxic crossover—the moment or season when what was tolerable suddenly became poisonous—was, in fact, much lower than biologists suspected in the wake of the early Kesterson discoveries. The learning process was still in its comparative infancy, however, when our search began in the spring of 1985.

The enormity of the challenge became painfully apparent, that hot, cloudless day in August, after I thanked the lab chemist and told him we looked forward to receipt of the final written report. Now the numbers were all in. But what did they really reveal? How much did they tell us about other potential Kestersons? What story did they tell? Was the "Kesterson Effect" merely a biological blip, a bizarre oddity? Or was it truly a West-wide phenomenon?

Nothing was immediately clear . . . except that we could be confident with our lab's analytical results. Government chemists compared the independent firm's results with the numbers they got when doing the quality control tests on splits of the same samples we had sent them. They said the private lab's results were "within acceptable scientific standards and show uncommonly good conformity." By analyzing samples spiked with a known amount of selenium, a standard laboratory practice, chemists are able to determine what percentage their methods are recovering. That confidence level is given another boost when other regular samples are split between different labs and the results compared.

The West Sacramento company did well on both counts, but we still groped for the *meaning* of these numbers. There was at least some selenium at nearly every site sampled. It was marginal in some places but incontestably elevated in others. There were "less than 35 ppb" findings, the lab's lowest level of detection in biological samples, for places like Desert Lake and Vernal, at opposite ends of Utah, and at Bosque del Apache NWR in New Mexico and Laguna Atascosa NWR on the Gulf Coast in Texas. But the other fourteen samples had concentrations of this unique natural element as high as—or higher than—those then accepted as thresholds for toxicity.

If the pace quickened when we learned the test results by phone, it became absolutely frantic in the days that followed. Helpful Fish and Wildlife field biologists and researchers, from a field station at Oahe Reservoir in South Dakota, from the parent Patuxent Wildlife Research Center in Laurel, Maryland, and from Harry Ohlendorf at its Pacific Field Station in Davis, filled in a lot of gaps about the thresholds for toxic effect. But none of them did more than the federal wildlife agency's top expert, Dr. Dennis Lemly at the National Fisheries Research Center in Columbia, Missouri, or Felix Smith, the courageous whistleblower.

It was becoming abundantly clear that *The Bee*'s sampling had turned up evidence of potentially toxic levels of selenium in sites from Utah, South Dakota, Idaho, Montana, New Mexico, other parts of California, and the southwest corner of Arizona. Moreover, from Doc's voluminous files and a growing pile of other research by Beath, Love, and others, we compiled an impressive array of evidence from which it could logically and confidently be inferred that dozens, if not scores, of other areas in virtually every state of the West—and three Canadian provinces—could be similarly afflicted.

Telephone interviews were completed with those missed on the West-wide odyssey. Stories were written and then rewritten. Quotes were checked, and rechecked, for accuracy. *The Bee*'s Pulitzer Prize-winning photographer, Michael Williamson, was dispatched to retrace the more productive steps of the reporters, capturing the unfolding drama in telling photographs. Copy editors, the silent figures who hold all good newsrooms together, pored over the stories that made up a three-day newspaper package, checking facts, making sure the stories were consistent with one another, cleaning up the grammar, tightening the focus. No one did more of that, or did it better, than the project's editor, Terry Hennessy.

Artists doubled as cartographers, reproducing the work of a variety of maps, from Beath, Love, Hubert Lakin, and others, on soil and vegetation selenium levels throughout the American and Canadian West. They also produced effective illustrations showing how selenium cycles both geologically and biologically from source to sink. There were almost daily conferences to update the paper's metropolitan editor, George Baker (now managing editor of the company's *Fresno Bee*), and, toward the climax, the paper's executive editor, Gregory Favre.

Everything was in place. The page proofs were read closely in the last round of checking. Nothing was missed. Editors and reporters read and reread headlines, picture captions, and map and illustration text, and the makeup editor arranged it all in a striking layout that gave readers of *The Bee* an unexpected jolt on Sunday, September 8, 1985.

"Selenium: A Conspiracy of Silence" read the Special Bee Report logo, just over the main Page One headline: "Toxic Trace Element Threatens the West; Massive US Water Projects Blamed." And the results of six months of often agonizing effort unfolded:

> *Selenium, the lethal natural poison that has killed and deformed birds, fish and other wildlife in the San Joaquin Valley, is poisoning wildlife, livestock and even some rural families over thousands of square miles in 15 Western states, a Bee investigation has disclosed.*
>
> *At fault, in most cases, are massive federal water projects.*
>
> *Built to make the parched West bloom through intensive irrigation, scores of these projects are robbing waterfowl and wildlife habitat of limited fresh water and returning it laced with selenium—and other toxicants—to taint wildlife refuge areas, lakes, rivers and reservoirs used for drinking water, irrigation or recreation.*
>
> *The Bee probe, backed by independent laboratory testing, has found alarmingly high levels of selenium on or near almost every federal water project it checked throughout the West.*

*The widespread poisoning is similar to that which is forcing the federal govern-
ment to close Kesterson National Wildlife Refuge in the San Joaquin Valley after
it suffered the most severe outbreak of bird deformities ever recorded in the wild.*

Other key findings of the four-month Bee investigation are:

- *The federal Bureau of Reclamation, whose empire of water projects is the suspected cause of the contamination, is trying to cover up the scope of the problem
by stalling a plan to search for selenium and other toxic trace elements, like arsenic, in drain waters from as many as 470 of its projects.*

- *Warnings about the dangers of selenium—contained in volumes of historical
reports, some nearly a century old—were ignored or overlooked by those who
sponsored or built the massive water-diversion works in areas where selenium
was known to exist.*

- *No government agency is testing food raised in high-selenium areas and some
doctors warn that farm and ranch families in those areas—and perhaps others
in nearby cities that rely heavily on locally produced grain, meat, milk and other
foods—may be in danger.*

- *Selenium contamination also has spread much farther than imagined in California, contaminating water as far north as Stony Creek in the Sacramento Valley and as far south as the Salton Sea and the Imperial Valley.*

- *Wildlife refuge managers throughout the West, fearing their once raucous and
healthy sanctuaries are being turned into silent "death traps," are reporting
rapid declines in bird and fish populations and serious loss of nesting and feeding
vegetation.*

*"Being at the garbage end of this thing is terrible," said Ray Rauch, manager
of a national wildlife refuge along the Gulf Coast in Texas.*

*A plan for a massive and detailed search for selenium, recommended by gov-
ernment scientists, has been stalled for nearly five months in the office of Robert
Broadbent, a former commissioner of the Bureau of Reclamation and now assistant secretary for water and science in the Interior Department.*

*Instead, the reclamation agency claims its regional offices have conducted a
"broad reconnaissance" that found only "minor problems" and "no direct evidence of wildlife impact."*

*In sharp contrast, The Bee sampled project areas in the West and discovered a
widespread pattern of selenium contamination.*

*Samples analyzed by an independent laboratory found dangerous levels of the
toxic element being flushed from drains in project service areas into or near waterfowl refuges in seven states: California, Idaho, Montana, South Dakota, Utah,
New Mexico and Arizona.*

Evidence of similar contamination and damage in eight other states was found through a combination of testing, reviewing government documents and interviewing dozens of ranch and farm families, federal and state biologists and geologists, physicians and pathologists.

Those states are Nevada, Texas, Wyoming, Colorado, Nebraska, Kansas, Washington and Oregon.

Indications of potential contamination also were found in the lower parts of three prairie provinces of Canada: Alberta, Saskatchewan and Manitoba.

The Bee collected samples from nine states and had them tested by California Analytical Laboratories, Inc. of West Sacramento. The independent lab is certified to do such work by the U.S. Environmental Protection Agency.

The tests showed that 14 samples from refuges and farm drains in seven states were high enough in selenium to trigger death and deformity in migratory waterfowl, shore birds, fish, frogs, insects and other marsh-related wildlife.

Although scientists still are trying to establish a threshold level at which selenium damage begins to occur, a new study by the U.S. Fish and Wildlife service at the Oahe Reservoir in South Dakota found that 564 parts of selenium per billion parts of sediment is a level of concern for toxic effect in fish and birds.

By comparison, Bee samples averaged nearly three times that level in sediments—1,634 ppb—more than enough to build up to lethal levels through the aquatic food chain.

The selenium danger level varies from soil to water to wildlife.

Sites where The Bee discovered selenium sediment concentrations in the danger zone, above 600 ppb and ranging up to 7,500 ppb, include:

The Salton Sea National Wildlife Refuge in Southern California.

The Imperial Valley NWR, on the Arizona side of the Colorado River.

The Bosque del Apache NWR in New Mexico.

The Desert Lake and Stewart Lake waterfowl management areas in Utah. A catfish from Stewart Lake had 7,114 ppb of selenium, far above the level needed to cause reproductive damage and low survival of young.

The Bowdoin and Benton Lake NWRs and Freezeout Lake waterfowl management area in Montana.

The Deer Flat NWR in Idaho.

The Belle Fourche and Cheyenne rivers, upstream of the Oahe Reservoir in South Dakota.

Selenium once was believed limited to localized "hot spots" in a few northwestern states. But a 1941 report by the federal Department of Agriculture obtained by The Bee states that selenium at levels high enough to make vegetation toxic to animals exists over "thousands of square miles" of Western land.

In addition to the higher, dangerous levels found elsewhere, The Bee found sediment concentrations approaching the danger point—from 200 to 600 ppb—in Rio Grande and Laguna Atascosa national refuges near the Gulf Coast in Texas; in the Imperial Valley and near a drain leading to the Salton Sea in Southern California; in seepage running into the Green River near Vernal and in Desert Lake, in southern Utah; in the Stillwater Waterfowl Management Area near Fallon, Nev.; and near the Bosque del Apache refuge in New Mexico.

Less hazardous, but elevated sediment levels—between 100–200 ppb— were discovered in Yuma Valley, Ariz., again at Stewart Lake in Utah and in a bird egg from Lassen County in northeastern California, near Termo.

Those discoveries come in the wake of an alarming decline in waterfowl and other wildlife populations on national and state refuges throughout the West.

The Fish and Wildlife Service's annual migratory bird census this year is the lowest it has been in the 30 years the counts have been made.

The number of ducks on the Pacific Flyway, generally from the Pacific Coast to the western flanks of the Rocky Mountains, has declined 20 percent from last year—down about 3 million, according to federal records.

In the Central Flyway, which covers the rest of the West to the Mississippi River, the decrease is much steeper. Last year there were 26.3 million ducks. This year, experts estimate there are only 18.5 million, a 30 percent loss.

Biologists say that the biggest single factor in those losses is the destruction of wetland habitat where the birds breed and nest. To make matters worse, what little habitat is left—as farmers turn more and more wetlands under the plow to offset declining profits—is being tainted by increasingly saline water and lethal contaminants.

Indeed, more than selenium is involved in the death threats now emerging at marshes, wetlands, refuges and other waterways throughout the arid West.

Although Bee sampling analyzed only selenium, federal studies have turned up dangerous levels of arsenic in refuges in Texas and Nevada. Toxic amounts of heavy metals, such as mercury, cadmium, chromium and others, are being studied at scores of refuges throughout the nation.

Numerous dissolved salts and minerals in irrigation return flows are seriously degrading waterfowl habitat throughout arid regions served by the federal water projects. Cropping and cultivation practices compound the problem. Millions of acres of native grassland that once held the water in place have been broken for cultivation, increasing tainted runoff and seepage. That drainage has been increased greatly by irrigation that flushes salts and toxicants from the ground that otherwise would remain in place or be leached out slowly, and harmlessly, over hundreds or thousands of years.

The extent of that problem is detailed in one of the many important govern-ment studies left to gather dust on a library shelf. The report, by the state of Mon-tana, identifies more than 2 million acres of farmland from which saline seepage high in both selenium and arsenic is endangering livestock, driving farmland out of production and poisoning ponds, reservoirs and streams.

Nowhere is that more evident than around the Benton Lake, Bowdoin and Freezeout Lake wildlife refuges in northern Montana, and many other smaller satellite ponds and marshes nearby, where the seeps proliferate.

Benton Lake refuge, 12 miles northwest of Great Falls, is a prime example. It gets some of its water directly from Muddy Creek, into which drainage from farms served by the federal Sun River project flows.

A mud sample from a pond there had the highest sediment level of selenium re-corded in The Bee sampling, 7,500 ppb. That is higher than some Kesterson sed-iment levels.

That came as a shock to refuge personnel, who didn't know that that much of their water supply was from farm drainage nor that it was laced with selenium.

"There is no agricultural waste water used in the refuge," said assistant refuge manager Tom Tornow, "although we do get some seepage from right here in the basin.

"I've read about Kesterson but I don't think the subject has ever come up here. I don't think we've ever tested for selenium here," said Tornow.

Although Tornow says the refuge has a "high nesting success ratio consis-tently," the current estimate is for a crop of only 12,000 young, half the number of ducks normally produced. Most of that has to do with low water supply, a time when selenium is concentrated to much higher levels.

Freezeout Lake, about 20 miles west, is a former national refuge now managed by the state of Montana. Bird production is down there, too, but no effort has been made to test for causes, even though several state agencies suspect that selenium is the cause of cattle and fish kills in the area.

In fact, no testing to discover the kind of death and deformity in waterfowl that occurred at Kesterson has been done anywhere else in the nation.

Sediment samples from drainage ditches feeding into Freezeout Lake exceeded 1,400 ppb, nearly three times the level needed to harm fish and waterfowl, and a selenium-accumulating weed called an Astragalus contained 74,760 ppb, enough to be highly toxic to cattle.

The picture at the Bowdoin refuge, fed by drainage from the federal Milk River Project, in the northeast corner of Montana, is more dismal.

Starved for fresh water to stave off the steady intrusion of salt that is killing off the needed nesting and feeding vegetation, refuge mud showed 3,136 ppb of selenium.

Other samples showed selenium in the water itself at levels at which fish begin to suffer or die.

Once the scene of a thriving commercial carp fishery, the refuge no longer supports fish life of any kind. "It's too salty now," said refuge manager Gene Sipe.

Similar conditions and findings are the rule, rather than the exception, in parts of Nevada, Texas and New Mexico, too.

Rauch, the manager of the 45,000-acre Laguna Atascosa ("muddy lake") NWR in South Texas, wonders where all the redhead ducks have gone.

Sampling of sediment and algae by The Bee indicated selenium levels on and around the refuge of from 215 ppb to 224 ppb. That is about half the sediment concentration found to trigger damage in fish and wildlife in the South Dakota study, but elevated enough to cause long-term accumulation to danger levels.

One of the reasons Rauch isn't seeing so many redhead ducks at Atascosa anymore is that fewer of them are being hatched at places like Stillwater refuge in Nevada, and others like them near Vernal and Price, Utah.

Once considered one of the most prolific producers of redheads on the Pacific Flyway, Stillwater now is turning into a bitter saline sink on the Nevada desert. The state's biggest wetland, Stillwater once produced an average of 30,000 birds a year, the majority of them redheads.

By 1983, that figure was less than 10,000. Elevated levels of selenium were found there by The Bee.

High arsenic levels, too, have been found there, high enough, according to Fish and Wildlife sources, to cause serious bird losses.

Stillwater also has a long reputation for major outbreaks of botulism, an avian killer-disease that researchers now believe may be directly or indirectly related to elevated selenium levels.

Similar problems seem likely at the Bosque del Apache NWR in central New Mexico. About 80 percent of its water is from agricultural drainage where selenium is known to be in both source rock and the soil.

The Bee's sediment and algae samples there, and about 15 miles north of the refuge, showed selenium from 308 ppb to 420 ppb, within the range where they could contribute to dangerous food-chain accumulation.

Brent Giezentanner, assistant refuge supervisor for the Fish and Wildlife Service regional office in Albuquerque, said Bosque loses "200 to 500 birds a year to disease; they've lost as many as 2,000 in one year."

Bosque del Apache covers 52,000 acres. Like most of the refuges in the South-

west, it is a wintering ground for species such as Canada geese and mallard ducks.
The resident population includes sandhill cranes and whooping cranes, as well as
wild turkey and quail.

There is no consensus on the subject of selenium toxicity in New Mexico.

Said David Coss, a water specialist with the New Mexico Environmental Im-
provement Division in Santa Fe:

"You can get in a lot of trouble out here for suggesting that agricultural irri-
gation causes water pollution. It's technically complex and politically fraught
with emotion." Countered David Teague of the same agency's water pollution
control bureau: "I don't consider it (selenium) to be a problem in New Mexico."[1]

Jim Morris and I combined our own sampling results with other
more extensive efforts conducted by California agencies trying to determine how widespread the problem was there. We found indications
of potential peril throughout California, from almost one end of the
state to the other, in water, fish, birds, other wildlife, and a variety of
plants and insects. State and federal scientists found elevated levels of
the toxic trace element leaching from mine tailings and geological formations and in discharges from farms, sewer plants, oil refineries, and
chemical plants. The place-names for the discoveries stretch from
Stony Creek in Glenn County and Termo, in Lassen County, to the San
Francisco Bay, the San Joaquin River, and the Tulare Basin, between
Fresno and Bakersfield, to Santa Monica, the Imperial Valley, and the
Colorado River, near the very southern tip of the state.

So far, biological damage has been detected only where it has been
specifically looked for in California: in Kesterson and the private farm
evaporation ponds in the Tulare Basin. But levels high enough to cause
damage also have been found in a huge seasonal wetlands adjacent to
Kesterson—the Grasslands area of Merced County. The same potential
exists in various reaches of the San Francisco Bay complex.

Wildlife experts warn that at many of the discovery sites, the levels of
selenium are high enough to cause similar problems for aquatic insects,
fish, waterfowl, and other wildlife. South of Kesterson, the State Water
Resources Control Board staff found selenium levels in fish in the Salton
Sea and the Colorado River at 3.1 ppm. Toxic effect and the possibility

of reproductive harm are believed to begin at levels above 2.5 ppm. And, as part of its own western selenium search, *The Bee* confirmed a buildup of selenium in the sediment of farm drainage ditches leading to the Salton Sea NWR, in the refuge itself, and in silt from the Colorado River. Levels in these two places ranged from 1,760 to 2,240 ppb in mud and from 216 to 1,360 ppb in algae. Both concentration ranges carry the potential for long-term biological accumulation and the damage that goes with it.[2]

Some biologists think that only time and size stand between the Salton Sea and substantial selenium toxicity. The vast inland sea, 36 miles long and 14 miles wide, was created in 1905 when a temporary diversion dam failed, allowing the entire flow of the Colorado to sweep into the historic Salton Trough, filling the large but shallow depression in the southern California desert. Since then, however, nearly all of the sea's inflow has been agricultural drainage from the Imperial Valley or sewage- and pesticide-ridden flows from the New and Alamo rivers that drain into the Salton Sea from Mexico. A big push for more efficient irrigation has reduced seepage of both fresh canal water and tainted drainage from the fields. As the sea steadily shrinks, its salt and trace element load is being increased in the process.

Federal biologists collected fifteen each of the four predominant species of fish—corvina, tilapia, sargo, and croaker—from the Salton Sea and two dozen heron and egret eggs in the marshes around it for analyses. The state water quality board staff collected twenty-eight fish for its own study. A state report suggests selenium is accumulating to levels of concern in fish. The flesh of a corvina from the Salton Sea and the liver of a catfish from the nearby Colorado River both had selenium readings of 3.1 ppm. That is high enough to impair the fish and approaches the 8 ppm level at which reproductive failure occurs. Fish-eating waterfowl also could be at risk from such food-chain contamination. The refuge there encompasses about 35,000 acres and is primarily a wintering ground for large flights of Canada geese, snow geese, and pintail and other ducks.

Concentrations of selenium that are potentially dangerous to fish, waterfowl, and those who consume them have been reported in the San Joaquin River and some of its tributaries by the Central Valley Regional Water Quality Control Board and the state Department of Water Resources. The DWR has found fourteen farm drainage sumps, ditches, ponds, or canals in the San Joaquin Valley and Tulare Lake Basin, both north and south of Bakersfield, with selenium levels as high, or higher, than in Kesterson water. At fifteen other reporting stations, including several in the San Joaquin River and its tributaries, the state has recorded levels consistently above the 2–5 ppb once believed safe for most wildlife but now considered a definite long-term accumulation threat to fish, waterfowl, and many of the other organisms that occupy links in the food chain upon which they depend. Two of those stations even exceed the safe level for drinking water of 10 ppb.

Near the south end of San Francisco Bay, the U.S. Fish and Wildlife Service has detected as much selenium in the livers of ducks as its researchers found in waterfowl from Kesterson. The source is community sewage treatment plants where there are selenium-using industries—particularly in the discharge of sewage plants that serve scores of large semiconductor plants in Silicon Valley, between San Jose and Stanford. More selenium is coming from glass and tire plants, photo shops, and other industries in other cities around the bay. But the biggest combined contribution, greater even than the upstream flows from the tainted farm fields, is from the string of huge oil refineries along the eastern shore of the northern part of the bay system, mainly in Contra Costa County.

Two environmental groups, Citizens for a Better Environment and the Bay Institute of San Francisco, working with data from the water quality board and others, discovered that industrial discharges from just six oil refineries accounted for 2,479 pounds of selenium every year in the bay system. And an unknown amount flows into the bay from a variety of other industrial dischargers, including printing, painting, dye, and glass operations. The damage isn't limited to waterfowl. Dungeness crabs near Redwood City and clams near refinery discharges contain selenium well above levels known to impair survival in most aquatic species. They discovered selenium levels up to 9.8 ppm in the crabs and 7.4 ppm in clams.

Among the several seemingly mysterious aspects of selenium that Jim Morris and I uncovered in our travels and readings was the disturbing evidence of conflicting interagency roles being played out. Nearly a century ago, one hand of the federal government was guiding the manifest destiny of western deserts to make them bloom like the proverbial rose with massive irrigation. At the same time, another federal agency was uncovering the poisonous threat of the natural trace element selenium to people, livestock, and crops raised on those same arid lands.

But the agencies—Interior's Bureau of Reclamation and the Department of Agriculture—shared neither mission nor findings. As a result, extensive evidence of the selenium danger was ignored and major water diversion projects that now threaten serious selenium contamination were built where or how they shouldn't have been. The failure to communicate continues to haunt these agencies . . . and a lot of innocent ranchers, farmers, livestock, and wildlife.

"The major reason that one hand didn't know what the other was doing is that the toxicity of selenium is hidden in obscure journals," said pathologist Dr. Jerry Simmons, chief of the clinical laboratory at the Veterans Administration Hospital in Sioux Falls, South Dakota, where he studies how selenium works its lethal damage. "It is amazing what we find when we go back and read some of the literature," said Simmons. "I guess that's why they call it re-search."[3] In the wake of the dreadful deformities discovered at Kesterson, what "re-searchers" at the USGS in Menlo Park found was stunning indeed. Dating back nearly a hundred years were a series of reports on the potent toxicity—and proliferation—of selenium throughout the West, centered in the Rocky Mountain belt but extending to the Plains States of the Dakotas, Nebraska, and Kansas, and beyond.

From Kansas in 1891, Wyoming in 1893, Nebraska in 1904, and South Dakota in 1910 came studies packed with evidence of the fateful toll of selenium on livestock, its contamination of a wide range of grain and other crops, and its bizarre botanical affiliation. The historical vaults yielded much more, most from repositories of the Agriculture Department and its various experiment stations that funded and did the fieldwork. There are extensive bibliographies, incisive geological mapping of the host-rock formations, complicated biochemistry reports, and dramatic accounts of the poisonous effects on a wide range of animals. While the differing missions and hierarchies of the two bureaucracies may have accounted for part of the communication gap, World War II was another factor. According to those unearthing many of the valuable volumes, all but war-related research was interrupted in the 1940s, just as scientific interest in selenium was cresting. "This was a very hot subject around here back then," said Doc Kilness. "But it was dropped after World War II broke out and it never started up again. It just dropped through the cracks."

Other researchers say the field suffered as experts retired or moved to other subjects. In 1961, fearful that many of the original selenium experts had either died or soon might, Cecil Wadleigh, then chief of research for the federal Soil Conservation Service, pulled together all of the historical work in one publication while there was still time. Even then, most of the original reports were either out of print or in very short supply. There were dozens more technical journals to be found and checked. The biggest clutch came from 1930 to 1940, when the scientists were proving that the toxicant in what some ranchers called locoweed, but which Orville Beath later correctly identified as *Astragalus* plants, was selenium—and that it was poisoning crops and animals and probably people throughout a number of western states. Unfortunately, history repeated itself.

The compendium produced by Wadleigh's five-member team, *Selenium in Agriculture,* published as Agricultural Handbook No. 200 in Janaury 1961, also was largely ignored by those who might have benefited the most: the Interior Department and Reclamation Bureau. Ironically, the Interior Department was a participant in compiling the

1961 handbook, along with the Agriculture Department's research service and the Geological Survey. But that document, too, eventually went out of print and without much fanfare. It came to light again only in the wake of the Kesterson discoveries. When Ivan Barnes of the Geological Survey went to the agency's Menlo Park library file, he found twenty-five pages of historical literature references totaling 325 separate reports. Most of those reports were quickly circulated among a new cadre of "re-searchers"—biologists and geologists, mainly—as rapidly as copying machines could reproduce them.

There were companion pieces in *The Bee*'s series, as well, stories the reporters and editors call "sidebars," drafted to fill in some of the obvious gaps for readers. One of those sidebars, headlined "Two-Headed Monster of Destruction on Loose," was another basic primer on the unique nature of the element. "Selenium is a Jekyll-and-Hyde element," it started out:

> *Too much causes poisoning or toxicity, with painful, sometimes swift death or horrid, twisted deformity. Too little turns muscles to putty, makes bones fragile and severely damages offspring. Just enough in livetock and some wild animals produces healthy growth. There is scientific division about whether it does the same for humans or plants.*
>
> *As a human poison, selenium hasn't been studied much outside South Dakota, even though there have been reports of human toxicity from it in Nebraska, Wyoming, Colorado and New Mexico. There are parts of China where infant death has been blamed on Keshan disease, or selenium deficiency. In another nearby province, however, more than half the people in five villages suffered impaired health when a drought ruined the rice crop and forced heavy reliance on locally grown crops high in selenium. The element was leached out of nearby coal deposits into the soil and groundwater.*
>
> *There are other puzzling contradictions.*
>
> *Selenium once was suspected of causing cancer. Now, most experts have discarded that notion because the early research work was seriously flawed. Instead, the National Cancer Institute, Harvard University and others think selenium blocks, not causes, some cancer and are doing studies to prove it.*
>
> *The same schizophrenic personality appears in selenium's interaction with members of the toxic heavy metal family. In some cases, it blocks or impairs the*

potent toxicity of cadmium, mercury and arsenic by somehow neutralizing the poisons or by protecting cell membranes against assault. But at other dosage levels, it magnifies the cell damage in what scientists call a synergistic effect, where the simultaneous action of separate components is greater than the sum of their individual effects, a case of 2 times 2 equaling 7, or 9 or 26.

The issue of safe or correct dosage is a matter of continuing discussion. For most adult humans, medical researchers have narrowed the maximum safe range for tolerated exposure to about 200 micrograms (written as "μg" in the scientific short form) a day. But that varies with age, health and genetic makeup of the individual. (The federal Food and Drug Administration in 1990 affixed a Recommended Daily Allowance—RDA—and set it at only 76 μg for healthy males, 50 for females and only 10 for infants.)

For the very young, old or weak, those numbers may be far lower. For stronger or even just physiologically different people, they might be as high as 1000 μg (millionths of a gram).

The FDA believes humans usually begin to suffer ill effects at dietary levels of 800 to 1000 micrograms (μg). Other experts, including those in the National Institutes of Health (NIH), feel that poisoning starts sooner, at 500 μg. Severe toxicity occurs when exposure reaches 3000 μg, the equivalent of 3000 ppb, or 3 ppm.

The most likely early effects are skin sores, loss of hair and distinct changes in both fingernails and toenails, which become excessively brittle or show unusual bumps or ridges. But if exposure persists, or worsens, symptoms can rapidly progress to extreme lethargy, nervousness, numbing and tingling of the extremities, headaches, dizziness, paralysis, motor disturbance and even birth defects. Though there is suspicion of birth deformities in humans, none has been looked for, or found.

While it takes much larger doses to impair the health of exposed adults, selenium takes an awful toll at the reproductive stage of life. Among its many other bizarre or discriminatory characteristics, selenium has a profound affinity for protein, and the makeup of the male sperm and female egg is, largely, protein.

There is another reason why its worst effects are visited upon the young, old and weak. "At the reproductive stage and with infants," says Dr. Arthur Kilness of Rapid City, S.D., "that happens for two reasons: the prevalence of protein and the immaturity of the body's immune system. In the case of the old or ill," said Kilness, "it is just as obvious. The body defenses are low and unable to ward off attack."[4]

The newspaper was not content just to share its discoveries with its readers. Hennessy suggested, and Favre and Baker, his superiors, quickly approved, a release of the full series to the national wire services and put the package out on the company's McClatchy Wire Service, whose nearly 200 clients included the *New York Times* and *Los Angeles Times*, the *Washington Post*, and other notable newspapers nationwide. And Hennessy made sure that tearsheets from all three days of the series were transmitted to every major western paper and many smaller ones, especially in the areas cited in the stories.

The response was swift and dramatic. Nowhere was that more true than the powerful water and power subcommittee of the House Committee on Interior and Insular Affairs chaired by Congressman George Miller (D–Contra Costa County) of California. The panel summoned Interior Secretary Hodel and his top aides to congressional hearings to comment on the newspaper's findings. Despite Interior's response that their own supposed in-house study had found nothing to be alarmed about, Miller and his fellow committee members insisted on a thorough investigation and report back to the committee.

Miller and ranking Republican committee member Congressman Dick Cheney, who went on to become secretary of defense in the Bush administration, cosigned a letter September 17, 1985, to Hodel, stating:

> *A recent series of newspaper accounts in the Sacramento Bee has raised new and serious concerns regarding selenium contamination in the West resulting from Federal irrigation projects. Specifically, drainage from lands irrigated in 15 Western states is alleged to contain high levels of selenium, much of it apparently linked to irrigation on lands included within Bureau of Reclamation projects.*
>
> *Contamination from subsurface agricultural drainage has been documented at several locations in California over the past few years. Kesterson Reservoir is the best known example, but dangerous levels of selenium and other contaminants have also been found in the Grassland Water District, in Kern County, and in the Imperial Valley.*
>
> *The Congress has been assured by Departmental officials and representatives of the Bureau of Reclamation that contamination problems such as those found at*

Kesterson are isolated and are unlikely to be duplicated elsewhere. The press accounts referred to above, however, suggest that the problem may be more widespread than was originally thought. We are concerned that contamination from intensive irrigation development in the West may pose a major problem for wildlife, the agricultural economy of the West, and possibly public health.

We are writing to request your continued attention to this problem. We need answers to some very basic questions, and we need those answers quickly. Simply put, we need to know whether irrigation drainage from Bureau of Reclamation projects is or is not a problem which requires our attention.

We request that you immediately direct the appropriate Departmental officials to undertake a preliminary assessment of the general nature and extent of this apparent contamination problem, to follow up on previous departmental actions.

By February 1, 1986, we ask that you submit a report to the Congress which clearly identifies: (1) where contamination has been found, and whether the contamination can be traced to drainage from irrigation development; and (2) whether the contamination has been, is, or might pose a threat to public health, livestock, wildlife, groundwater, or other resources.

We are certain that you share our conviction that a prompt assessment of this potentially critical situation is in the best interests of everyone. We would be happy to discuss this request in detail with Departmental officials.[5]

The probe began in October. And it was met with both excitement and apprehension at *The Bee*. It was one thing to uncover a problem dramatic enough to warrant congressional attention and action. It was disquieting, in the extreme, to wait while a team of federal scientists pored over your work to verify its accuracy.

In the Sacramento newsroom, things got especially tense. Concerned editors kept asking how solid the foundation was, how secure its interpretation, how accurate the analyses, how reliable the lab, how trustworthy the government sources who helped explain what levels constituted potential danger points. And, more than once, they wanted assurances that the protected "anonymous sources" were real and trustworthy and, above all, had no personal axes to grind, no venal intent to serve. Of course, all of that had been done before. But it was done again.

By early December, the waiting was over. Before the formal report made its way to Congress, *The Bee* heard from its confidential sources that the three-member teams—one each from the geology, wildlife, and reclamation branches—had finished a thorough audit of every site examined by the newspaper. "The U.S. government has confirmed most of the discoveries of a Bee investigation that uncovered a buildup of toxic selenium on or near wildlife refuges throughout the West," our subsequent story stated. "The trace natural soil element has been identified as the cause of death and deformity of waterfowl, fish and other wildlife at Kesterson NWR in the San Joaquin Valley," it continued.

> *Biologists fear that its buildup in widely scattered parts of at least six other states could wreak similar havoc there.*
>
> *Although the federal government's report drew no conclusions, the newspaper's investigation found that massive federal water projects are at fault in most cases. Scores of these projects are robbing waterfowl and wildlife habitat of limited fresh water and returning it laced with selenium—and other toxicants.*
>
> *The formal Department of Interior report, demanded by a congressional committee after The Bee published its findings in September, is scheduled to be released in Washington, D.C. on Dec. 9 or 10.*
>
> *In what essentially was a detailed audit of The Bee investigation, the government found that 18 of 23 sites tested by the newspaper are either confirmed or suspected "high-selenium" sites. There was virtual agreement on the number of sites with low potential for selenium toxicity. The government listed five and The Bee six. Both found high levels of selenium in California, Arizona, Nevada, Montana, New Mexico and South Dakota.*
>
> *Despite the strong agreement of the two studies, there are important differences. The Bee defined "high" as sediment levels at or above 600 parts per billion, based on new Fish and Wildlife Service studies showing that selenium can accumulate from comparatively low levels in mud and sediment to dangerously high counts in wildlife as it travels up the aquatic food chain. Interior set "high" levels at 1,500 ppb, or 1.5 ppm, however. As a result, six Bee sites in the "high" range were classified as potentially high by the government and needing further study.*
>
> *Another difference was the number of states where high levels exist. The Bee claimed seven, the government six.*
>
> *Both agreed on two sites in California, the Salton Sea NWR and the Imperial Valley NWR on the Colorado River. The reports also agreed on a site in Arizona's Yuma Valley and another in Poison Canyon, N.M., upstream from two national wildlife refuges.*

Others include Nevada's Stillwater refuge, that state's largest marsh; several sites in South Dakota, including an Edgemont ranch and farm drainage canals flowing into the Cheyenne and Belle Fourche Rivers; and several in Montana.

The government study excludes a state waterfowl management area—Stewart Lake—in Utah, but recommended further study there.

The 11-member task force was drawn from three agencies of Interior: the U.S. Geological Survey, the Fish and Wildlife Service and the Bureau of Reclamation.

The Interior document is only the first phase of the selenium study reactivated by the department after The Bee reported it had been derailed because of budget restrictions and fears over potential expensive government liability for cleanup.

The next stage is a full-scale sampling at the 18 "high" or suspected high sites, and, perhaps, at other locations not visited by the newspaper but which have been identified by others as likely selenium trouble spots.[6]

The waiting was over for the newspaper. There was more to come, of course, more testing, more complicated interpretation, and more reports. More important, the besieged wildlife at the known and suspected selenium target sites would now get some serious attention. The concern to make sure that selenium's lethal effects would be dealt with, however, didn't stop there. *The Bee* republished the series in a tabloid format and mailed out hundreds of copies to every member and affected committee of Congress, to governors of all the western states, and to the bureaucracies with jurisdiction there. It made thousands more available to environmental groups, schools, and the general public.

Finally, the "dark side" of Doc's moon would get a definitive look. Barnes's selenium genie was going to get all the way out of the bottle this time.

| # FORGOTTEN CRUSADERS

Ivan Barnes was not the first geologist to make the stunning prediction that the selenium shadow would spread over vast tracts of the semiarid West. Fully thirty-six years earlier, on February 25, 1949, J. David Love sent an astonishing "memorandum" to his superiors in the U.S. Geological Survey. Love was one of the foremost western geologists of his time and one of the agency's two or three most prominent field geologists. In nine pages and accompanying maps, he outlined to chief USGS geologist W. H. Bradley a program that would "bring geology, geobotany and geochemistry to the homes of farmers, ranchers and other property owners throughout vast areas of the western United States. If this program is properly effected," Love continued, "it will save these people millions of dollars by preventing livestock deaths, preventing livestock and human debility, preventing the raising of poisoned crops, eliminating poisoned pastures, and preventing unwise investments in land and livestock."

Plainly stating that he had "no axe to grind" and "no personal ambition" to serve with respect to such work, Love proposed that the Geological Survey dedicate the "best geologists, best administrators, best coordinators, and best diplomats" at its command. Then he added in his own wry manner that he did not consider himself to be "in any of these categories, and feel sure that my long-suffering superiors in the Fuels Branch will agree that this statement is made with no sham attempt at false modesty."

His branch chief at the time, Carle H. Dane, had directed Love to prepare such a proposal after a major international geological conference in Salt Lake City dealt, at length, with the threat of selenium, molybdenum, tellurium, and other such poisonous trace elements and the need to bridge a growing gap between geology and public health concerns. But the proposal never surfaced again, officially or otherwise, and Love still is not certain how high up the USGS ladder it went. "All I know, for sure," he recalled during a November 1990 interview in his office at the University of Wyoming in Laramie, "is that it was never acted upon and that its sequel has virtually disappeared from the face of the earth."

For Love followed up what certainly must have looked like a political bombshell to his superiors—and to theirs—with an even more explicit proposal in 1951. In it he urged the USGS to establish a new and separate section devoted entirely to the study of a wide range of impacts to public health from an even wider array of geological threats. "That one just disappeared altogether. It has vanished, entirely, from the Survey files," said Love.

It's not surprising that someone might have gone a bit weak at the knees over Love's frankly stated objectives in the 1949 memo or subsequent blunt explanation of the threat to livestock and humans from consuming vegetation tainted by poisonous soil elements. But nothing could have prepared them for Love's "conservative estimate of the magnitude of the problem confronting the economy of the western United States" on the second page of his 1949 proposal.

There, in his stark fashion, Love wrote: "In Montana, approximately 30 percent of the state has, at the surface, seleniferous rocks that are actively or potentially poisonous. The figure for Wyoming is 20 percent, for Colorado 30 percent, for the northern half of Arizona 20 percent, for the northern half of New Mexico 40 percent, for Utah 25 percent. In short, thousands of square miles of land in these regions are now, or may become, poisonous to livestock that graze there and to human beings that live there, and crops that are raised there may be poisonous."

He recounted a threat of progressive debility for the regional economies involved and warned of acute cases of rapid poisoning that could cause "several million dollars in livestock losses per year" in the Rocky Mountain region alone. "The losses in terms of debilitation, sterility, crippling, and suffering," he added, "cannot be estimated. More tragic still are the wasted years of hard work, the broken homes, the blighted lives, and the abandoned farms and ranches of those people who homesteaded or bought places without realizing they never had a chance to succeed because of these poisonous elements in the ground. They fail without knowing why."

Nowhere, Love warned, was the threat greater than to reservations of the Navajo, Hopi, Apache, and Kaibab Indians in Arizona, 60 percent of whose lands he estimates are pocked with outcroppings of seleniferous formations that are "actively or potentially poisonous." He says that the entire Navajo Reservation in New Mexico is similarly afflicted. And, now well beyond the tight parameters of the passionless geologist, he adds: "It is no wonder that the economy of these Indians is in terrible condition and their health and that of their livestock is poor. The government has poured hundreds of thousands of dollars into the support of these Indians, yet it has totally disregarded the fact that more than half of the land allocated to them is now or probably will become poisonous."[1]

Love is retired now but remains active in his fieldwork, writing, and lecturing. During the interview in his windowless, basement office he chuckled at the apparent brashness of his warnings. "You could say that the language was, oh, rather direct, I guess."

I asked whether he had any doubts about the accuracy of his selenium assessments, any frustrations at the lack of response to his warnings, so many decades and discoveries later. The swivel chair in his Laramie office creaked as he tilted back and ran a hand through richly
textured, snow-white hair. He paused to adjust the wire-rim glasses
that framed sparkling blue eyes and a complexion that defied so many
years in the rain, snow, and ceaseless high-country winds of Wyoming.

"Doubts? Do I have any doubts about the toxicity of selenium to cattle and other livestock, or even to people in the West?" he repeated.
"No. I don't have any at all, especially about the validity of the mass of
anecdotal information about it in the historical literature. There is just
too much of it to be ignored, even though that is what many in Wyoming still want to do. Politically, we are still ignoring the whole problem. Sooner or later we are going to have to face up to the fact that we
have poisoned ground in our state . . . and many others."

There was a long pause as he watched the words reappear on my
notebook. The chair swiveled slowly, and creaked again, as he picked
up the conversational thread. "Do I feel frustrated by the lack of response to these warnings?" he paraphrased the inquiry. "Oh, my, yes.
You try to impress the importance of vision on these young people today, some sense of long-range impacts, and it just doesn't take. I would
like them to think of the future and the importance of the need for co-
ordination of the various scientific disciplines involved, the botany, the
geology, the chemistry, specifically on this selenium problem. I have
given lectures on this subject and on this need all over the West, on the
relationship of geology to human health and disease. There has to be an
interrelationship of the sciences. No one person can know it all. It is too
complex for that."

J. David Love should know. His connections to selenium go way,
way back . . . to some of his first recollections, stories told around the
roaring hearth of the Love Ranch, 12 miles from the exact geological
center of Wyoming and 13 miles from the nearest neighbor. David and
his older brother, Allan, were the only two children within a thousand

square miles, and Love still laughingly tells how they outnumbered the native trees in that part of the Wind River Basin's sea of buffalo grass and grama grass and nutritious salt sage.

His earliest recollection about the dangers of selenium? "Well, no one knew what it was back then, as far as the name goes, but they sure knew its effects. I remember the ranchers talking about the Lysite Buttes. As a youngster, I remember hearing them talk about having to put range riders out there all the time, on patrol, to keep the sheep and cattle away from the poisonous grass. And that was only 25 miles from our place."

He told the story with a verve and touch that his great-uncle, John Muir, the founder of the Sierra Club, would have appreciated. "It was in the 1890s, at the peak of the Mormon persecutions," Love recalled, "and a couple of Mormon sheepherders came through with 4,000 sheep and found this huge range and camped there to graze. Doug Fuller was the range rider then and his son, who worked for us later, told us the story about how some cowboys just happened to ride through and see them there and warned them about the poisoned ground. Unfortunately, the drovers took it as just more anti-Mormon bias and insisted they had a right to use it as free range. The next morning, when they awoke, 2,800 of the sheep were dead. And in the next few days, as they trailed what was left of them out of there, another 800 died, leaving them with only 400 of the 4,000 they came with. That was a terrible tragedy for them."

Such accounts often are reduced to the stuff of myth and legend by the passage of time. Love, however, saw much of selenium's misery firsthand, as did Kilness. The geologist recalled another experience with the toxic legacy of the Lysite Buttes. "About every generation or so, someone goes back in there," he recalled. "They see all that grazing land and just can't resist. I guess they figure the old stories are just a myth. The last time that happened was about twenty years ago. A well-known sheep rancher from Lysite went in there with his flock and it was a disaster. He lost a lot of animals."

The same rancher didn't remember anything about that when Doc and I spoke with him in 1988. We had been on the way to the Lysite Buttes and, by pure coincidence, selected his house to seek directions. Well, it wasn't as random as all that. There were, after all, only a handful of houses in the tiny hamlet of Lysite from which to choose. Doc briefly outlined our mission, then asked whether he had ever heard of selenium or suffered any losses from it to his sheep. "Nope. Can't say as I ever heard of that word. But we steer clear of the Buttes anyway," said the rancher. "We never graze our animals anywhere near there."

His firsthand experience with the effect of selenium came more than twenty years after University of Wyoming research chemist and leading selenium researcher Orville A. Beath had scientifically validated the potency of the Lysite threat. Soil samples he collected there contained among the highest soil selenium concentrations ever found: upward of 119 ppm.

Tales of similar massive herd kills in the region, and the isolation of being one of only two children in such a vast sweep, gradually pulled Love toward a lifetime of kicking over rocks to watch what crawled out (and looking closer at what didn't). "Well, there weren't any girls for a thousand miles, so what else was there to do?" he laughed while recalling those early days. Despite the isolation, he didn't lack for proper and creative schooling. When his Scottish father, Johnny Love, wasn't reciting poetry he was singing the lads Scottish ballads or imparting wood lore and astrology while camped under star-studded skies. What the boys didn't learn from him they picked up on their own while running trap lines, riding roundup, and trailing herds, or during five-day wagon trips to the nearest wood lot at the foot of the Medicine Bow Mountains. The family supplemented its meager wood supply with hand-dug coal and the boys did their share of digging, not only for the coal but on the family well, too. That still left plenty of time for studying clouds, snaring rabbits, collecting arrowheads, and rousting the occupants of the nearest rattlesnake den.

The more formal part of their schooling came from David's

Wellesley-educated mother, Ethel Waxham Love. She started out as the "marm" of a log-cabin school 60 miles away, on Twin Creek, near the mouth of Skull Gulch. But after a courtship with determined Johnny Love, she wound up teaching David and Allan years later, in the spacious living room of the ranch house, on a converted roulette table from Joe Lacy's Muskrat Saloon.

A more thorough and glorious description of the Loves and their lifestyle graces the masterfully crafted pages of John McPhee's *Rising from the Plains,* but I can't conclude here without at least a summary of the mother's reference library. Among its volumes were the 1911 Encyclopedia Britannica, the Redpath Library, one hundred volumes of Greek and Roman literature, including the *Iliad* and the *Odyssey,* and works by Shakespeare, Dickens, Emerson, Thoreau, Longfellow, Kipling, Twain, and many, many more.[2]

Love's selenium schooling may have started at the fireplace, but it didn't begin to bud until he enrolled at the University of Wyoming. There he had the respected head of geology, Dr. Samuel Howell Knight, as his mentor. Knight was close, personally and professionally, to Orville A. Beath, the school's chief research chemist and also one of the world's foremost selenium researchers. It wasn't long before Love was hired by Beath to do "odd jobs" in the summer. One of them was to journey to Jackson Hole in 1934, when Love was just nineteen. There, with one of Beath's long-time aides, Harold Eppsom, he looked for *Astragalus* plants, the aboveground flags of the belowground presence of selenium. There, in the shadow of the Grand Tetons, Love's curiosity about the "freaky" trace element and quirky *Astragalus* would take on new dimensions.

He remembers the experience and its significance well. "We camped out for about a week—you can imagine what Jackson Hole looked like back then, absolutely magnificent country—and found one area with a few *bisulcatus*," said Love. "But there were no woody aster at all. Today," said Love, speaking of his most recent visit there in the summer of 1990, "there are hundreds of thousands of asters all over that area and a lot more *bisulcatus*, too." The daisylike woody asters, or *Xylorrhiza*, resemble, but are shorter than, the common oxeye daisy. Like other primary selenium indicator plants—Beath has identified twenty-four species and three varieties of *Astragalus* in this category—they require high levels of soil selenium to grow.

But these unusual plants are more than warning flags of the danger below. Their deep taproot systems, perhaps aided by distinctive soil microbes, are uniquely able to absorb from the surrounding soil the elemental form of selenium that is apparently essential to their growth but otherwise unavailable to other plants and grasses. Once taken up into the plant, the metalloid is metabolized into water-soluble selenate—so that when the converter plants die, they deposit an enriched halo of water-soluble organic selenium around them that can be readily taken up by nearly all other forms of vegetation. And, as so often happens with other hazardous elements, the methylated daughter compounds often are more potent than the parents. Research by U.S. Fish and Wildlife scientists has proved that the organic compound selenomethionine is ten times more toxic to some forms of wildlife than even selenate, widely regarded as the most potent of the inorganic forms.

The passage of time and Love's astute powers of observation in the rich Teton meadows near his summer home have revealed a chilling but little understood role that unwitting human endeavors may have played in spreading the impact of selenium toxicity. The virtual explosion—Love calls it an invasion—of primary indicator and converter plants is slowly turning the Upper Gros Ventre Basin (pronounced "gro-vaunt" from the French name "Big Gut" for the Sheepherder Indians of that region) into a very real selenium threat. On the southern doorstep of Yellowstone National Park, the basin is a popular summer range for 6,000 head of Wyoming cattle and 15,000 elk.

Love grew clearly agitated as he recalled the scene and thumped the top of his ancient oak desk with a thick, weathered palm. "Many of those cattle now come out of that range with the distinctive 'paddle hooves,' low birth rates, and low fat content common to selenium-poisoned livestock—despite grazing on what used to be some of the most nutritious grass on God's green earth," he said. "And they are up there for only a few months of the year." Again, he paused, waiting for my scribbling to catch up. "But that's only half the story. The Gros Ventre is the year-round range for the Yellowstone elk herd and the Gros Ventre mountain sheep herd, the largest mountain sheep herd in North America. They are increasingly in danger of being wiped out by selenium. But it won't be anything dramatic. They will just fail to reproduce successfully and, slowly, the herds will die out."

Love's years of fieldwork in the region define the scope of the risk. Nearly the entire Gros Ventre range is on seleniferous soil, and he estimates that up to 60 percent of it may now be covered by the converter plants that change the selenium from latent to lethal. "The plants are expanding all over that country, year after year," said Love. "I can't prove how it happened but I strongly suspect it is the result of trucking cattle in from areas where the indicator plants were common and from this relatively recent practice of trucking hay all over hell and gone. Those big hay trucks are going up and down those highways all the time, carrying cut-up *Astragalus* plants—and their seeds—along with the hay. I think that is how they have been spread."

There was no pause this time. Love played both roles in the pre-Thanksgiving interview. "The question, now," he preempted, "is at what point does that process convert and mobilize enough of the native selenium so that it becomes toxic to those animals? I don't know the answer to that and I don't think we can afford to wait any longer to find it. I have taken U.S. senators, governors, cattlemen, and three different heads of the U. S. Forest Service through there and showed them the problem during the last thirty years. It keeps getting worse but nothing ever gets done."

But how did the selenium get there in the first place? And how did it spread over hundreds of thousands of square miles of the rest of the West and so many other parts of the world, too? It is a complicated answer. Love said the process started millions of years ago with the magma flows and volcanic eruptions associated with formation of the earth's crust. The gaseous emissions of selenium eventually were scrubbed from the atmosphere by rain and snowfall, concentrating wherever the downwind plumes took them. The rest spewed out in volcanic ash, some of which straddled the globe and added volcanic selenium in places where no volcanism occurred. Love believes the remainder was brought to the surface by flows and surges of superheated lava.

But what didn't reach the surface then, millions of years ago, has emerged since, through the intervening periods of uplift, subduction, other volcanic episodes, and more thrusting, faulting, and uplifting of the earth's surface. Erosion and weathering carried selenium-laced sediments into the beds of ancient lakes and seas, especially over much of the West. There, layer upon compressed layer, concentrated in the remains of billions of aquatic organisms and in the detrital ooze they comprised, the selenium was incorporated in the shales that are present at the surface. Those same seleniferous outcroppings are present throughout much of the West today, and many of them contain enough of the element to produce toxic vegetation.

But there is more to the selenium distribution than marine shale formations. Dozens of researchers the world over have reported extremely high concentrations of the poison in everything from deeply buried coal seams and oil formations to limestone, sandstone, and, especially, sulfide ore bodies, some of which contain so much of the element that concentrations are expressed as percentages—up to 23 percent in some cases—rather than mere parts per billion or even million. By comparison, 1 percent is 1 part per hundred—four orders of magnitude greater than a 1 ppm level. Even the wintertime snowfall over Cambridge, Massachusetts, in 1964 contained 270 ppb, according to a report by USGS researcher Hubert W. Lakin.[3] The selenium fallout from the area's coal smoke in 1964–65 was almost as high as the selenium load flowing into Kesterson.

Love had at least three firsthand experiences with selenium cropping up in ore bodies and other rock formations, and two of them have serious public health implications today. One of those was selenium's almost constant presence in uranium ore formations, many of which Love discovered as a government geologist. Another case of guilt by metallic association was selenium's combination with vanadium. During World War II, Love supervised government efforts to mine and mill vanadium from organic-rich black shale formations at eight different sites in the West because the Department of Defense needed the element as an alloy to strengthen the armor on U.S. tanks being ventilated by superior German Panzer firepower. Those same vanadium-rich shales held selenium levels of from 20 to 119 ppm . . . and it still taints mine tailings decades later.

Love talked also of reports written about health dangers to uranium miners and millers constantly exposed to both the toxic and radioactive effects of the uranium. "But," he added, "they almost never mention selenium, even though it is probably more dangerous." One of those documents made only a one-paragraph mention of the potential health effects of incorporated selenium dust, although others often refer to common occurrences of a "red slime" on the surface of spent uranium ore tailings. That, said Love, is the reddish-colored elemental selenium.

The veteran geologist also spent years studying the West's prolific phosphate formations, from which some of the nation's largest firms now mine phosphate rock for fertilizer. "We know that selenium is present in most of that formation," said Love, "sometimes at hundreds of parts per million."[4] Its presence, he believes, is related to the high organic content of phosphate deposits from marine organisms that would have concentrated the selenium from the water around them.

The veteran geologist cautioned: "I worry about whether we are spreading selenium all over our lands in this country, today, from the use of phosphate fertilizer. We are spreading millions of tons of phosphate on our farmlands every year and most of it has at least some selenium." He said the same thing occurs in many other countries, too, including Morocco and Turkey, where phosphate rock is extensively mined and also tainted by selenium. "This absolutely needs to be looked into," said Love. "I have screamed and yelled about this for years because we need to know the risks. But, I warn you that if you do raise this issue, you will run into an industrial roadblock from people who mine and process it here in the West." The historical research literature is full of references to phosphate formations containing substantial levels of selenium.

Love's third concern, about selenium leaching from the uranium tailings and other mine waste deposits with which it is often associated, is not being ignored, however. The federal Office of Surface Mining has commissioned studies of abandoned mine wastes and their selenium potential and also is funding recovery and archival preservation, in the University of Wyoming Library, of volumes of early and unpublished selenium research by Love's mentor, Orville Beath, and his colleagues. Some of the historical research has already documented especially high levels of selenium in the outwash of old silver, gold, lead, and zinc milling operations at Park City, Utah. Some ore samples there held as much as 540 ppm selenium, and the Weber River carries elevated selenium levels today.

Beath and noted Columbia University botanist Samuel F. Trelease, coauthors of the first selenium textbook in 1949, discovered similar problems in the southwestern corner of Idaho. Of a mining district which once produced large quantities of silver and gold, not far from where the Jordan River flows through Owyhee County, the authors stated: "One of the most abundant of the silver ores in the district was naumannite (Ag_2Se) containing 23 percent selenium." That is a remarkable 23 parts per hundred, or 230,000 parts per million. Beath and Trelease say the selenium moved into the downslope grasslands, where floodplain silts were found to contain from traces to 25 ppm selenium—and the grass growing in them up to 116 ppm.[5] For comparison, the highest level found so far in the alluvial outwashes of California's San Joaquin Valley is 4.5 ppm selenium in the soil and some edible crops with levels from 10 to 12 ppm.

Beath became the preeminent selenium researcher of his time, though there were dozens of others probing into its unique properties in the 1930s and 1940s. He was born and raised on a small farm in Wisconsin, graduated in chemistry from the University of Wisconsin, and earned his master's there in 1912. After a two-year stint as a chemistry instructor at the University of Kansas, Beath joined the University of Wyoming faculty in 1914, becoming head of its Department of Research Chemistry, a post he retained until his retirement in 1955.

Perhaps because he had done postgraduate work in plant chemistry at Wisconsin, Beath was especially interested in persistent reports of mass sheep deaths on the high plains of Wyoming and some ranchers' claims that the cause was some kind of toxic agent in the vegetation. The most dramatic of those events was the loss of more than 15,000 sheep in the summers of 1907 and 1908 north of Medicine Bow, Wyoming, where the animals grazed an area profuse with woody aster and what the ranchers then called Gray's vetch (later identified by Beath as *Astragalus bisulcatus*).[6]

Other researchers, including Dr. K. W. Franke and coworkers at the South Dakota Experiment Station, found toxic levels of selenium in wheat and other grains grown in high-selenium soils as early as 1929. Franke's report was considered highly controversial by his superiors and it was withheld from publication until 1934 because of the same kind of economic and political pressures commonly experienced by current selenium researchers. Love said he had heard Beath agonize about Franke's problems with reports censored or withheld because of their economic and political implications, a quandary he was not altogether unfamiliar with himself. Concentrations in some grain samples were as high as 12 ppm, high enough to be toxic to humans, and the gluten contained up to 90 ppm.[7]

But Beath, moved by the tragedies of area ranchers whose livestock continued to suffer inexplicable death on the open range, concentrated on the unique native plants suspected as the cause. Before his work was over, he had combed known and suspected selenium host-rock formations throughout the West and closely studied the work of other researchers in nearly every western state and the prairie provinces of Canada. Thousands of samples of both the host-soil formations and the vegetation growing on them were collected and analyzed. Sam Trelease, the biochemist, conducted detailed research on the internal chemistry and metabolic functions and properties of the plants.

Beath separated the samples into three categories: *primary selenium indicators,* plants that accumulate (and need) high concentrations, often in thousands of parts per million, from high-selenium soils; *secondary selenium absorbers,* plants that take up only moderate concentrations from highly seleniferous land; and *nonindicator species,* those plants which grow in the presence of selenium but absorb only tiny amounts, less than 1 ppm. He conferred the pretentious title of "Beath's Primary Selenium Indicators" on twenty-four varieties of the pealike *Astragalus* plants and three other plant genera—*Xylorrhiza* (woody aster), *Oonopsis* (goldenweed), and *Stanleya* (prince's plume), twenty-seven in all. But the plethora of *Astragalus* species—there are 300 of them in North America and 2,000 worldwide—and how much of the several forms of inorganic and organic selenium they can or will absorb makes biological flagging more art than science. K. C. Beeson, in a valuable summary of selenium research work by the Agricultural Research Service wing of the U.S. Department of Agriculture (*Selenium in Agriculture*) expanded the list of primary indicators to forty-seven, including thirty species from seven different groups in the genus *Astragalus,* eight species of the genus *Stanleya,* four of *Xylorrhiza,* and five of *Oonopsis.*

Beath was captivated by the unpredictable interplay of the element's geology, botany, and chemistry. Some plants pick up the majority of selenium present as the inorganic and water-soluble selenate (usually the dominant form in predominantly alkaline western environments). Others yield more organic forms, such as the potent selenomethionine or selenocystine. While most of that selenium was what the plant probably metabolized itself, some researchers think organic forms also can be absorbed directly from decayed plants that already have completed the chemical conversion. It is that potential—to be miniature chemical factories—that makes the primary indicator plants so critical to the whole poisoning process, especially in places like the Gros Ventre Basin.

Neither Beath nor his cohorts knew it then, of course, but a new generation of scientists is discovering that a similar conversion process is carried on by different strains of soil fungus and bacteria. Those which operate in an aerobic environment—that is, oxygen-rich—can oxidize the elemental and inorganic forms to gases like dimethylselenide. Anaerobic bacteria, which thrive in an oxygen-free environment, reduce the inorganic selenate and selenite back to the more stable and relatively unavailable elemental form. Either conversion might someday serve as an economic and safe way to treat existing and more dangerous forms of selenium.

Beath prospected an overwhelming number of selenium leads during nearly forty years of active research on the topic, ranging from personal and historical accounts, news stories, and even tales of the Old West to scientific reports and the unpublished findings of others. While his personal files are laced with tragic anecdotes drawn from ranchers in search of answers and assistance, his texts are chock full of the science, pathology, and toxicology of the substance.

His work triggered great controversy—and still does—in Wyoming because of its obvious potential impact on property and livestock values. The university was supportive of some of his work but, especially toward the end, in the 1960s, he had to fund much of it himself. Outside help was almost nonexistent. In fact, Beath and Trelease, the respected chief of Columbia University's botanical department, had to pay for publication of their first text. And Beath himself had to publish a pamphlet in which he summarized some of his two books for circulation among ranchers and others threatened with selenium's toxic impact in his home state. "No one—around here, especially—was interested in what he was finding out," said Love. "The more evidence he collected, the more people worried about the economic impact. No one would touch that first book. He had to pay to get it published himself. The obstacles he faced were tremendous, but he just pushed ahead anyway. He showed true courage."

Many of the ranchers he tried so hard to help wound up hating him, sometimes ordering him off their land at gunpoint. That part of Beath's legacy has been passed on to others. Stephen E. Williams, one of the new generation of selenium researchers and a plant physiologist at the University of Wyoming, recounted the story of how he and his colleagues were digging a series of pits beside selenium indicator plants that virtually covered parts of a ranch, northwest of Laramie, near Bamfort Lake. I interviewed him right after my luncheon with David and Jane Love.

"It was this spring," said Williams, "We were digging pits, next to *Astragalus* plants, so we could examine the root structure and its interface with the underlying soil. We got the permission of the owner's son, who managed the place, and were out digging when the owner came by and asked, 'What the hell are you guys doing?' We told him we had received permission from his son to be there and that we were trying to authenticate some of the early Beath work on selenium. Well, he ordered us off the place, right then," chuckled Williams as he flashed slides of the pit on his classroom projector screen. "He didn't do it at the point of a gun, exactly, but there was a rifle in his cab and his hand was uncomfortably close to it. He was really angry. He gave us an hour to pack up our stuff and get off. Someone asked him whether he had ever heard of Beath and the research he had done with selenium and he replied: 'Oh, I remember, all right. I really hated that Beath.'"

Earlier that day I had met with Beath's daughter, a retired art teacher, only half a block from the campus where her father had spent most of his academic life. Mary Elizabeth Beath was rummaging through scrapbooks and a growing file on her father's selenium work. She had heard many stories like the one told by Williams. "I have heard that some of the ranchers Dad helped actually grew to hate him for the effect his work had," she related. "But he loved ranchers and was deeply hurt by their economic and animal losses to selenium. That was how he got started, at the request of ranchers who kept having these losses and couldn't understand why. They wanted him to do the chemical work to find out what was causing all the death and deformity in their livestock. Later, I know, he was kicked off or ordered off some of those same ranches because the owners didn't want their land devalued by any talk of selenium contamination."

Stephen Williams is one who shares Love's concerns that the converter plants will mobilize otherwise unavailable selenium in places where it will threaten Wyoming's elk herds, antelope, and mountain sheep. "I think it could be a real threat to them," said Williams. "I am not sure just how much damage it does to the wildlife out there," he added, gesturing westward from his campus office, toward the sprawling high plains country. "But I would really like to see some research which addresses what happens to people who eat the antelope that eat on these ranges constantly. We don't know whether the antelope have built up a resistance to selenium or whether they avoid selenium-bearing plants, but clearly they have high potential exposure."

Wyoming wildlife biologist Bill Hepworth had expressed similar concerns two years earlier, in 1988, when I talked to him about the state study for which he was the research director in 1976. That report found high selenium levels in lake water and fish. Hepworth had since transferred to the state wildlife agency's big game branch, but he was aware of the evolving flood of research triggered by the Kesterson episode. "Frankly, I am concerned about hunters who eat antelope," said Hepworth. "Those animals live out there and graze the land continuously. They could have high levels of selenium." The possibility of tainted big game is an issue he raised with some trepidation. "They make a lot of money in Wyoming from antelope hunters," he volunteered, "so it will not be a very popular idea to test some animals and, if necessary, warn hunters of any risks."

Doc Kilness, for one, always thought antelope either had a built-in distaste for seleniferous vegetation or had developed resistance to its toxic effects over generations of genetic coding. But he had doubts because he kept seeing reports of high levels of selenium in antelope fawns and moose in Wyoming that had died of unknown causes. Those doubts were reduced considerably one cold and windy day in May 1988, west of Laramie, during the last selenium research swing Doc made through his beloved West. He and I were on the way to one of the Laramie Plains lakes to collect trout that were rumored to have elevated levels of selenium (they did, later tests proved) when the hawk-eyed Kilness shouted to me to stop the car.

He pointed to a couple of dark clumps on a slight knoll a few hundred yards away. Minutes later, the carcasses of two yearling antelope were kicked over. We found months-old remains of five others in the next fifteen minutes of inspection over just a few hundred yards of the wind-swept prairie. We also found those of two calves. "This doesn't prove anything," grumbled Kilness, his words trailing off in the brisk wind. "They could have died in some big storm during the winter. But it sure makes me wonder about all this talk about resistance and avoidance." The reason for his concern was obvious. Sprouting from the closely cropped carpet of buffalo and grama grass were thousands of woody aster, one of the more potent of Beath's "converter" plants. We collected several of the plants for analysis. Tests showed the composite sample to contain 271 ppm.

Ironically, Williams, the Wyoming University plant physiologist, thinks that one returning form of Wyoming wildlife—buffalo—may hold at least a partial answer to ranchers whose land is so high in selenium they can't safely or profitably raise livestock on it. "We have seen buffalo on one large ranch chomp off an entire adult *Astragalus* plant and never show any ill effects from it. And some of those plants we know have up to 10,000 ppm selenium," he related. "That's enough selenium to drop them dead in their tracks if they were affected by it. It may be that since that species has grazed seleniferous range for centuries, they have built up an immunity to it."

If that turns out to be the case, it could be the salvation for places like a large Laramie-area ranch that is so thick with selenium accumulator plants that Williams calls it "Selenium National Park." High-selenium soil covers nearly half of the massive cattle ranch. "There is a small herd of buffalo there now, and we've seen them eat the *Astragalus* plants with apparently no ill effects. It gets me to wondering if the animals have some immunity to selenium," said Williams. That ranch sells hunting rights to the buffalo. They and others could do a lot more of that, and a lot more profitably, if the buffalo and other wildlife turn out to be reasonably immune to selenium's effects. Even if the immunity theory proves out, however, and it is only that, a theory, close monitoring would have to be done to ensure that the meat, especially the liver, kidney, and heart, which concentrate much higher levels of selenium, is safe for humans to eat.

Some of those close to the controversy in Wyoming firmly believe that political opposition is trying to stifle efforts to resurrect selenium research efforts there. Love is convinced of it. So is Beath's daughter, who has bequeathed most of her estate to the University of Wyoming's American Heritage Center to fund the restoration and cataloging of thousands of pages of her father's unpublished work.

But their skepticism doesn't come close to that of Kilness, the crusty South Dakota physician who vigorously resisted Wyoming efforts to acquire his own files. Two years earlier, during his last selenium work, he told how some Wyoming officials had made overtures to acquire his voluminous files. He then added testily: "I would never, never, never allow them to get their hands on that stuff. They would destroy it in a minute if they got the chance. They are afraid of the truth in Wyoming, at least the ones making all of the decisions. They are afraid of the light and the only thing I am afraid of is the dark. It's what you don't know about selenium that could kill you."

Stephen Williams, taking up where Beath and others left off decades ago, is sensitive to concerns that the university will be unable to resist political pressure to go lightly on selenium. After listening to Mary Elizabeth Beath broach her fears and suspicions, he interjected: "Some of the old work and the facts *are* being hidden. Some of it on purpose by those who really do fear the consequences but most of it by accident because they just don't know all that is involved. If people in this state are ignoring the selenium problem or even trying to sweep it under the rug, it's because they fear that solution of the problem will require that we abandon grazing use of some rangelands and farming of some irrigated land. The state certainly is not eager to tackle the problem." Then he added: "Ultimately, it involves abandoning some range and farmland in the state. That's what it all comes down to. The new governor's task force report is an attempt to sweep it under the rug, but that isn't going to make the problem go away."

Wyoming officials only recently conceded there is any evidence, at all, of selenium's toxic effects in their state. And all of that, so far, has been supplied by the U.S. Fish and Wildlife Service and U.S. Geological Survey in a 1987 reconnaissance study of fish and waterfowl in the Kendrick Project, a federally funded irrigation system near Casper, to the north of Laramie. Selenium levels in water, waterfowl, fish, and other parts of the food-predator web are much higher there than those at Kesterson. Even so, some members of the governor's Selenium Task Force in Wyoming continue to insist that neither Beath nor any of the scores of other selenium researchers have delivered "actual hard evidence" that selenium has killed or harmed any livestock in their state.

That recent assertion, by Wyoming Geological Survey geologist James Case of the task force, prompted this measured reply from Williams: "The only way for Jim Case and I to agree on this subject is not to talk about it. He prefers to doubt there is any evidence that selenium has or continues to harm livestock. I am not convinced that is the case yet. But there is clearly something going on, something we have to come to grips with. I am not a doubter, but neither am I a convert. I am just a very, very curious and interested scientist looking for answers."

Love grimaced when he was asked why he thought that some members of the governor's task force claim there is no hard evidence of livestock impact. Neither rudeness nor contempt is part of his personality. "The trouble with people like that," he said gently, "is that they just won't take the time to read all they should on the subject, even just the work on this campus. If they did, they would know there is ample evidence and most of it from highly respected scientists." Nevertheless, Love believes that one member of the task force, Case, has helped advance selenium research in Wyoming by mapping potentially seleniferous ranch lands in the state and for what Love called "the evenhanded way he chaired the governor's task force on selenium, before that was taken away from him."[8]

But to deny there is evidence in the historical literature of livestock poisoning is to ignore or reject not only the scores of anecdotal accounts listed in study after study but dozens of livestock feed tests in which animals were fed both artificially added selenium and selenium-tainted *Astragalus* plants of known concentration. Those same peer-reviewed studies, many by some of the leading researchers in the Department of Agriculture at the time, reported on the pathology of the poisoned animals along with graphic descriptions of the symptoms they suffered at each successional stage.

The historical accounts are highlighted on the opening pages of Beath's first text on selenium with Columbia's botanist Sam Trelease, published in 1949. That was the same year that Love proposed his major selenium project to the USGS. In addition to the Wyoming State Board of Sheep Commissioners report of 15,000 sheep lost near Medicine Bow, in 1907–1908, the book cites reports of the overnight death of 275 sheep that grazed on poisonous *Astragalus* (then called "two-grooved milk vetch" because of the obvious indentations in the seedpod) near Rock River, Wyoming, in 1919. Other tragedies were recounted as well: the 1930 loss of 340 sheep near Elk Mountain, for example, and the death of all but three of a flock of 200 sheep in an *Astragalus*-laced gulch near Pueblo, Colorado, where 71 more died the next year after a similar episode with the vetch. There are references, as well, to the "poison strips" near the Book Cliffs town of Thompson, Utah, where losses of sheep and cattle "ran into the hundreds . . . on numerous occasions."[9]

But all of those cases were identified, then, as victims of "alkali disease." It wasn't until the early 1930s that researchers began to pin down the evidence that it was not the mineral salts associated with the prairie's ubiquitous alkali crust that were doing the poisoning, but selenium. Thereafter, the noose of responsibility was drawn tighter and tighter around selenium. That was true not just in the texts by Beath and cohorts, but in pioneering work by Franke at the South Dakota Experiment Station and others. Feeding and field tests were done on stricken animals, everything from rats and chickens to sheep and cows, and they were followed by intensely detailed pages of microscopic examinations of the pathological effects to all organs of the animals. The cause and effect were stitched tightly together. Beath reported the surprising discovery that the chronic "alkali disease" poisoning resulted when livestock ate selenium-contaminated grains and grasses. The acute "blind staggers" ailment, a misnomer because the animals stricken did not always live long enough to either go blind or stagger, was more often the result of consumption of the wild *Astragalus* and other indicator plants. Beath subsequently identified poisonous levels of selenium in a wide variety of the often colorful and showy native *Astragalus* plants. And South Dakota feeding tests with toxic grain from seleniferous areas confirmed that "alkali disease" and "blind staggers" were, in fact, cases of chronic and acute selenium poisoning, respectively.

Franke, Beath, and Kilness each warned repeatedly that not just cattle but humans, too, were at risk from selenium toxicity. Ironically, each of them died during or just after intensive investigations of selenium toxicity. Franke's death, in the summer of 1936, was the result of a secondary infection while being treated for bovine undulant fever he contracted while studying poisoned cattle in seleniferous areas of South Dakota. Beath died less than a year after completing his second and more definitive text with colleague Irene Rosenfeld in 1964. Kilness was stricken with leukemia just months after completing his last selenium swing through the West in 1988 and died in March 1989.

Some of those familiar with Beath's work think that selenium played more than an ironic role in his death. "Beath almost died from it once," said one former colleague. "He had been up in the Lysite Buttes, getting samples for his second book, and brought two fist-sized rocks home from there with him. He took them to the lab and ground them down to the consistency of a fine powder. But he didn't wear a mask or anything and he must have inhaled some of the dust because he got terribly sick and had to be taken to the hospital."

Years earlier Beath had experienced a brief but virulent bout of stomach problems from a meal of duck livers later found to be high in selenium. This time, however, according to associates, he suffered major liver and kidney problems and never really fully recovered. Those rocks were loaded with water-soluble selenium. The dust poisoned him and he never got over the exposure. He was never healthy again.

There was far too soon an ending for Ivan Barnes, as well. The USGS geochemist, the man who touched off the West-wide hunt for selenium, died in his sleep on May 11, 1989, still deeply troubled by his fate and exhausted from the long hours he spent trying to compensate for it as researcher and adjunct professor at the Oregon Graduate Center.

Chapter 8 | # SHATTERED DREAMS

Almost everywhere it outcropped, on the farms or sprawling cattle ranches of the West, selenium wrote a painful chapter of human misery. Doc was ecstatic with the success of our 1985 sampling venture together. But he constantly reminded me of the promise I had made to come back some day and see how tough things were for the farmers and ranchers who lived in the selenium belt but knew virtually nothing about the element or its harmful effects. We linked up again, in the summer of 1988, to visit some of his patients and others he knew of with similar problems.

For Sam Bennett and his family, the tale of frustration and failure started almost the moment they set foot on their new sheep ranch on the border of North and South Dakota, near the tiny farming village of Watauga, in 1957. On the second day, one of his four pregnant brood sows died. Next, it was the bait minnows he kept in the stock watering tank for when he wanted to go fishing.

The death and disconnected events kept happening all through the first year. In the second year, sixty-five ewes died. Lambs and calves were stillborn. Lambs and chickens were born with abnormalities. Neither cats nor dogs could reproduce. Everywhere, hardly without end, livestock were dropping dead. Sam didn't know it then, but his pasture grass, hay, and grain were loaded with lethal levels of selenium.

Nothing had been said about selenium when he bought the remote ranch on the rolling, windswept prairie, about halfway between the Grand River National Grassland and the massive Lake Oahe on opposite sides of the Standing Rock Indian Reservation. He had sunk everything they had, every penny of their life's savings, and mortgaged as much as he could to leverage some revenue for stock and equipment.

He could take the losses, frustrating though they were. What he couldn't take was the "dumb farmer" label that went with them. "Oh, it was pretty subtle at first," he said, that cold spring afternoon in 1988 when recounting those tough, early days on the lonely land. "The neighbors would shake their heads and say, 'Tough luck, Sam.' But you could see it in their eyes. They thought I was just a bad farmer, a dumb rancher who couldn't look after his stock." Before the family nightmare ended in 1961, Bennett had lost more than $40,000 worth of livestock, including 1,100 sheep . . . and, finally, his ranch.

He didn't take it lying down. He turned to almost every government agency for assistance, even the governor of South Dakota. Finally, university researchers pinpointed the cause of the death and deformity: selenium. "It was a new word to me," said Bennett, "and no one else around here seemed to know anything about it. But I think most of them did. They knew all about what it did, at least—that there was something wrong with the land—if not what was causing it."

However frustrating and painful the inexplicable stock losses and the murmuring of their neighbors, these were not the worst that happened, either to the Bennetts or to the many others like them throughout the West. "It was bad enough to lose everything, like that," said Bennett, decades later while resting at his new home in Sturgis, nearly 200 miles away, in southwestern South Dakota. "But when it started ruining our health, that was real spooky."

Bennett's skirmish with selenium struck his family hard. "There were constant skin rashes, especially for Loretta and the kids," said Bennett. "And we had stomach and indigestion problems all the time." Those problems were worse—and, apparently, permanent—for their youngest daughter, Sandra, who was conceived on the ranch. "I can't recall Sandra getting any normal sleep for the first six months. She cried every day until we took her off our own cow milk and put her on store-bought," said her father. "She had colic constantly and when her teeth came in, there were black rings around where they came out of the gums and the teeth were spotted black, just like an overripe banana." Dental studies have detected similar symptoms among people known to have high levels of selenium in their system. Later studies by South Dakota's Dr. Raymond Lemley, who almost single-handedly pioneered the field of diagnosing and treating cases of human selenium poisoning, confirmed in both blood and urine tests that most of the Bennett family had sharply elevated levels of selenium.

"We were so full of selenium that our breath was just awful with garlic odor. We had so much in us we were exhaling the stuff," said Bennett three decades later. And the family's brush with selenium still lingered. "Sandra still has a little of what we call the nerves," said her father. "She is very high-strung. Things upset her pretty quick. And the older girl, Sharrey, still has a lot of stomach trouble." Most of the worst symptoms disappeared not long after Bennett's doctor diagnosed the problem and urged the family to leave the ranch and its tainted food. Most of the selenium poisoning came from the milk, meat, and eggs they ate.

Bennett worries, as well he should, about the legacy the land passes from owner to owner. "That ground should go out of private ownership," he says now. "The problem won't change. It's in the soil. I was told not to eat the livestock because they had too much selenium and not to sell grain locally but to a terminal from where it could be shipped to Chicago."

The ranch has changed hands five times since then. Each successive owner has suffered similar problems. No one lives on the lonely, isolated spread now but Stanley Rye, who owned it in 1988, still grazed his own livestock there, and harvested hay and grain for his dairy herd at a headquarters ranch about 17 miles away. He, too, was losing cattle—ten or twelve every year—but didn't know why. Despite the tainted hay and silage the herd's milk still was being shipped to commercial dairies. Attempts to obtain samples for selenium analysis were unsuccessful.

"Selenium? I've only heard the word," said Rye at the tiny general store he operated with his wife, on the side, in Watauga. "Nobody will tell us anything about it. Is it some kind of plant?"

The answer is more than academic. Rye had had increasing indigestion himself, as well as more—and more painful—stomach problems. "It has been a chronic problem for the past five years, along with general tiredness and muscle weakness, which have been getting worse every year," he said. He is not alone in his suffering, though virtually nothing has been done to pin down the cause of such general malaise throughout the selenium belt. He and the Bennetts are two of only hundreds of known farm families who have suffered hardship and heartache from similar exposures.

Doc and I had driven back to Rapid City after the unsettling meeting with the Bennetts, battling roads made skittery by an unexpected spring blizzard. The next day brought a steady dose of sunshine as we headed east on Interstate 90, splitting endless miles of prairie farms checkerboarded by alternating strips of green wheat and earth-tone fallow. The only visual break in the patchwork of monotony was the sight of the eerie Badlands National Park, twisting north out of historic Pine Ridge Indian Reservation, home of the mighty Oglala Sioux and their famous Battle of Wounded Knee.

On and endlessly on we drove through the wheatbelt of the state's midsection, through the fractured and storied Missouri Breaks, where so many movieland desperados made their getaways from determined posses; across the sprawling historic river and on to Sioux Falls. The next morning we passed through Vermillion, home of the University of

South Dakota where Doc had earned Hall of Fame status with four un-
beaten performances in the pole vault at the Dakota Relays, and turned
back west, again, along State Route 50, to the tiny farming hamlet of
Meckling.

Just outside of town, we watched the rich, brown earth of the Missouri bottomland spiral up behind the tractor of native son Gerald
Jepson as he made his way in from the fields for a morning chat. He was
another of Doc's far-flung selenium patients. Prairie-born and prairie-
raised, Jepson had forged his life around the rhythms and patterns of
the land and a see-forever sky. But that bucolic lifestyle had been rudely
and painfully jolted in 1978.

Jepson kicked off his mud-crusted boots and led us through the back
door of the comfortable clapboard farmhouse to where all good farming talk occurs, the kitchen table. He looked as robust as the rich earth
on which he farmed, his blocky build crowned with a slight fringe of
white around a tanned head. Friendly, sky-blue eyes crinkled a warm
greeting and a thick, calloused hand reaffirmed it with a vigorous
shake. "C'mon in and sit down. Good to see yah again, Doc. Been quite
a while." The pleasantries out of the way, Doc primed him with a leading question or two about his "experiences" with selenium to get him
going. It didn't take much.

Jepson knew full well why we were there and he was eager to tell his
story. He had been working the mixed farming operation for years
without the least hint of health trouble, he said, raising a mix of cattle
and hogs and enough silage crop to feed them. But it all began to change
in 1978, when some of his prized Hampshire hogs started to die. His
veterinarian suspected white muscle disease and, later, mulberry heart
disease. He urged Jepson to start feeding his hogs an enriched selenium
mixture to pull them out of it.

The trusting farmer purchased hundreds of small bags of the rust-
red sodium selenite powder and mixed it almost daily for his pigs and
livestock. He ground the supplement into his silage in a small feed mill
housed in a windowless structure next to the barn. The room would fill

up with choking dust, Jepson recalled, layering his head, neck, and bare arms with a powdery red coating and rose-coloring his spit. He wore no protective clothing. In fact, he said he was usually in his shirt-sleeves because the mill room was so hot and dusty. Neither did he have a respirator to guard against inhalation.

Gradually, the exposure took its toll. He had less and less energy. His hair started coming out in clumps until he was almost bald. Then his eyebrows and eyelashes fell out, along with assorted toenails. The growing numbness in his fingers and toes progressed to partial paralysis, alternately striking opposite sets of legs and arms. It got so bad that Jepson could barely manage his chores and became a wallflower while others danced with his wife at the popular town square events that once gave them both so much pleasure. The symptoms peaked in 1982, when his left leg "went absolutely numb dead." Tests by the family doctor failed to reveal a cause. The specialists he saw in Yankton, then in Omaha, Nebraska, and, finally, the Mayo Clinic in Rochester, Minnesota, fared little better.

At last, a family friend suggested contact with a Rapid City doctor he knew, a man who had treated similar cases. That man was Kilness. Doc visited the site, talked with Jepson's doctors, and, then, had his own samples taken, and not just from Jepson's blood and urine. He collected samples of soil, crops, water, and some of the "red powder" from the mill room.

"It was Doc Kilness that made the diagnosis," recalled Jepson, between sips of strong, black coffee at the kitchen table, "and when they tested my blood and urine for selenium, it was really high." The soil, crops, and water also contained potentially harmful levels. The supplement had so much selenium in it that each gram—each twenty-eighth of an ounce—subjected Jepson to more than he could safely tolerate in a day from all sources combined. On Kilness's orders, he discarded the supplement and changed his water supply. Within weeks, selenium levels in his body plummeted.

"I began feeling better and better," said Jepson, "but I still have the numbness from time to time." He worries about his neighbors, and about his son, who still used the supplement in 1988. "There are other people in this area who have health problems just like mine," he said. "But they don't want to talk about it. I think it's related to selenium. They all are using the supplement. They are exposed to it all the time, just like I was. Sooner or later, they are going to have worse problems than me. It's just too damn bad. Money, I guess, is behind it. But I'd quit farming before I'd ever use it again," he vowed, "and I love farming."

About 30 miles further west, just across the state line, near Fordyce, Nebraska, another hog and cattle man was reliving part of Jepson's nightmare. Only it had just begun for Alfred Haberman Jr. In 1987, during a weekend softball game in nearby Yankton, South Dakota, where he managed a cattle feedlot, Haberman started having physical problems he couldn't accurately describe, or understand. "I was running the bases, and I was a damn good ball player," he said, "and I just started stumbling . . . and fell down." He would get "deathly tired," at other times, without having worked that hard. And stumbling or losing his balance without apparent cause happened on more than the base paths of the local ball field.

The vague symptoms progressed steadily until the loss of strength became something far worse. Alternately, he would, like Jepson, lose the use of opposite limbs: right arm, left leg; left arm, right leg. Not only could he no longer grip a softball bat or ball, he was having trouble negotiating steps and handrails, and holding a cup of coffee. In between, there was stomach cramping, indigestion, excessive gas, numbness, and other symptoms often associated with selenium poisoning. His wife, Mary, began to experience some of the same problems, though to a lesser degree. More than a year of intensive examinations and tests raised—and discarded—as causes everything from multiple sclerosis to amyotrophic lateral sclerosis, Lou Gehrig's disease.

"I'm getting desperate," said Haberman in mid-1988, when he was forty-six and no longer a husky, powerful man. In fact, he was reduced to shuffling along, hardly able to raise his feet off the floor. Mayo Clinic doctors kept testing his blood and urine for selenium. It remained dangerously elevated. In fact, test results showed that his levels, and Mary's, were three to four times higher than normal.

I collected samples of Haberman's beef, especially the liver of which he was so fond, and samples of his water and vegetables. They were bagged, tagged, and put into the ice chest for shipment back to the laboratory for selenium analysis. The water exceeded safe drinking water levels and the beef, especially the liver, was high enough to cause toxic insult. Even the bottled tomatoes from the Habermans' huge garden were so high that a large helping would deliver more selenium than the total daily safe limit. Haberman said he ate beef "nearly every day of my life and liver sometimes twice a week." Samples of his soil, too, and the grain raised on it, contained elevated levels.[1]

But Haberman's biggest surprise, like Jepson's before him, was to be found in the commercial livestock feed he used for his cattle. At Doc's suggestion, he knelt down next to a bag of it on the cement floor of his mill room, read the label, and grunted in surprise. "Yup, by damn. It does have some. Sodium selenite. Right here on the label." He was exposed to the supplement dust routinely in the mill room but suffered additional daily exposure to it at the Yankton feedlot he managed, both in the selenium-tainted dust from the corrals continually stirred up by the cattle and in the gaseous forms of the element they exhaled and vented.

Desperate to halt what he saw as a relentless downward spiral in his life, Haberman made dramatic changes in his diet. He ate beef only sparingly (and only when the cattle had been kept off selenium supplement) and tried to make sure that the chickens he ate did not come from the area. The new meat supply was tested and the samples contained ten times less selenium than his prior supply, selected from prime stock at the feedlot. Al and Mary began eating more fresh fruits and vegetables, and switched to bottled water for drinking.

But it was too little, too late, at least for Al. The symptoms worsened steadily. He got irreversibly weaker, month by agonizing month. His mother called one day, sobbing quietly as she tried to learn everything she could about selenium toxicity, its symptoms and treatment, if any. "He was so big and healthy and active all of his life," she confided. "But, now, he can't even walk. He has no strength at all and I think he is going."

She was right. Her son died two months later, on February 14, 1990, at age forty-eight. The initial diagnosis was pneumonia. But specialists who treated Haberman in Houston said later they believed the cause of death was ALS, amyotrophic lateral sclerosis. Though there was never any proof that selenium was the cause of death, Doc Kilness insisted to the end that the symptoms were "strongly suggestive" of it.

What made Haberman's case all the more unusual was that Kilness had found, and written about, earlier experiences with the terminal muscle disease. Walt and Yvonne Ehlers had a mixed farm and ranch near Presho, South Dakota, on soil formed by an ancient seabed just west of where the Missouri River now flows. There, more than fifty years ago, the federal government had bought up 200,000 acres of land and turned it into a research preserve because the soil was dangerously high in selenium and the grain raised on it was lethal to livestock.

The Ehlerses know all about the Haberman experience. Both Yvonne and Walt have had tragic illness in their families and some of the symptoms have been traced back to excessive selenium exposure. "My dad and Yvonne's first husband both died of ALS," said Walt when interviewed in 1988. They were two of a cluster of four cases that occurred in an area with only twenty families and within an 8-mile radius of each other in south-central South Dakota's rural Lyman County. They all died of the ravaging muscular disease within a ten-year span and three lived within a mile and a half of each other.

Kilness could not prove selenium was the cause, but tests on one of the patients before death revealed excessively high levels of selenium: 450 ppb, or 0.45 milligram per liter, in the urine and 750 ppb (or 0.75 mg/l) in the whole blood. The recommended maximum safe urine level is 100 ppb and the average for U.S. citizens is 30–35 ppb. Average

U.S. blood levels of selenium range from 135 to 200 ppb, with anything over 400 considered evidence of toxicity. None of the patients were related. None had a family history of ALS. But all shared common selenium links. They lived in an area with high soil selenium that grew vegetation, including garden produce, with toxic levels of the element and all of their herds suffered from acute or chronic forms of selenium poisoning.

What made the cluster uncommon, other than the fact it was only the fourth known incident of ALS clustering when reported in the *Journal of the American Medical Association* (*JAMA*) in 1977, was that it occurred in such a small population. The normal incidence rate is 1.4 cases per 100,000 people, five times lower than the Lyman County cluster, even when compared to the total county population of just over 4,000. Kilness concluded his *JAMA* paper thusly: "We have reported an unusual clustering of cases of ALS occurring in a farm locale where chronic selenium intoxication had been noted to be endemic in farm animals as early as 1936. The occurrence of a cluster of cases of ALS implies that an environmental factor may be present. The presence of selenium in toxic amounts in the Cretaceous soils of this area warrants examination of selenium as a possible environmental factor."[2]

The sensitive subject was raised again during an afternoon interview Doc had arranged with the Ehlerses in their Presho home. It would become another of those tense joint interviews in which we often became embroiled during two separate rounds of searching and sampling for selenium in the West. They almost always occurred when Doc was loyally trying to protect the interests of his patients from prying, personal questions. I scribbled down Ehlers's account of some of his own children, by a previous marriage, who had suffered prolonged bouts of skin rashes and cases of numbness in both the hands and feet, symptoms commonly linked with selenium poisoning according to Kilness.

Throughout the mid-afternoon interview in the front room of their farmhouse, Yvonne had remained resolutely quiet, letting her husband and Doc do all the talking. Her only contributions to the conversation were a knowing or rueful smile, marking agreement or remembrance, and the occasional vigorous, affirmative nod . . . until Walt recounted his family experiences with the kinds of kidney problems Doc had said sometimes went with selenium poisoning. Without warning, Yvonne leaned forward in the comfortable rocker, near the spacious front-room window, and broke the conversational flow. "A lot of the families around here have had kidney problems," she interjected. "Why, in my family, alone, my sister and my niece, my daughter's two girls, and the wife of one of the ALS victims all had to have kidney transplants because of chronic kidney problems."

Kidneys are a major target of insult from selenium poisoning, and blood and urine tests among Ehlers family members over the years have confirmed routinely high selenium counts. That sent Kilness off on another of his recountings of the many medical faces of selenium. Sometimes his observations seemed almost purposefully staged to provoke an opposite response. It seemed that way, again, as Yvonne listened carefully to his explanation of how some medical research had indicated that selenium sometimes appears to have a buffering or protective effect against certain forms of cancer and how *that* prognosis was occupying nearly all of the medical research community's interest.

"Well, my best argument against that," said Yvonne, "is my family. Let's see, there was Annie and Bill, Ewald, Elmer, and, oh yes, Marvin. They were all from my first husband's family. They all died from cancer so I can't see it was any cure or protection for them."

That evidence, any researcher would be quick to point out, was purely anecdotal, as are most selenium reports because of the lack of scientific studies about its human health effects. But it was a pattern that is often repeated in the selenium belt, where many members of the same family either died from cancer or were diagnosed as having it.

It was near the end of this interview that the interests of the family doctor and the inquisitive journalist clashed yet again. Walt had detailed how the selenium had once ravaged the area on which he and many of his neighbors farmed and ranched and still poisoned many of the animals and crops raised there. An awkward silence followed. Then, finally, came the question: "Well, do you eat your own produce? How do you feel about it being sold to others? Should there be some kind of government monitoring and notification program?"

Sure, it was blunt, prying, even offensive. Yet it was a point that had to be raised. Doc flushed almost at once. There was nothing subtle about the man. Angry or pleased, he wore his emotions openly for all to see. Ehlers, however, didn't miss a beat. Neither did he seem unduly upset with the query. "Well," he drawled, "if you ever go down to Texas, and bump into any of those rich people who breed and raise expensive thoroughbred horses, you might ask them why they never buy oats from South Dakota."

It was as close as he would get to a direct response. There was an awful lot of foot shuffling and nervous throat clearing after that, an obvious signal that the interview was over. Doc held his peace, but only until we were in the car, safely out of earshot from the Ehlerses. "I told you before, I won't stand for that kind of offensive questioning of my patients. I will not have them embarrassed or held up to ridicule. I absolutely don't want it to happen again."

If the silence in the Ehlerses' home was awkward, the one that followed in the car was absolutely icy. I couldn't afford not to get access to these people and Doc was the man with the key. Clearly, they would not open up to me if he weren't around, even if I did have their names and addresses, which I didn't. Doc and I kept having these conflicts pitting his desire for patient protection against mine for details and candid answers. "Look, Doc," I started out, kindly enough, "we need each other. You want the selenium issue out in the open. You want people to know and understand what a danger it is. Well, so do I. And we can't do that if we don't tell the whole story. I didn't ask those questions to offend them, but they have to be asked, and that kind of directness will be repeated everywhere we go. We have to accept it or do this some other way."

Doc could take a punch as well as give one. He thought it over quietly, again turning his body so that he was facing away from the driver's side. Finally, he started tracing an imaginary map on his side of the windshield. "This whole region has been suffering from this problem for decades and nobody, nobody at all, will do anything about it. It is just terrible." That was the last time we clashed over that particular issue. There would be others, however.

Once, after we had collected samples from Sweitzer Lake, south of Grand Junction, Colorado, our tour almost came to an abrupt, angry end. Kilness always wanted to be in on any information exchange . . . with anyone. I, on the other hand, sometimes had to arrange separate interviews to avoid his innocent but distracting interruptions. One of those was with the resident ranger at the lake. Despite having read a state circular noting the presence of selenium in the fish and warning about the possibility of adverse effects if too many of them were eaten, the ranger acknowledged a steady diet of fish from the lake. Excited about the bulletin and the obviously understated threat, I came back to the car, started up, and drove out of the park. But before I could share a word, Doc snapped: "Stop the car! Right here. Right now. We have to have this out once and for all."

Stunned, I pulled over and parked. The tirade continued: "We agreed to share all information and I have given you everything, patients, case histories, access to files I have never opened up to anyone before. But you keep what you get to yourself. If that doesn't change, this is going to stop right here and now. I will get on a plane and head home tomorrow." My wife was dying a slow death in the back seat. She was used to the occasional clash, but this was major league confrontation. Until now, I had been as diplomatic as possible. It was more than just not wanting to lose critical access and a valuable source. I truly liked and respected the man, pugnacious as he could be at times. But my patience too was worn thin.

"Look, Doc. I've had it. I'm tired of the threats, the interruptions of my interviews, of you treating me like a little kid. I respect your knowledge about this issue and the fact you have probably forgotten more than I will ever learn about it. But I am every bit as good a journalist as you are a doctor. I know what I am doing. I know how to question people, how to get information with or without you. I would prefer it to be the former, but I'm not going to put up with any more of this haranguing. End it if you want. But I demand to be treated just as professionally as you want to be."

Now I had done it. Sure, I could go on alone. I had maps and reports and a few contacts. And, by now, I had been pretty well schooled in *Astragalus* identification and knew how to spot marine shale formations from a moving car at 60 miles an hour. But Doc had been over this ground before and his storehouse of anecdotal information was invaluable . . . and very tightly controlled. He would spring some intriguing little nugget at the most unexpected times. While I might not be totally lost without him, it was certain my prospects for success would be greatly diminished. The exchange continued, but more calmly, until we each felt our point had been well enough made. Then Doc turned, winked, and said: "Well, what the hell did he say? What did you find out?" How could you stay angry with a guy like that?

In two separate years of interviewing rural families in areas known to be highly seleniferous, the kinds of stories he led me to surfaced again and again, from Wyoming to Colorado and Utah to Nevada. Hundreds of miles further south of Presho, on the Ute Indian Reservation, south of Durango, where Colorado shoulders into New Mexico, there are dozens of cases of family wells being tainted with unsafe and in some cases dangerous levels of selenium.[3] One of those was at the trailer home of Jolene Hopper. What passed for a lawn out front was crusted with alkali, as was the small garden plot behind. The well water was sampled in 1988 and measured 36 ppb of selenium. She and her husband had been battling bouts of gastrointestinal problems, another telltale symptom in the selenium belt, along with excessive lethargy, irritability, and numbness in both hands and feet.

Nearly every home from which a well water sample was collected that day showed evidence of selenium contamination, ranging from 17 ppb to 400. But no sample was more dramatic than the one in the small, plastic bottle drawn from the now-abandoned domestic well on the Harmon Ranch. There, the selenium level was 6,200 ppb. But for Paul and Irene Harmon, there was more than one path of exposure. The meat, eggs, vegetables, and milk they ate were later found to be heavily contaminated as well. The pasture was covered with *Astragalus* plants that grow only where high levels of soil selenium are present. "Paul died three years ago from brain cancer," said his 79-year-old widow Irene in 1988, just a few months before she remarried, sold the place, and moved away. She sat in the tiny kitchen of the wooden farmhouse, nervously drumming her arthritic fingers on a well-worn wooden table as she recounted a list of other health problems the pair had suffered, including skin cancer, heart and kidney troubles, and severe, persistent stomach distress.

"We both had a lot of sour stomach and lost all our hair and toenails," said Irene, now living near Grand Junction, further north. She laughed, nervously, when she told of one year that they tried to raise chickens from dozens of chicks purchased in town. "They never lived long enough to reproduce. They just got real sick. All of their feathers fell off and they had trouble standing up. So we killed them and took them to market," she said. But they kept some at home for eating . . . and every time they did, "sour stomach" problems followed.

There are similar historical accounts in Utah, where a family briefly drank well water with 9,000 ppb selenium. Their five children suffered total or partial hair loss, general weakness and low energy, and discoloration or loss of fingernails. Because theirs was a single-source exposure, the health problems disappeared after the family converted to another water supply. The selenium was coming from deep-seated shale beds underlying almost their entire ranch.

That was not the case in the tiny New Mexico hamlet of Lemitar, where the Rio Grande is pinched between the Magdalena and Los Pinos mountains. There the dangerous element is shallow enough to have concentrated in the vegetation. But only its effect, not the element itself, is well known to ranchers there. Mention the word "selenium" to Chuck Muncy and all you get is a blank stare. Talk about the third-stage, paralyzed tongue symptom of acute selenium poisoning, however, and the response is without hesitation.

Muncy fairly blurted out the local name for the malady before the symptom's description was complete. "Woody tongue," interjected Muncy, who knows it all too well. The selenium-laced mustard plants on his ranch, and on many others around him in the arid heartland of New Mexico, about 75 miles south of Albuquerque, take a heavy annual toll on livestock. Muncy runs only a small herd of cattle, usually about fifty head, and so his profit margin is razor-thin. In a good year, one with no deaths, the worst his livestock will suffer is loss of weight gain. But most years he loses between two and five head to the strange malady. "But even if they get well," says Muncy, "you have to sell them at a loss. It's just something about them . . . they never raise another offspring." But neither he nor his neighbors had ever heard about selenium.

Twenty-five miles to the west, near Magdalena, Ross and Pat Ligon own a large ranch and have suffered similar ravages for more than thirty years. Like their neighbors, they know the symptoms of the element's impact only by their more colorful, westernized nicknames. Asked about cattle deaths from the selenium accumulator plants, "I'd say we have some every year or two," replies Pat Ligon. "Some years seven or eight die. It's tragic when a horse gets it. They just roll around and get real sick and can't even drink. It's real pitiful."

Ranchers throughout the West are all too familiar with what selenium does, but very few of them know what it is or where it comes from. For the lack of hard science, they are forced to deal in anecdotes. And few anecdotes are more disturbing than those that Montana scientists attribute to concentrated levels in stock watering ponds of the rolling ranches and farms along the state's northern tier. The problem with saline springs was so severe in the 1970s that researchers were summoned by a consortium of government agencies to identify the cause and, hopefully, a solution. Dr. Paul Brown, who worked in the agriculture experiment station of Montana State University, was one of them. During a telephone interview, he told me about problems he believes were caused by selenium around the southeastern city of Billings and, farther north, in a massive triangle of undulating prairie farms between Great Falls, Havre, and Shelby called "the Great Falls seeps."

"Cattle kills have occurred at various times," said Brown. "It is hard to pinpoint exactly what killed them but selenium appears to have been a factor. And, possibly, high nitrates too." The seeps, many of which were more saline than ocean water, were caused by a change in farming practices. Historically, the native grasslands of the northern prairies absorbed the available subsurface moisture. But when the soil was broken for cultivation, and alternating strips of it left fallow for a season to guard against using up the soil's nutrient content too rapidly, the unused moisture built up and leached out of the soil, flushing a potent load of salts and toxic trace elements to the nearest swale or pond.[4]

One dramatic example was caused by the subsequent concentration of selenium by evaporation, according to Dr. Marvin Miller, a soil physicist and hydrogeologist at the Montana Bureau of Mines and Geology. "I can't tell you the name of the rancher," recounted Miller, almost in a whisper, even though we had the privacy of a telephone between us. "He is terribly embarrassed and would not admit it publicly. He had five prize bulls shipped from Omaha. They had been on the road a long time and were really thirsty when he turned them out onto his rangeland. They ran straight to the nearest water—one of those ponds—and tanked up on this bad water. He told me they got only 50 to 100 yards away and dropped like a shot . . . dead in their tracks, within minutes. It must have been a horrible sight, and a very expensive loss, for him" said Miller.

Many of the cattle deaths stopped about a decade ago, when the land fallowing stopped. But there are nearby regions where the losses continued and ranching had to be abandoned altogether. Some of that land has been converted to dryland grain farming instead, although no agency has any program for testing the crops for selenium content.

"Gradually, the cattle would get in extremely poor condition and go blind," said Miller, describing some of the symptoms where that happened in a lonely stretch of Big Sky country called the Highwood Bench, east of Great Falls. "Then they would start staggering around and many would die. Some would recover, once the farmers put them on fresh water," he said, "but we are not exactly sure of what killed them. We encouraged necropsies but none were ever done."

Not just cattle suffered. Ranchers in the Montana triangle also lost prized fishing holes—watering ponds stocked with rainbow trout that grew so plump so quickly on the rich nutrients from the field runoff that their girth was out of all proportion to their head size. "Nearly every rancher has . . . or had . . . his own trout pond," said Miller. "It was a bragging point with them. But we saw a complete die-off in dozens of ponds we visited."

Selenium was suspected, though never proved, as the cause because no tests were done. In 1981, however, the Environmental Protection Agency was asked to study the quality of well water in the area because of general complaints of ill health among many rural families. An extensive sampling program showed startling results: many of the wells had higher selenium levels than the inflow to Kesterson. More than 30 percent of the wells exceeded the EPA's own safe drinking water standard of 10 ppb and some were as high as 1,800 ppb. By comparison, the highest selenium level in Kesterson water was 1,400 ppb and the average just under 300. In every case, the common link is the underlying geology. If the source rock is there—and it *was* there in every place the geologists Barnes and Love had predicted—the whole bitter suite of selenium problems are likely to follow.

That was certainly the case hundreds of miles away, in the middle of Nevada's Basin and Range country. There, John Shanahan and his family paid a much higher price for their dream ranch than they bargained for when they fled the smoggy skies of Los Angeles for the wide open spaces of Nevada. The Shanahans are gone, now, their trailer-home headquarters towed away to another starting point in Montana. All that is left to mark their unwilling ransom is an empty tool shed, some dead fruit trees, and a meticulous concrete food cellar, still lined with bottles of home preserves from a garden plot that grows rhubarb high enough in selenium to be a consumption threat.

It is unlikely that anyone will ever know, for sure, exactly what happened to turn the once-sweet water of Newark Valley sour, but it became the wellspring of bitter failure and bizarre effects for the Shanahans sometime in the early 1980s. This is how Jim Morris set the scene for his readers in an October 1984 story in *The Bee*, months before the newspaper's selenium project was born:

> EUREKA, NEV.——*The hair, a youthful brown not long ago, has turned white. The voice is deep, the speech halting. There is a dullness to the eyes; it is the look of someone who has lost hope.*
>
> *John K. Shanahan, this slow-talking bear of a man, is 47 but could pass for 60. He lumbers along at half-speed, cursing the government, the oil industry and life in general. He considers himself and his family to be victims of bureaucratic indifference. And he is terribly bitter about it.*

Though the account surfaced before we had forged such links to selenium, the Shanahans' experience took on the same contours as many other rural selenium victims in the West. First, the family's health deteriorated swiftly and in fairly bizarre fashion. Morris described the suite of symptoms graphically:

> *Two years ago, he, his wife and two children contracted a strange and potent ailment. It sapped them of energy, ruined their appetites and shortened their tempers and attention spans. It killed Shanahan's livestock and crops and nearly killed him. The symptoms began disappearing when the family moved into the small mining town of Eureka, 20 miles east, but some continued to linger. Sixteen-year-old Shannon was hyperactive and acquired a severe case of asthma. Eighteen-year-old Will had severe pigmentation problems, not unusual in cases of severe selenium toxicosis, and also had difficulties in school because of*

nervousness, irritability and attention span problems. John's wife, Virginia, had not recovered her strength even months after an operation that removed her uterus, ovaries and non-cancerous tumors. And John remained mysteriously sluggish, slow in speech and slower to move.

The father was convinced the troubles were tied to nearby government seismic exploration and underground explosions that either shattered the integrity of his well or created fissures through which bitter, saline water from shallow, subterranean formations seeped into the higher-quality well water below. He will never know whether it was the seismic work or the natural drawdown from pumping to irrigate crops and garden that drew the poisons to his well. Once protected from shallow aquifers of salty water by an unbroken layer of semi-impervious clay, the sweet, deep water turned suddenly very sour.

By May 1982, the combination of total dissolved salts that water quality people measure as TDS had reached 440 ppm, still well below the state safety level of 1,000 ppm. But just two months later, as the health problems worsened, other tests were done and the results were shocking. The TDS count had soared to 4,079 ppm. Although those involved did not know it then, the selenium levels were dangerously high too: 350 ppb, or thirty-five times above the EPA safety level of 10 ppb. That was when the poisoning began in earnest.

"It was like waking up drunk every morning," Shanahan told Jim Morris two years later. "You couldn't remember what you did the day before. You were sick, throwing up." Their appetites disappeared. They became dehydrated. Shannon suffered partial paralysis and cried out in pain at the slightest touch. John's hair turned from brown to black to white in just a few months. Dogs and cats died. The family's health worsened. Sheep died. The barley and alfalfa crops withered, coated with a chalky-white powder. Goats gave birth to fetuses that lacked hair, eyes, and in some cases even bones. Shanahan said they looked more like "gobs of jelly."

The garden plot still is tainted by selenium. When sampled four years later, volunteer flower and rhubarb plants contained toxic levels of selenium. No one knows whether the selenium was always there and just took years to accumulate to poisonous levels, whether it was pumped up from the mysteriously tainted well, or whether pure capillary action naturally wicked it to the surface from the shallow, saline aquifers beneath the 320-acre ranch that sits on the bed of an ancient lake.

But Bill Robinson, a Bureau of Land Management geologist based in nearby Ely, thinks it was simply a case of a bad well gone worse. "We don't know why the family quit using the deep irrigation well for its domestic supplies because it was good quality water," said Robinson in February 1991. "We tested it for selenium and it contained only 3 ppb, and the TDS was well within safety limits." But as a quid pro quo for access to his land, Shanahan had a private seismic testing crew doing site-related work for the MX (Peacekeeper) Missile program drill him a new well closer to the home, for free. "The well was only 75 feet deep and was not fitted with the required 50 feet of casing to seal off any bad water formations it might have penetrated on the way down," said Robinson. "We think that's how the Shanahans got into trouble. Either they drilled into a saline aquifer underneath that old lake bed or they penetrated one on the way down and didn't seal it off. Either way, the selenium got to them and 350 ppb is very high."

About 400 miles due north of Shanahan's now deserted and sagebrush-covered spread, in the sun-baked southeastern corner of Oregon, selenium played out its most lethal, if bewildering, role on Burns area rancher Girard Perkins. There, somewhere south of Poison Creek and west of Stinking Water Pass, where the Paiute Indians once roamed freely, Perkins ran a cattle ranch of his own, just north of the Malheur NWR.

The rolling, high-country plains region is more desert than farmland, a natural condition overcome by the irrigation ingenuity of its settlers. Every depression traps the melt from the spring freshet, gradually shrinking to salt-encrusted playas, or dry lake beds, by early summer. Lake Malheur is the region's sink, nourished only by occasional wet-year overflows not siphoned off by upstream diversions from the Silvies River that drains out of the scenic Blue Mountains, to the north, and the Blitzen River that twists down and northward from the Steens Mountains.

No one will ever be sure what started Girard Perkins on his irreversible downward spiral. In his prime, he was a hulk: 6 feet 3 inches and 250 pounds, none of it wasted flab. He was so strong—says best friend (and doctor) Burt Campbell of Burns—that "he didn't have to rope a steer, he could just lean over and grab one." That was in 1972 when Perkins, a transplant from California's southern San Joaquin Valley, was forty-one years old.

Within months, however, he had shriveled to only 90 pounds, was completely bed-ridden, and couldn't even lift a spoon to feed himself. Nothing could change his course. Doctors were pumping 3,000 calories a day into him intravenously but, said internal medicine specialist Dr. Paul Burgner, "he just wasted away . . . unrelentingly." He died January 29, 1973, in a Portland hospital.

A respected internist, the crusty Burgner was baffled by what seemed to him as the onset of very uncommon symptoms. But he was even more bewildered by the cause of Girard's death. In frustration, he finally listed more the symptoms than the cause: "hyponutrition, due to idiopathic atrophy of the intestine and inability to assimilate intravenous hyper-alimentation regimen." Lay translation: Perkins's body mysteriously had lost the ability to assimilate nutrients from the intravenous diet, or any other before it, and literally starved to death. "It was just a damn shame to see a guy like that—a man's man in every way— waste away," said Burgner, recalling the puzzling episode fifteen years later in his clinic office.

A month after Perkins died, Burgner came across an article in a medical journal about selenium toxicity in humans that listed one of the classic symptoms of acute poisoning as "overtly garlicky breath." In effect, the body, in its rush to excrete the poisonous burden, converts some of it to dimethylselenide and exhales it.

"Damn! It just jumped right off the page at me, especially the part about garlic breath," said Burgner, who months later suffered a stroke that left the right side of his body paralyzed but his speech and brain functions unimpaired. "Every time I saw that old SOB," the rough-hewn Burgner said, "I told him to quit eating so much garlic or it would kill him . . . or me. His breath would drop an ox." And almost every time, Perkins would respond, just as profanely, that he "didn't eat any of that damn, smelly stuff."

Burgner mused about the selenium toxicity article for several days. He just couldn't get it out of his mind. He hadn't taken kindly to losing Perkins, because he had felt so entirely helpless with the way it happened. Nothing he did had any effect. Finally, in desperation, he collected samples of body tissue which had been preserved after Perkins's autopsy and took them to chemists at nearby Reed College to be analyzed for selenium.

The results were shocking. Selenium counts in the bowel, liver, brain, muscle, heart, and kidney were among the highest ever detected in a human, said Burgner. They ranged from 3.15 ppm in the heart to 10.15 ppm in the kidney. Muscle tissues contained 5.95 ppm, five times higher than normal.

"What made this thing so tragic," said Burgner, "is that I read that story a month too late. Hell, it just made me sick. If only I had seen it sooner. I had never heard of selenium poisoning." But even if he had, a cure would have been difficult. Detected early enough, before the toxic effect of heavy body burdens shows up, merely changing the diet to avoid excessive intake will give the body time to purge itself and repair the damage. But in Perkins's case, as with the cattle who die in much the same manner, once the toxicity threshold is overwhelmed, there is no turning back.

To this day, the exposure path that prompted those toxic concentrations remains a mystery. One theory is that Perkins came across just one tainted batch of pothole water too many. Like the cowpokes of an earlier generation, when he was out on solitary range rides, checking his herd, he would quench his thirst by scooping his Stetson into one of the numerous ponds, creeks, or seeps that dot the undulating plains. Doc Campbell, his range-riding buddy, says Perkins "could guzzle more water more quickly than any man I ever saw." And some of that which he guzzled could have been lethally contaminated with selenium.

Nearby "Poison Creek" didn't come by its name accidentally. There is a history of livestock deaths along its twisting course. And there is, among the maps and works of the Wyoming researcher Orville Beath and others, ample evidence of elevated selenium in both soil formations and vegetation in the region.[5] Several kinds of selenium indicator plants can be seen on the ranch of Perkins and his neighbors. But, in each case, the levels are generally lower than those commonly associated with such stunningly adverse effects in humans.

The big rancher had no uncommon dietary quirks. He ate most of the same foods that everyone else in the family ate and none of them suffered any unusual ill effects. The only other potential pathway for poisoning that was unique to Perkins, at least in *his* family, was his constant exposure to alfalfa that might have contained elevated selenium counts. Perkins not only cut and baled his own hay crops but did custom cutting for many other ranches around, often working shirtless in the arid summer heat. Burgner, Campbell, and others have postulated he easily could have inhaled selenium-tainted dust or microscopic bits of hay or even absorbed it by constant skin contact.

Campbell, the prototype "country doctor" who first treated Perkins, was just as puzzled, and frustrated, as the Portland specialist to whom he referred his friend and patient. "I never heard of this [selenium poisoning in humans] until after Girard died," said Campbell a few days after my interview with Burgner. "Oh, I knew about things like the blind staggers in livestock. It is well known around here," he said of that acute form of the poisoning. After reading a proferred list of selenium poisoning symptoms, in humans, livestock, and wildlife, Campbell gasped: "My gosh! I've probably treated more of this than any doctor in the country and didn't even know it. I have been seeing and treating symptoms like these for forty years and never knew they might be linked to selenium."

Campbell is not alone in his ignorance. "I doubt seriously that doctors know enough to recognize the symptoms of selenium poisoning in humans," says Dr. Bruce Furst, now professor emeritus at the University of San Francisco and an internationally noted researcher of the toxic and cancerous effects of trace levels of heavy metals. "It is such a recent problem, up to now most of those who have looked at this whole issue have spent too much time on deficiencies of a lot of trace elements but not enough on their toxicity," he said when interviewed in 1988. It is an ignorance that could exact a high price. "Selenium has the narrowest range of any element I know between what is safe and what is toxic," said Furst. "With selenium, you only need two or three times more than what is safe—somewhere around 200 micrograms—to go beyond the gray level and into the toxic range."[6]

Researchers are growing increasingly uneasy about the health risks of selenium exposure, especially in the wake of scientific findings about what the compound, in just microscopic doses, does to everything from waterfowl, songbirds, and fish to livestock, poultry, and pigs, and even to domestic animals like cats and dogs and rabbits and mice.

In both laboratory and field experiments, birth either has been prevented altogether, aborted prematurely, or resulted in grotesque abnormalities. Central nervous systems have been irreparably damaged. The body's natural defenses against disease and infection have been impaired. Growth, even when successful in poisoned species, often is severely stunted or followed by blindness, lameness, irritability, or extreme weakness and lethargy. Little has been done to give medical practitioners exposure to what the wildlife biologists are learning almost daily about how, why, when, and where even minimally elevated doses of selenium work their poisonous and debilitating effects. Until recently, little has been done to follow the earlier recommendations of South Dakota's Dr. Robert Lemly, who warned western physicians, especially, half a century ago to be concerned and diligent about human poisoning. Nor have similar cautions by the late Dr. Kilness been given serious heed.

Part of the human exposure pathway has been addressed by California health officials. Alarmed by the spread of wildlife poisoning—and the obvious health consequences to hunters, anglers, and recently arrived Southeast Asian refugees who routinely supplement their food supply with wildlife—they have ordered the posting of places like Kesterson, the Tulare Basin, and Salton Sea areas with multilingual health advisories. There the selenium levels in fish and waterfowl are high enough for them to have cautioned women of childbearing age and children under age fifteen to avoid them altogether. Other healthy adults have been warned to limit their consumption to no more than 8 ounces a month in some cases.

The people behind that initiative were Dr. Kenneth Kizer, then director of the state's Department of Health Services and an environmental toxicologist, and Dr. Anna Fan, chief of the agency's epidemiological and environmental health unit. Together they also published a comprehensive article in *The Western Journal of Medicine* spotlighting not only symptoms but potential exposure pathways.[7] Today there are other initiatives to bring not only western health professionals but a wide variety of other disciplines together on selenium through a regional network operating within the framework of the Western Governors' Association.

Finally, the veil of Doc's "conspiracy of darkness" was being lifted.

Chapter 9 | CALIFORNIA
POISON

    While biologists, geologists, plant physiologists, and microbiologists learned more about the elusive trace element and how to bottle it up before it did any more harm, the federal government poured millions of dollars into what they hoped would be a prototype for correction in the San Joaquin Valley. There were many reasons to focus their experimental and research energy there. One of the principal ones was the legendary productivity of the valley. Another was the considerable political leverage exercised by the major corporate farms there. And a third justification was the obvious fact that the San Joaquin was where the contaminating effect of selenium resurfaced after a long research hiatus. The Geological Survey's extensive soil mapping already had proved that the problem was widespread in the valley and not just confined to the Kesterson region.

    The Department of Interior faced the unthinkable prospect that both its western reclamation and wildlife refuge missions were rushing toward a costly bureaucratic head-on collision. Neither was likely to survive if the unfolding pattern of tainted reclamation project areas created more Kesterson nightmares. Interior needed a way out, fast. So the department chose a massive research effort, pouring more than $40 million into the San Joaquin Valley Drainage Program that it hoped would become a prototype for selenium solutions throughout the West. From the time it started, in 1986, until it concluded as an active research program, in the fall of 1990, the huge effort was coordinated from a cluttered and unpretentious office on the second floor of the same federal office building in Sacramento that housed the reclamation and wildlife agencies.

Edgar Imhoff looked an unlikely commander-in-chief of such an auspicious undertaking as he settled into the high-back chair behind an oversized desk loaded with stacks of reports. Slightly built, with a wispy shock of graying hair, he looked overmatched, but wasn't. His seventeen years in the Department of Interior came after a long stint in state and private employ during some of the most hectic years of the western water wars. At Interior, his career was marked by ascending levels of responsibility. From senior hydrologist, he graduated to environmental planner, director of the Office of Water Information and director of the Midwest Region in the Office of Surface Mining before he took over the California post.

He sighed with resignation as he viewed an overflowing In basket, swept aside a jumble of maps, reports, and correspondence that had piled up in his absence, and replaced them with a thick sheaf of briefing papers and reports.

Imhoff had just returned from a tiring December trip to report on the five-year study of irrigation-induced drainage problems to key congressional committees and to the National Research Council and National Academy of Science in Washington, D.C. His return home would be short. In another week, he would give similar briefings in Denver and other parts of the West repeating his warnings about the selenium danger to top regional officials of the Bureau of Reclamation, the Geological Survey, the Fish and Wildlife Service, and numerous state officials. It was part of a plan to ensure that discoveries about selenium and its toxic elemental companions, arsenic, boron, molybdenum, chromium, lithium, uranium, and others, would be shared with those facing similar threats in parts of every western state. From the start, Imhoff had headed the joint federal-state effort to investigate the source, mobilization, transport, and distribution of selenium in the San Joaquin Valley, south of Kesterson NWR, and closely study the chemical, biological, botanical, and other characteristics of the uniquely dangerous element.

Scientists had surveyed, mapped, and scrutinized the distribution of selenium and experimented with most of its physical and chemical properties to characterize the threat facing the vast and fertile San Joaquin Valley. In the five years of that program, a hundred scientific reports were produced and nearly a thousand conference papers presented by scores of federal, state, university, and private scientists. Some of that work was conducted by University of California researchers from the Berkeley, Davis, and Riverside campuses, and some by private consultants to various irrigation or drainage districts. But the great bulk of it—about $40 million worth—was done under the auspices of the federally funded San Joaquin Valley Drainage Program headed by Imhoff. Jointly coordinated by Interior and California's Department of Water Resources, the interagency effort was a logistician's nightmare.

Imhoff adjusted his wire-rim glasses, bent over the document-covered desktop, and picked out the final report issued in September 1990. His thin, bony fingers traced down the rosters on the eleventh, twelfth, and thirteenth pages as he counted off just the number of agencies, committees, technical panels, and scientific review bodies involved in the huge effort. "Just look at this," he said, pointing to the lineup and description of the full study team. "We had three full committees, seven subcommittees, and the National Research Council reviewing all of that, through five of its subcommittees, plus a staff of thirty-one. This was a legitimate full-court press. All the way."

More definitive than any similar contaminant search ever mounted, the five-year probe defined everything about the element's nature, from origin to impact, along the whole sweep of one of the world's most prolific growing regions. The lineup of those involved was impressive, to be sure. One hundred and fifty-seven different people were involved in policy and management, citizen advisory, and interagency technical committees and subcommittees. And the subjects they covered included agricultural water management, aquatic and fishery biology, data management, groundwater, public health, treatment and disposal, economics and systems analysis, quality assurance, and water quality issues. The process generated more paperwork than solutions, however, a point Imhoff made graphically by pointing to the chest-high pile of reports stacked in the corner of his windowless office. Their volume and complexity befit the geological history and setting of the productive San Joaquin.

The great Central Valley, of which the San Joaquin is the southern end, was formed more than 150 million years ago along a continental margin down what is now the middle of California. Covered by seawater, it was framed on the east by an arc of volcanoes and on the west by an elongated marine trench and subduction zone, where the massive Pacific tectonic plate collided with and slid under the continental plate. Over millions of years, erosion of the volcanic arc gradually covered the sea bottom, filling it with tens of thousands of feet of erosional outwash: interbedded layers of sand, gravel, clay, loam, and minerals.

Between 150 and 65 million years ago, the trough was alternately covered and bared, each episode leaving thick layers of ancient mud and the remains of aquatic life forms on its seabed. When the greatest of these seawater invasions retreated 70 to 65 million years ago, it left behind two dominant geological formations on the west side of the valley floor: the Cretaceous Panoche Formation and Moreno Shale. Between 65 and 2 million years ago, a valley was created from the sea-washed trough, uplifting the granitic Sierra Nevada, where the volcanic arc once stood, on the trough's eastern flank and raising the Coast Range along its western side.

The ceaseless surge of erosional deposition layered the valley with fossil-laden sandstone and organic-rich shales formed from layers of sea bottom muds compressed by the weight and pressure of the overlying formations. The sea retreated for the last time, about 2 million years ago, through the only remaining gap in the Coast Range. The seismically driven folding, faulting, and uplift subsequently created a valley 400 miles long, from Bakersfield to Red Bluff, and 40 to 50 miles wide, from the toe of the Coast Range to the foothills of the Sierra Nevada.

The San Joaquin is a fertile layer cake of loam, sand, silt, and gravel on a base of tightly packed clay. But it is as saline as it is fertile.

What salt was not left behind by the retreating sea as separated ribbons or aquifers of saline water in the soil has been wicked up to the surface from underlying groundwater by capillary action. That solar-driven evaporation and plant transpiration accounts for more than 7 feet a year in water loss, a continuous natural pumping process that concentrates the residual salts as a crust on or near the surface. In an enclosed basin where rainfall seldom exceeds 8 inches a year and daytime summer temperatures consistently top 100 degrees Fahrenheit, that evapotranspiration creates a saline burden of nearly 2 million tons of salt a year in the valley, most of it along the poorly drained west side that is skirted by the divided four-lane ribbon of concrete that forms Interstate 5, the main route to Los Angeles.

The natural accumulation of salts was compounded when irrigation came to the San Joaquin, especially the massive kind provided by the construction of the vast federal and state water projects in the 1950s and 1960s. Even though their diverted river water carries only 350 parts of total dissolved salts in every million equal parts of water (seawater, by comparison, holds about 31,000 ppm TDS), the enormous quantity applied—3.4 million acre-feet a year—adds another incredible salt burden to the soil. Imhoff's study estimates that imported burden at 1.6 million tons . . . each and every year . . . spread out over the San Joaquin's 2.5 million acres of irrigated land.[1]

But the underlying and tightly packed clay layers—some only 10 feet beneath the surface—significantly impede the downward migration of flushed saline water. Thus farmers must criss-cross their fields with buried, perforated pipes to carry the poisonous drainage away or watch the saturation process waterlog their land and poison it with tons of dissolved salt.

Those who planned and constructed the gigantic water import systems made a fateful mistake, however. They overlooked early soil studies that reported elevated levels of selenium in the valley soil and raised the specter of potentially harmful levels of it being leached into the drainage. One of those studies, in 1941, was authored by U.S. Department of Agriculture soil researchers H. W. Lakin and H. G. Byers. But those who designed and built the federal Delta-Mendota Canal and the state's California Aqueduct mistakenly assumed the drainage canals would carry only the expected sulfates, chlorides, carbonates, and bicarbonates of common elements like sodium, calcium, magnesium, and potassium.

Escalating costs prompted California to abandon its plans to jointly fund and build an earthen ditch to transport those salts out of the valley. The federal government decided in 1964 to go it alone. But they changed the design of the proposed 207-mile-long master drain to a concrete-lined canal that would stretch from between Bakersfield and Fresno all the way to the confluence of the San Joaquin and Sacramento rivers, about 50 miles upstream from San Francisco Bay. Environmental opposition mounted in the wake of fears that the nutrient-rich drainage would trigger damaging algae blooms in the world-famous bay and pollute it, and its meandering delta, with pesticide residues as well. So Congress, in 1965, added a special rider to the appropriations bill for the San Luis Drain, requiring that the discharge comply with state water quality standards approved by the administrator of the federal Environmental Protection Agency.

The Bureau of Reclamation began construction in 1968. Two years later, it added a temporary terminus to the initial 85-mile-long segment that ended at Kesterson while it planned the last but most controversial leg of the line to the delta. In 1970, the evaporation ponds designed to concentrate the drainage became the Kesterson National Wildlife Refuge, to be jointly managed by the Reclamation Bureau and the Fish and Wildlife Service. The canal and temporary terminus were complete by 1975, along with 120 miles of subsurface collector drains in the Westlands Water District. The Bureau of Reclamation and California's two water agencies—the Department of Water Resources and State Water Resources Control Board—formed the San Joaquin Valley Interagency Drainage Program to find a solution to the environmental, economic, and political obstacles of salt disposal.

The multi-agency's recommendation in 1979 was to complete the San Luis Drain to a point in the delta, near Chipps Island, where they thought maximum flushing action would dilute the saline drainage and carry it harmlessly out to sea. But no such discharge could be made without a permit from the water quality board. In 1981 it directed the bureau to undertake a full study to learn what was *in* the drainage and how it would affect a wide range of aquatic organisms and other wildlife. The state needed that kind of information to set water quality standards, both for the discharge and for the delta into which it would flow. That was the genesis of the historic nesting survey that Harry Ohlendorf undertook at Kesterson and the reason for his fateful 1983 spring trip through the then-silent marsh with Felix Smith.

More than a year later, the interagency drainage program was reborn with a series of meetings between department heads of the federal and state water and wildlife agencies. But not until early 1986 was the formal search for a solution begun. By the fall of 1990, the quiet-spoken and diplomatic Imhoff had conducted dozens of public hearings and hundreds of committee meetings to fold the last of the hundred scientific studies and a full range of public comments and changes into the final report. Although the threats from the accumulating burden of dissolved salts and other toxic trace elements were addressed, the main emphasis was on selenium.

To those who felt Kesterson was only a bizarre exception, including top Bureau of Reclamation officials, it was a rude awakening. Government geologists had found a serpentine band of groundwater dangerously high in selenium trapped between the surface and the irregular clay layers beneath. In some cases, the poisonous subterranean lake was inundating the root zone of crops. In others, it was as deep as 150 feet.

Imhoff was so familiar with the report, by now, that you could mention the topic and he would flip, almost automatically, to the section describing it. The worst of the problem, he pointed out, stretched along more than 180 miles of the narrow valley trough between the San Joaquin River and the eastern toe of the Coast Range hills. On the maps of the final report, purple shading traces the distribution and concentration patterns. What they show is an almost uniform band of contamination that twists and bends from south of Bakersfield to just north of Los Baños . . . with selenium counts ranging from 5 to 50 parts per billion. Substantial zones between the fanlike erosional outwashes from Panoche and Cantua creeks, in the midsection of the valley, are almost uniformly contaminated at 50 to 200 ppb selenium, and three separate sections held groundwater laced with more than 200 ppb. For comparison, the poisonous flows entering Kesterson averaged 290 ppb. Unless the amount of irrigation was drastically reduced or a more ambitious drainage effort was devised to prevent further soil saturation, the study warned, the rising water table would waterlog 40 percent of the irrigated farmland. A million acres of the San Joaquin's most productive land would be poisoned within a decade.

The options are severely constrained. The concentrations of toxic trace elements dissolved in the underlying groundwater are too high, primarily in selenium, to be safely disposed of aboveground. The estimated 628,300 acre-feet of "problem water" would create a wildlife death trap more than 523 times the expanse of Kesterson, just where millions of migratory waterfowl and shorebirds winter. But the buried poisons can't safely be left where they are, either. Without intervention, they could migrate slowly downward through the so-called Corcoran

Clay and pollute the underlying rich deposits of pure water. That prospect made Imhoff squirm uncomfortably in his oversized chair. Those aquifers are pumped by many valley cities for drinking water.

The federal-state study proposes a novel, if complicated, solution: reduce the amount of applied water through more efficient irrigation and pump some of the least contaminated shallow groundwater— above the relatively impervious clay cap—for blending with imported irrigation flows. That way, they reasoned, the high water table could be lowered enough to protect the root zone and a balance struck to reduce, if not stop, the threat of continued percolation.

Imhoff scratched his head. Deep in thought, he was searching for a more simple explanation of the complex interplay of actions needed to keep the selenium genie confined in the subterranean formation. "Well . . . it's sort of like creating a safe, underground reservoir for it," he volunteered. "Pump out enough to lower the water table well below the root zone and cut down irrigation to avoid pushing this stuff any deeper. It may not be the most scientific or exotic solution in the world, but there isn't any safe place to put it. Nobody wants it in their backyard."

That does not guarantee the safety of the deep drinking water supply aquifers below. Hundreds of old gravel-packed wells, drilled to provide irrigation water before the big water projects were built, already penetrate the Corcoran Clay, providing a free-fall path of contamination to the untainted water beneath it. That protective cap, however, for all its reputed "impermeability," is not totally continuous. Its clay lenses vary dramatically in thickness, from 20 to 200 feet, and in some places the most contaminated water is within only 50 feet of it. Moreover, much of the valley, like most of California, is underlain by the scars of seismic activity, criss-crossed with fissures, cracks, and earthquake faults that already provide escape hatches for the poisoned drainage or could do so sometime in the future.

But even if Imhoff's underground lake stays put, continued pumping from the deep aquifers, to meet the future needs of a rapidly increasing valley population and offset the effects of prolonged droughts, will continue to draw the contamination zone downward. In any event, the decision to abate as much surface disposal of the drainage as possible will force dramatic changes in crop selection for an area world renowned for the volume and variety of its agricultural produce.

California's $13.92 billion worth of agricultural output in 1987, $9.27 billion of it in crops, was 10.2 percent of the nation's total. And 49 percent of that came out of the San Joaquin Valley, which, alone, accounts for one-fifth of all U.S. irrigated land. The worsening salination problem could also put more pressure on America's deteriorating balance of payments position. California is the leading agricultural exporting state in the nation and the San Joaquin accounts for much of that, including nearly half of the nation's total cotton export and all of its walnut and almond exports.

The approved plan has eight major strategies:

1. Reduce the amount of applied irrigation water, cutting back on both deep percolation and the volume of contaminated drainage generated.

2. Reuse drainage on progressively more salt-tolerant crops, say from carrots to tomatoes to cotton and, finally, eucalyptus and saltbush plantations, dramatically reducing drainage volume. Smaller ponds could be completely isolated with netting and are cheaper to build and operate.

3. Channel remaining drainage into smaller on-farm evaporation ponds specifically designed and maintained to prevent their use by wildlife. Ponds receiving drainage with less than 2 ppb selenium would be without design or operation restrictions. Those receiving drainage with between 2 and 50 ppb must include wildlife safeguards and set aside an equivalent amount of nearby safe freshwater habitat. More toxic flows would be routed either to fully contained ponds with enhanced spray evaporation or fed into ponds that generate electricity from the low-grade heat stored by concentrated brines in which the poisons are locked up, out of reach of any wildlife.

4. Abandon irrigated farming, altogether, on land that is difficult to drain and underlain by the most contaminated water, an option that could ultimately sentence at least 75,000 acres to early retirement.

5. Pump groundwater from above the confining Corcoran Clay where the water table is within 5 feet of the surface and the water low enough in salts and trace elements to be safe for both farming and wild-life.

6. Continue discharging drainage to the San Joaquin River through a completed San Luis Drain, as long as receiving water standards set by the state and approved by the EPA can be maintained.

7. Mitigate existing wildlife damage by providing enough fresh water and untainted land to protect and restore damaged fisheries and wetland habitat.

8. Permit tiered water pricing, improved water delivery schedules, and the sale or transfer of saved water to help offset the cost of drainage management.

The plan is long on ideas and goals but short on authority and fund-ing. The drainage program can't order anyone to undertake any of the steps. Only the state legislature and regulating agencies can do that. And little is said about who will fund the plan's estimated costs of $42 million a year. Spread over the project's proposed fifty-year lifetime, that amounts to $2.1 billion.

But even if all of the plan is implemented, the substantial change in operating procedures will merely buy a few more decades of continued productivity, at most, for the increasingly saline valley. The plan ac-knowledges what experts have warned about since intensive irrigation began there: without a huge out-of-valley conveyance system to export the salts to the ocean, intensive irrigation is doomed. But that same prospect—dumping toxic farm drainage into the headwaters of San Francisco Bay—is what foiled the drainage disposal plan in the first place nearly twenty years ago.

One look at the plan's "Future-Without" alternative—that is, the option of doing nothing—offers dramatic incentive to make sure that this latest valley salt management study does not gather dust on the shelves of the bureaucracy the way its predecessors did. This "none-of-the-above" option is included in the study not to coerce selection of the preferred alternative—though it well could—but to comply with the long-standing requirement for such comparisons in all federal planning studies. While its stated goal is to give those involved common ground for judging what (if any) action is needed or justified, its most likely effect is to give them nightmares about what will happen if they don't act . . . and soon.

The "Future-Without" alternative is based on some common assumptions. One is that federal money for major water projects will remain tight. Another is that public pressure for environmental protection will continue to increase. A third is that the state's population—and water needs—will keep growing. Such suppositions raise these unsettling scenarios:

▪ Increasing soil salinity and trace element contamination would force abandonment of 460,000 acres of irrigated farmland by the year 2040.

▪ The volume of poisoned drainage would more than double, from the current 100,000 acre-feet per year to 243,000.

▪ Economic impacts would ravage the valley's farm belt. Annual crop value would plunge $440 million. Farm employment would dip by 4,000 jobs, with a subsequent 5,000-job loss in supporting agricultural industries. Personal income would fall $123 million, causing a domino-like reduction of retail sales in surrounding communities of $63 million.

▪ The availability of healthy wetlands in the valley, already slashed to less than 10 percent of historic levels by conversion to farmland, would plummet from only 90,000 remaining acres to 55,000. Populations of waterbirds would continue declining as crowding increased their vulnerability to predators, hunters, and the ravaging effects of cholera and botulism epidemics.

▪ Increasing use of evaporation ponds would elevate the danger of trace element poisoning not just to water and shorebirds but to endangered predator species like the San Joaquin kit fox, the American peregrine falcon, and the bald eagle. Too, as ponds filled and dried up, their toxic, wind-blown dust could become a public health threat if people inhaled microscopic particles or absorbed them through the skin.

But even if all the recommended management options are followed, question marks will remain. One of the key assumptions is that state water quality standards would allow continued discharge of tainted drainage into the San Joaquin River at the northern end of the valley. In fact, regulatory agencies already are under pressure to tighten existing standards, especially for selenium and boron. The EPA, in 1990, rejected the state's allowed levels of discharge for both and announced an effort to impose tougher limits of its own.

Another presumption is that thousands of acres of agro-forestry plantations, of deep-rooted eucalyptus trees and the saltbush called *Atriplex,* would be a safe sink for toxic elements. Biologists, however, have warned that the seeds, nectar, and leaf litter of such extensive plantings could carry the Kesterson effect to songbirds, to land mammals, and to honeybees and other pollinating insects. And the proposed use of these crops as livestock feed and firewood raises prospects of further and little-understood exposure pathways.

Nor does the passage of time offer any likelihood that the selenium source will be depleted by natural processes. In fact, an authoritative new Geological Survey study indicates that selenium will continue to be carried from the Coast Range to the valley below for centuries to come. This report, *Geologic Sources, Mobilization and Transport of Selenium from the California Coast Ranges to the Western San Joaquin Valley,* shows how the element moves from its source to impact the area. Authored by Theresa Presser and reconnaissance partners Walter Swain, Ronald Tidball, and R. C. Severson, the study illustrates the primary modes of mobilization and transport to valley soils.[2]

Presser, the same delicate, admittedly bookish, Easterner who labored with geochemist Ivan Barnes in the eye-catching orange "Rhino" on Kesterson's searing levees, looked much more at home in the laboratory of the USGS western headquarters in Menlo Park. Flipping through the pages of the study, she patiently explained how part of the toxic burden is dissolved and carried downstream in hydrological pulses from infrequent winter storms in the rain shadow of the Coast Range. More selenium is introduced when infrequent heavy storms undercut the steep, unstable hillsides and trigger large landslides, slumps, and mudflows. Erosion subsequently carries the undissolved source rock itself down to the large alluvial formations that fan out from the tributary mouths, most notably Panoche and Cantua creeks, into the valley. Although both are ephemeral streams, drying up through summer and fall, they have transported large volumes of such material to the valley for millions of years . . . and those nutrient laden, fan-shaped wedges are intensively farmed and irrigated.

But there is yet another source of selenium introduction, Presser explained. High levels of the element are leached out of the soil by percolating rainwater that, in turn, gradually seeps into the shallow underground water zones of the San Joaquin. While there was initial doubt about the source of the selenium when Kesterson's contamination was first discovered, there is none now.

The study, Water Resources Investigations Report 90-4070, pinpoints the location of source rock in eleven small basins of a 1,000-square-mile study area between Cantua and Panoche creeks. Moreover, it traces the complex chemistry by which the element is formed, dissolved, and transported. The findings carried an unwelcome message for those who had hoped that the source rock would be more confined. Instead, Presser's team collected and analyzed hundreds of samples, with disquieting results. The seleniferous shales contained a mean concentration of 7.3 ppm selenium. Even the nonseleniferous rocks averaged 0.8 ppm, far higher than the national average. The highest levels found were 45 ppm in the Kreyenhagen Shale and 35 ppm in the Moreno Shale. By comparison, Lakin's earlier work on marine shales throughout the United States showed Niobrara and Pierre formations to hold the highest selenium counts and the medians for those were 6.5 ppm and 2.2 ppm.

If the mean levels are unsettling, some of the concentrations found by Presser and coworkers in the seasonally ephemeral pools of creekbeds and in acidic groundwater seeps emanating from the Coast Range are stunning. They found concentrations up to 420 ppb in seeps and from 2,100 to 3,500 ppb in pools of an ephemeral stream in Tumey Gulch. Both EPA and California standards require designation as a hazardous waste of any liquid with more than 1,000 ppb of selenium.

As the source rock is exposed to rainfall, sunlight, and oxygen it is geochemically weathered from the insoluble selenide into two forms of the poison: the water-soluble selenate and an insoluble form, selenite, which then moves with compounds of iron and aluminum. Both of these forms are transported to the valley floor, where selenate moves directly into the water column. The selenite, once into the extensively cultivated and irrigated alkaline soils, is further weathered and made water-soluble. Sodium selenate salts then appear on the crust of valley soils as evapotranspiration takes place.

Unfortunately for those trying to manage the selenium already washed down to the valley floor, there is a lot more of it entrained in four separate water sources that form a significant hydrological reservoir poised upslope of the San Joaquin. According to the USGS reconnaissance, those sources are:

- Ephemeral, or part-time, streams in which selenium often exceeds the hazardous waste criteria of EPA.

- Runoff waters from winter flushing in which surface deposits of selenium, left as a crust on mineral soil by capillary pumping and evaporative concentration, are remobilized.

- Relatively low but sustained releases of selenium carried in near-surface fluids that flow through subsurface cracks, crevices, and small tunnels in the hillsides.

- Enough dissolved selenium in the deeper regional groundwater system (watersheds and wells show concentrations up to 153 ppm) "to represent a significant source" for years to come to the valley's groundwater basin.

The combined transport of soluble selenium, the report concludes, "remains high enough to pose a threat in the San Joaquin Valley to water quality and, hence, to the wildlife, fish, human health and beneficial use supported by that water."[3]

That finding isn't likely to reassure those who had hoped the poisoning presence of the element was the result of a one-time episode that could be managed or at least isolated. In fact, it raises the uncomfortable prospect that similar, long-lasting source and transport mechanisms are at work throughout the West, especially in places like the geologically similar western slope of the Continental Divide, along Colorado's western flanks. There, south of Grand Junction, much higher levels of selenium have been found in the soil, vegetation, and running water but a definitive inventory study has only just begun to determine how wide its toxic footprint may be.

If the same natural capillary and erosional mechanisms are in place there, and at more than a score of potentially troubled areas already undergoing preliminary screening elsewhere, the West could find itself with yet a third Superfund program to go along with those already mounted to handle man-made hazardous wastes at industrial sites and Department of Defense facilities.

Chapter 10 | # COMING FULL CIRCLE

The company Ford edged cautiously through the dense tule fog shrouding the San Joaquin Valley. It was late February, in 1991. Caution was not just prudence but survival. Just the week before, seventy-two cars had smashed together under similar conditions in a chain-reaction collision just a few miles to the east, along narrower Highway 99, the valley's older main drag. We were cruising safely, if slowly, down Interstate 5, the shortcut to Los Angeles, tracing the toe step of the Coast Range down the valley's west side. We drove in and out of pockets of the thick blanket of ground moisture south of Stockton, past the cutoff to San Francisco, and headed for Highway 140. There we would turn east, toward the tiny dairy town of Gustine, the doorstep to Kesterson, back to where the selenium detective work had started eight years before. The two-hour drive had been unusually quiet. The soft clacking of my passenger's lap-top computer punctuated the metallic drone of engine and tire noise.

Dr. Joseph Skorupa looked like something straight out of Hollywood casting for the well-turned-out research scientist. His trim build led up to a faintly angular face framed by high-set cheekbones and firm jawline. Deep-set, light-blue eyes blended with the sea-green hue of his turtleneck sweater and heavy denim field slacks. The gray half-vest picked up the subtle tones of a full shock of brown hair flecking faintly gray. Skorupa's clothing was stylish yet fully functional for a hard day at the marsh. Skorupa had spent five years in the evolving selenium issues, the first two out of the Wildlife Service field office in Sacramento and the last three with the Patuxent Wildlife Research Center's Davis-based Pacific Field Station. After Harry Ohlendorf resigned from the service in 1990, Skorupa moved out from behind Ohlendorf's considerable scientific shadow to become one of selenium's frontline wildlife field researchers.

Ohlendorf, like others, had seen his Wildlife Service career stalled in the bureaucratic wake of Kesterson. Mere name association with the prominent trouble spot, as well as his refusal to back away from his findings and sever ties with the outspoken Felix Smith, became professionally terminal for him. Long-promised promotions and raises receded inversely with the rate of each new Ohlendorf selenium discovery and report. Hurt and disillusioned, he left the service in 1990 and joined a prominent private firm doing consulting work for the state on the same issues. Smith followed him out of the service only four months later, in July, choosing early retirement over what for him was an even chillier administrative climate.

Skorupa and I were heading for Kesterson so that he and refuge manager Gary Zahm could retrace the path of Smith and Ohlendorf across the too-quiet marsh in June 1983. The cloaking envelope of fog closed in, again, as we swung south of Gustine and turned east on Gun Club Road, toward the marshy valley trough. Skorupa had finished updating his computer-stored data bank on valley contaminant levels and was now peering intently ahead, looking for the end of the narrow, two-lane paved road and the entrance to the refuge.

"There he is, over there in the beige van," he said, pointing to Zahm, waiting at the locked gate that barred public entry to the refuge. Minutes and handshakes later—there was no need for introductions—we were moving across the marsh. Only this time, there was no silent swish of the paddle, no mirrored surface to reflect the thick braid of cattails around the edge of ponds, no splattering parade of coots rocketing away from shoreline feeding sites to the comparative safety of the pond's midsection.

There was no water at all. Kesterson's 1,280 acres of evaporation ponds had been drained. Its maze of berms and levees had been leveled. The ponds had been filled. The cattails, with their enduring burden of assimilated selenium, had been swathed into a thick, contaminated carpet, left to rot in the searing summers and moist winters of the valley. Where Ohlendorf and Smith had once paddled toward fluorescent-flagged nesting sites, Skorupa and Zahm now wandered across a dun-colored layer of dead stalks. Instead of nests of twisted hatchlings, they looked for remains of deer mice, voles, shrews, and pocket gophers upon which half a dozen northern harrier hawks could be seen actively preying.

They paused to inspect mounded gopher burrows. "Look, here," said Skorupa, dropping to one knee and fingering shreds of cattail half-way down the opening. "No question they are feeding on this cattail litter." Further along, pointing out clearly depressed trails that busy rodent traffic had created in the hummocky layer, Zahm scuffed his boot into a furball that marked the end of the trail for one rodent. "Yes, and the hawks are eating them," he said. "Lots of them. Look, up ahead, there's a female making a pass now. Bang. She nailed something." The victim hung limply from her talons as she banked away to a safe eating perch. It was weeks before the arrival of the male harriers and the start of springtime aerial courtship displays and reproductive rites.

It was the offspring of that mating about which Skorupa was most concerned. "I am worried about the terrestrial contamination threat now," he said, watching the feeding hawks. "I don't know whether it is inevitable that we will end up having traded a poisoned water environment for a tainted land one," he added. "But look at the food chain. The selenium numbers are going steadily up and we know that anything above 4 ppm is a concern for toxic effect. Maybe what's happening right now is an artifact of the drought. But the bottom line is that we are a long way from having achieved any cleanup of selenium. It's still here and it still is cycling through the food chain."

The issue of selenium moving up the food chain in the dryland refuge, just as it had in the earlier aquatic one, had not attracted much attention when the federal reclamation agency was trying to figure out how to accomplish the cleanup ordered by the state of California in 1985. Those involved were much more concerned, then, with the potential $100 million cost of digging up all the contaminated mud and cattails and trucking them to one of the state's few remaining hazardous waste dump sites. A second and less expensive option—disposing of the same mud and organic load in a newly built and supposedly leak-free repository on an upland portion of the 5,200-acre refuge—also was rejected. Both wildlife and water quality experts convinced state regulators that at best it would only defer contamination. The thick plastic liners, they said, would be quickly breached by burrowing rodents or just wear out on their own in thirty years or so. Then the poisoning would start up all over again.

The Reclamation Bureau also lost its third bid to effect cleanup by switching to a clean water supply that, over time, would isolate the selenium inventory in an oxygen-free layer of mud and organic ooze at the bottom of the ponds. There was vigorous scientific debate before the State Water Resources Control Board about whether the process would work at all. But there was no disagreement that it would take too long to lower the levels of toxicity enough to stop killing the wildlife. Even the proponents of that "wet-flex" plan acknowledged that it would take more than a decade to reach safe levels.

After a series of prolonged hearings, the state board ordered the series of twelve ponds to be drained as the most effective and immediate way to end the waterfowl mortality and malformation and to comply with the international bird treaty. Meanwhile, the agency was directed to continue experimenting with more permanent solutions, including some promising ways to reduce selenium concentrations with natural soil fungi and bacteria. And they were ordered to conduct detailed monitoring of the soil, vegetation, insects, birds, and mammals that had replaced the mud, cattails, and aquatic organisms of Kesterson. At first, the monitoring was monthly. Now it was only a quarterly process . . . and the reclamation agency was pushing to have even that requirement canceled.

Skorupa had been studying the results of that monitoring closely and, like others, had watched the slow, steady buildup of selenium in the dry, upland habitat that replaced the wetlands. He was worried about the implications of the accumulation but still not certain whether it was the inevitable result of normal food-chain cycling or a consequence of the withering drought that had started in 1987 and persisted through the early 1990s. Without dilution and flushing from normal rainfall, selenium may have been unduly concentrated by increased capillary pumping induced by longer periods of evaporation and plant transpiration. Whatever the cause, it was clear that the upland food chain was growing increasingly toxic.

The "Kesterson Reservoir Biological Report and Monitoring Plan" reported by the Bureau of Reclamation in December 1990 showed just how clear. Virtually all the samples of nine major vegetation types analyzed were above the 4 ppm safety level for toxic effect. And four of those vegetation types—alkali weed, burning bush (summer cypress), prickly lettuce, and saltgrass—showed significantly higher levels than the previous year. The samples ranged from 0.2 to 82 ppm. There was one stunning addition to the collection in 1990: edible wild mushrooms were found for the first time . . . and they contained from 320 to 660 ppm.[1] Although there was no evidence that the fungi were being eaten by any of the refuge wildlife, mushrooms are known to be an occasional dietary target of a wide range of animals, from rodents and deer to skunks and game birds. But wildlife toxicity from the poisonous mushrooms was not the only concern. The state health department's top toxicologist, Dr. Anna Fan, considered them a definite health threat to humans. Less than an ounce of mushroom at even the lowest level of contamination, she said, would yield a dose of more than 3,000 micrograms (millionths of a gram), a level considered toxic to humans.

But even without the threat of that level of food-chain poisoning, researchers were finding ample evidence that selenium was accumulating at toxic levels in a variety of insects upon which birds, rodents, and other animals routinely feed. Concentrations in beetles, crickets, grasshoppers, spiders, and sowbugs ranged from 0.7 to 77 ppm. Soil litter, the rich organic duff that compares to the decaying animal and plant detritus of the marsh bottom, was dangerously high, too, ranging from 8 to 317 ppm. Both patterns of poisoning are predicted to go higher as the selenium bound up in cattails and other vegetation is released as the plants die and decay. Very little analytical work had been done on birds that frequent the filled pond areas. Selenium levels in some killdeer and western meadowlarks sampled there were nearly as high as those commonly associated with death and deformity in waterfowl. If there were no reports of death or reproductive problems as recently as February 1991, perhaps it was because there had not been any detailed effort to look for them. Nevertheless, selenium levels up to 14 ppm had been found routinely in the livers of meadowlarks and up to 24 ppm in the eggs.

Nowhere were the risks of food chain poisoning more apparent than in the rodent population, the same creatures on which the harrier hawks were feasting when I toured the refuge with Skorupa and Zahm. Western harvest mice contained from 2.1 to 15 ppm and averaged 6.5. Deer mice ranged from 2.6 to 13 ppm and averaged 6.3. The numbers were higher for California voles, 2.9 to 79 ppm, and averaged 9.3. Ornate shrews, a small, mouselike mammal, contained 7.4 to 44 ppm and averaged 19; house mice ranged from 1.7 to 24 ppm, a 7.2 average. Only one small mammal species was consistently below toxic levels, the valley pocket gopher. They averaged 1.8 ppm. But one of those sampled reached 6.8 ppm and the levels are expected to rise as the selenium is released into the rich duff upon which they are known to feed.

The rodent population has more to fear than loss by predation. Rates of reproductive failure among them ranged from 22.2 percent for harvest mice to 76.9 percent for voles. Those are higher numbers of reproductive failure than Ohlendorf first found among waterfowl in 1983. Researchers were not certain all of the breeding problems could be the result of selenium alone. Many species of wildlife curtail breeding when natural conditions like prolonged droughts make survival of young even chancier than usual.

Virtually no analytical work has been done, so far, on the larger predators of Kesterson, even though 1983 testing found disturbingly high selenium levels in raccoons. Those tested at Kesterson contained fifteen times more selenium than a comparable sampling at Volta NWR, the refuge that biologists were using as a clean, controlled site. Coyotes and raptors are the dominant large land predators at Kesterson now, but researchers and refuge personnel there have seen red and gray foxes, raccoons, skunks, and, more important, one or two San Joaquin kit fox. That species already is listed as endangered in both the federal and state protection programs. Blacktail hares and desert cottontail feed on seeds and grasses, barn owls prey heavily on rodents, and all are becoming more numerous in the refuge.

Skorupa thinks the harrier hawks should be monitored closely—not only because of the obvious rodent predation risks but because they could be used as an indicator species for similar threats to other predators that are harder to collect. "They are very difficult to trace back to their nests, but we could ease that problem by injecting bait rodents with tiny microchip radio transmitters," he suggested. "Then we could easily home in on the hawk nests when they go back to feed their young. That way," he added, "we could monitor both the adults and their offspring." If northern harriers hold the key to discovering whether a whole new population of land-based species is likely to recreate the poisoning experience of their water-based counterparts at Kesterson, they also have become an indicator of severe contamination at another drainage-tainted site in central Wyoming.

Federal wildlife researchers tracked fifty mated pair of harriers through the reproductive cycle of 1990 in the Kendrick Irrigation Project, near Casper, and didn't find a single fledged chick. But harriers are not the most extreme sign of selenium poisoning on the semiarid and wind-swept plains of Wyoming. Almost without exception, selenium levels in water, sediment, vegetation, and waterfowl there have set new standards of selenium contamination among those sites being studied throughout the West by the Interior Department. Fourteen of twenty-four water samples exceeded the known safety limits and some were higher than those at Kesterson: up to 300 ppb. Five of nine sediment samples exceeded the toxic threshold, ranging to 25 ppm. Every plant and invertebrate sample analyzed exceeded the 4 ppm food-chain safety level and ranged to 89 ppm. Fourteen egg samples exceeded the 20 ppm level that Skorupa now feels is a reliable indicator of embryo death or deformity in a general population. One of the eggs held more selenium—160 ppm—than had ever been found in a bird egg. Eight samples exceeded a similar threshold for lethal effect in bird livers: 30 ppm. And one of those, too, was the highest liver level ever reported: 170 ppm. Fish from several sites, including the North Platte River, which runs through Casper and is the city's main supply of drinking water, were higher than the 7.5 ppm toxicity threshold for fish. One of the fish livers contained 97 ppm, enough to deliver a toxic dose to any human consuming it.

The 120,000-acre Kendrick Project is something of a standard for contamination. It is the only one of thirteen sites in nine study areas for which final reports were available in early 1991 that exceeded all toxicity thresholds for water, sediment, food chain, eggs, liver, and fish tissue.[2] Montana's Freezeout Lake, a state waterfowl management area, and Benton Lake NWR, north of Great Falls, are both part of the Reclamation Bureau's Sun River Project. Sampling there revealed that the known safety limits for five of the six toxicity trigger points just noted were being exceeded. The same is true at Utah's Stewart Lake waterfowl management area.

More will be understood about the widespread nature of selenium-tainted drainage when the second and third rounds of the Interior Department's investigation are completed and final reports have been issued. But early in 1991, when twelve more of those documents were going through final review, the pattern of poisoning was on the rise—well beyond the minimal scope repeatedly claimed by top Interior officials.

Nothing makes this more clear than a brief summary. As they embarked on the congressionally ordered formal investigation prompted by *The Bee* series, Interior administrators insisted that no other Kesterson-like lethal effects would be found. They maintained that claim even after the preliminary sampling of the first nine sites, but admitted that selenium levels were high enough at several locations to require "careful vigilance."

But within months of the 1988 release of the final investigations at seven of those nine locations—which made no mention of lethal impacts or the prospect of them—confidential sources said dead and deformed hatchlings or embryos had been found at four more sites: Stillwater, in Nevada, where the impact may be caused more by mercury than selenium; the Tulare Basin, in central California; Kendrick, in Wyoming; and Ouray NWR, just downstream from *The Bee*'s Stewart Lake sampling site in northeastern Utah. (Interior officials confirmed that report weeks after the story appeared in the Sacramento newspaper). With the discovery of deformed waterfowl embryos at Benton Lake NWR, in Northern Montana, another site where *The Bee* found alarmingly high levels in 1985, the list of lethal impact sites, counting Kesterson, has since grown to six.

Victim searches have not yet begun at five other locations where researchers have found enough selenium in bird livers to indicate a strong possibility of death and deformity. Those sites include the Salton Sea

The expanding selenium threat

The map shows the progress of the U.S. Department of Interior's continuing investigation of selenium contamination throughout the West.

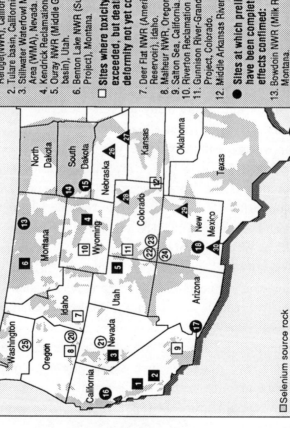

▨ Selenium source rock

Source: U.S. Department of Interior

Legend

■ **Sites at which dead and deformed waterfowl have been found:**

1. Kesterson National Wildlife Refuge(NWR), California.
2. Tulare basin, California.
3. Stillwater Waterfowl Management Area (WMA), Nevada.
4. Kendrick Reclamation Project, Wyoming.
5. Ouray NWR (Middle Green River basin), Utah.
6. Benton Lake NWR (Sun River Project), Montana.

□ **Sites where toxicity thresholds exceeded, but death and deformity not yet confirmed:**

7. Deer Flat NWR (American Falls Reservoir), Idaho.
8. Malheur NWR, Oregon.
9. Salton Sea, California.
10. Riverton Reclamation Project, Wyoming.
11. Gunnison River-Grand Valley Project, Colorado.
12. Middle Arkansas River basin, Colo.-Kan.

● **Sites at which preliminary studies have been completed but no toxic effects confirmed:**

13. Bowdoin NWR (Milk River Project), Montana.

14. Belle Fourche Reclamation Project, S. Dakota.
15. Angostura Reclamation Unit, S. Dakota.
16. Sacramento NWR complex, California.
17. Lower Colorado River Valley, Arizona.
18. Bosque del Apache NWR (Middle Rio Grande), N. Mexico.
19. Laguna Atascosa NWR (Lower Rio Grande Valley), Texas.

○ **Sites where investigations just beginning**

20. Owyhee-Vale projects, Ore.-Idaho.
21. Humboldt WMA, Nevada.
22. Dolores Reclamation Project, Colorado.
23. Pine River area, Colorado.
24. San Juan River area, N. Mexico.
25. Upper Columbia River basin, Washington.

▲ **Sites at which investigations recommended but not started, yet**

26. Central Nebraska Project, Nebraska.
27. Bostwick Division, Neb.-Kan.
28. Colorado-Big Thompson Projects, Colorado.
29. Fort Sumner, N. Mexico.
30. Rio Grande Project, N. Mex.-Texas.

Bee graphic / Lisa J. Smith

NWR in southern California; Deer Flat NWR in Idaho; the Riverton Reclamation Project in western Wyoming; several sites on the Gunnison River and Grand Valley projects that have been combined into a single study site in western Colorado; and numerous off-stream storage reservoirs along the Middle Arkansas River basin, on both sides of the Colorado-Kansas border, and in the river itself.

With the addition of three new areas in which selenium search teams will begin work in 1991, the list of places with enough of the toxic element to inflict death or deformity may soon grow to fourteen sites in ten different western states. Although sampling had not begun by mid-1991, there is ample evidence in historical studies to indicate selenium levels may be as high in those three sites as any already confirmed. The new sites include the Pine River Project on the Ute Indian Reservation of southwestern Colorado (where there also are major public health concerns because of dangerous concentrations of selenium in well water), the Owyhee-Vale Project along the southern Oregon-Idaho border, and the San Juan River area of northwestern New Mexico.

No one knows how many other sites will yield similar effects. Only moderately elevated concentrations have been found at six other locations where preliminary studies were drawing to a close early in 1991: Bowdoin NWR, along the Milk River in northeastern Montana; the Belle Fourche and Angostura projects in western South Dakota; the Lower Colorado River Valley in Arizona; and Bosque del Apache in New Mexico; and Laguna Atascosa NWR on the Rio Grande in Texas. But early work by Wyoming University researcher Orville Beath, USGS geologist David Love, and others indicates high selenium levels where two other studies are just beginning: the Dolores Reclamation Project of southwestern Colorado and the Humboldt River Waterfowl Management Area of central Nevada. There are similar historical reports of a high-selenium threat in or near five other sites for which study recommendations have been made but not yet approved by Interior: the Central Nebraska Project, the Bostwick Division Project in both Nebraska and north-central Kansas, the Colorado–Big Thompson Project in Colorado, the Fort Sumner Project in New Mexico, and the Rio Grande Project that straddles New Mexico and Texas. If all of these study sites are approved, it would raise the total number of investigations to twenty-eight, involving more than fifty individual areas in parts of all fifteen western states.

New discoveries about the nature and toxicity of the potent trace element, however, are raising the prospects of more unsettling discoveries. So far, the federal studies have been confined largely to direct reproductive effects of selenium in waterfowl and, to a lesser degree, fish. But serious population declines also may be occurring in dozens of other aquatic species, tiny insects, invertebrates, and aquatic plants that form vital links in the wetlands food chain. Their loss or decline would have a powerful secondary effect on the larger and more visible marsh populations. In addition, researchers only now are beginning to assess the secondary effects of chronic poisoning. In some cases, those impacts may be only lower birth weights or slower rates of development. But either impact would make survivors easier targets of predation. In others, the poisoning could damage or overload immune systems and make them more vulnerable to natural diseases like avian botulism and cholera.

Other discoveries are yielding unexpected results, too, including Skorupa's revelation that some species suffer toxicity when levels of dissolved selenium are far, far lower than originally believed. For instance, when the initial Kesterson discoveries were made, in 1983, the state had no safety limit for selenium and the federal Environmental Protection Agency limit to safeguard freshwater aquatic species was 35 ppb. But Dr. Dennis Lemly of the Fish and Wildlife Service's national fisheries laboratory found reproductive failure in fish when water levels were between 8 and 12 ppb and strong indications that toxicity resulted in concentrations down to 5 ppb. That 5 ppb level was adopted as the new safety standard by both EPA and California. But even that number may be too high for species, such as the eared grebe, that feed entirely on aquatic invertebrates. Because of the biological accumulation in that selective food chain, Skorupa thinks there is a potential for toxicity any time waterborne concentrations exceed 0.5 ppb.

Two factors—diet and the chemical *form* of selenium—are playing an increasingly important role as scientists continue their research. In Kesterson, it was initially supposed that destructive effects occurred only when selenium levels reached the hundreds-of-ppb counts measured in the water there and the tens-of-ppm range in the food chain. But only 100 miles further south, in the dead-end Tulare Basin, Skorupa and others reported double the amount of toxic effect when selenium counts were four to five times lower in the water and food organisms than at Kesterson. The Tulare version of the Kesterson effect was more lethal because birds either had no other clean sites at which to feed or because there was so much poisoned food available they wouldn't make the effort to look elsewhere. Skorupa says that the supply of brine flies and shrimp is so thick in some of the Tulare drainage evaporation ponds that even ducks will nest on bare ground just to be close to the rich—but deadly—food supply. This is such a rare event that waterfowl biologists who have spent a lifetime in the field still demand photographic evidence before they believe it. And Skorupa willingly obliges.

The other factor is chemistry. The biological transformation that selenium goes through is critical to how much effect its presence will have. In its elemental form, selenium is thought to be available only to the unique family of *Astragalus* plants that Beath labeled as selenium indicator flags. But once they (or soil-based microbes) metabolize it to an organic form, such as selenomethionine, selenium can be picked up by the roots of almost any vegetation. Like the inorganic selenate form, the organic forms are readily dissolved in the water column, where they pose a double threat. Not only are they more toxic to many species, if not all, than the inorganic forms purely on a gram-by-gram basis. But, because their levels are both absorbed from the water (bioconcentration) and multiplied when a large predator consumes the entire body burden of hundreds of smaller tainted prey (biomagnification), organic forms can bioaccumulate to as much as 100,000 times what is present in the original water column.

What started out as a bizarre episode at Kesterson has now become the equivalent of an agricultural Superfund in the West. Detailed studies leading to cleanup plans like those that prompted the dewatering of Kesterson and the recommended $40 million-a-year management plan for the San Joaquin Valley already have begun at six locations: the Salton Sea, Stillwater, Kendrick, the Middle Green River Basin, the Sun River Basin, and the Klamath Basin refuge complex, which straddles the Oregon and California border but may be more related to pesticides than selenium. Similar remediation plans are scheduled to begin in 1991 in the combined Grand Valley and Gunnison River project area in western Colorado.

Marc Sylvester, whose involvement in the spreading issue dates back to almost the earliest days at Kesterson, has been promoted to head a national water quality assessment team for the USGS. But he was still issuing and reviewing selenium status reports for his agency in January 1991 when he said: "Obviously, selenium is a prevalent problem when you find it at so many sites in so many states, especially at levels high enough to cause death and deformity in so many places."

There are other elements of concern at many of those sites, including arsenic, mercury, chromium, molybdenum, lithium, uranium, and boron. But Sylvester has no doubts that selenium is playing the lead role in the toxicity seen so far. "Selenium is the most common element at elevated levels and it most likely is the cause of the toxicity we are seeing. That organic forms are so much more toxic—up to ten times for some species and developmental stages—and bioaccumulate so high may explain what we are seeing at places like Stillwater, for instance," added Sylvester during an interview in his Menlo Park office.

In early 1991, compound concentrations still were being measured as "total selenium" at all sites in the spreading Interior investigation. At

Stillwater, those levels are comparatively low but death and deformity still occur. It took several years of intensive interlab cooperation for the agencies involved to agree on commonly accepted analytical methods just to correctly detect and report the amount of total selenium present. The work on identification and measurement of its various chemical forms, a process the scientists call "speciation," is only just getting started.

Skorupa is even more certain than Sylvester that selenium is not just the main culprit in the San Joaquin Valley portion of the West-wide poisoning but the only one. "A lot of people like to keep pointing to something else, anything else that hasn't been well enough studied, as the cause of these effects," said Skorupa during the fog-bound tour of the dewatered part of Kesterson. "But, so far, even though many of these other things are widely present, there is no evidence at all that any of them are responsible for the toxicity we are seeing. Selenium is what's doing the poisoning here. Period."

Not even those directing the evolving study are sure of its ultimate reach. Richard Engberg, who is the agency-wide coordinator for the Interior program, said he was "very surprised that we found this problem in so many places." But he worries whether there will be enough federal money to carry the program to its most logical conclusion. Acknowledging that there are a host of potential sites yet to be selected from the reams of historical literature available, Engberg added: "We have had to pick and choose which places we investigated pretty carefully because there is only so much money available. There may well be problems in places we haven't looked very closely at or at some we haven't even thought to look. I don't know what will happen there."

Nor is anyone certain about the eventual outcome of the selenium search. So far, it has consumed eight years and more than $100 million, the great part of it in federal funding and most of it spent on the prototype detailed studies in California. But even there, no clear solutions have appeared and federal officials say it may be ten more years before any of the promising treatment methods are proved effective enough to implement.

There have, however, been instances where recognition of the problem has helped avoid creating new troubled sites and encouraged the mitigation of existing ones. For instance, one proposed irrigation project in south-central South Dakota, the $180 million Lake Andes–Wagner Project, was denied federal funding in 1990 because high soil and plant levels of selenium were found in the proposed service area as a direct result of the federal probe.

And for all its ill omens, even Kesterson has begun to yield impressive offsetting gains. Forced to mitigate the negative effects of its poorly conceived experiment there, the Bureau of Reclamation has purchased the damaged adjacent ranches of the Freitas and Claus families and acquired other nearby holdings to virtually double the size of Kesterson to more than 10,000 acres. The selenium contamination was largely confined to about 700 acres of that holding, at the southern edge of the refuge. Now the reclamation agency has granted the refuge a firm supply of clean water—the first secured and guaranteed water rights for any federal wildlife area in the entire San Joaquin Valley.

There is a surviving irony, however. Even though it took a selenium disaster to secure the first water rights at Kesterson, the Kern NWR, at the southern end of the valley and in the very eye of a farm evaporation pond disaster, still must beg for water charity year after year, obtaining supplies only when there is a surplus beyond the needs of all other water project customers. Still, at Kesterson, the new water could turn the untainted parts of the refuge into the largest and most productive refuge in the valley.

The rest of the selenium news is not nearly so encouraging. Not a single site has been cleaned up yet. And the increasing presence of selenium in Kesterson's dry, upland areas raises serious doubts of such a favorable outcome anywhere else anytime soon. So far, too, little attention has been paid to any of the nongame species involved in the poisoning episodes. Gary Zahm unwittingly indicated how much remains to be done . . . and how difficult it will be to prod the agencies to do it unless attitudes at the top change abruptly.

We finished our tour of the rest of Kesterson and saw the promise of its untainted north and east quadrants, which Zahm called "classic California pothole prairie," where seasonal vernal pools would soon be ringed with brilliant bands of wildflowers and cluttered with all manner of waterfowl, from white pelicans to white-faced ibis.

We stopped near old Pond 1, where some of the highest levels of selenium had been found. Blacktail hares and desert cottontails hopped in and out of the burning bush, alkali weed, iodine bush, and such well-known selenium accumulator plants as aster, mustard, and *Atriplex*. Large clumps of the latter were scattered across the filled area and closer inspection revealed scores of smaller volunteer plants coming up through the dense understory of vegetation.

The sun was burning off the last tendrils of fog. The soft flutter of wings could be heard in the bushes. The sweet chorus of songbirds broke the silence.

"Look . . . there . . . in the *Atriplex*," whispered Zahm, pointing to one of the larger specimens only 10 yards away. "See how many songbirds use this stuff. They are in there for the seeds. Yet no one is sampling *Atriplex* seeds for selenium, even though we know this plant readily picks it up from the soil and serves as a major attractant for bird feeding." The bush was alive with savanna and white-crowned sparrows and finches. And the dust around them was laced with rabbit tracks. "The raptors will be in here soon, too, feeding on the young rabbits," said Zahm. "Maybe we just ought to blitzkrieg this whole place. Dig up all the tainted soil and truck it away and cut down all of the vegetation and burn it. Then we should put some buried drainpipes in to collect the tainted groundwater before it rises to the roots and collect it in sumps so we can keep it from poisoning this place all over again."

He stopped, abruptly, thought of the economic consequences of such a massive cleanup effort, and pondered aloud the possibilities of such a proposal coming forth.

"For all of the money spent on this problem so far, we still haven't come up with any real solution . . . and I don't think anyone up the administrative ladder is going to want to hear a suggestion like this. The field researchers have been right all along about this problem and I think they still are right to worry about the threat to terrestrial creatures. This is going to be with us for a long time to come."

EPILOGUE

It has been suggested by some that readers should be let down lightly at the end of a story like this: given hope that better days are ahead; urged to pursue constructive course corrections. Neither, alone, is an easy task. Together, they are purely daunting.

In mid-1991, as these final words are put in place, some final perspectives are needed. What follows, then, are purely personal positions, but they are based on hundreds of conversations with technicians, experts, politicians, biologists, and birders.

Researchers at a recent conference at the University of California campus at Davis concluded that "we have come a long way on selenium . . . accomplished a great deal." I am not so sure. Beyond dispute, we have learned, and more often relearned, much. Selenium research has become a new and thriving cottage industry in California. So far, nearly $100 million has been spent on selenium work since Ohlendorf and Smith made their macabre find in the cattails of Kesterson. But only a few million of those dollars, certainly little more than $12 million, has actually gone to cleanup work.

Even so, Kesterson is a very long way from clean. More and more it looks like an aborted tradeoff in which dead and deformed rabbits, songbirds, rodents, and hawks will soon retrace the tragic destiny of coots, ducks, frogs, and fish. There is enough selenium in the shallow groundwater beneath and beyond Kesterson's now-filled evaporation ponds to contaminate the surface soil and vegetation by capillary action for decades. And much more is tied up in the slowly decaying mass of cattails, an organic form of selenium that when laid down in the surficial organic duff will be a dangerous legacy for most of the land-based ecosystem.

Gary Zahm, who once managed the Kesterson refuge and now has been promoted to oversee the whole San Luis complex of refuges, and his colleagues at the Fish and Wildlife Service may have been right all along: that nothing short of removing the tainted soil and vegetation and collecting, treating, or removing the tainted water below will render Kesterson clean.

But there is one substantial bright spot at Kesterson. Forced to make amends for the damage its project did, the Department of Interior has purchased nearly 10,000 acres of adjacent and uncontaminated ranch and farmland that could make Kesterson the most productive and important wetlands in the San Joaquin Valley. Properly, this time, the Bureau of Reclamation is dedicating the permanent water rights that such lands need to fulfill their promise as mitigation sites.

A hundred miles to the south of Kesterson, in the semiarid heart of the Tulare Basin, another vital chapter of the selenium story is unfolding. On the one hand, the intensive, $40 million research effort mounted by the San Joaquin Valley Drainage Program there is a brilliant stroke of site characterization. Scientists have learned much about the source, mobilization, transport, and biochemical and biological cycling of this unique trace element. On the other hand, the program has fallen far short of discovering any magical formula to correct the emerging biological nightmare there.

There are more than 7,000 acres of similar but on-farm evaporation ponds in that basin, between Fresno and Bakersfield, on the valley's parched west side. More than half of them, equal to nearly four Kesterson pond systems, have selenium levels associated with reproductive toxicity in a wide range of waterfowl and shorebirds. Even worse, the ponds represent almost the only source of wetland habitat in the intensively cropped area, so the birds are almost continuously exposed to toxic food and exhibit far worse toxicity at far lower levels than was experienced at Kesterson.

For all of its impressive marshaling of information, the San Joaquin Valley study is long on imaginative plans to manage the selenium and wider salt balance problem but painfully short on implementation mechanisms. So far, no law or regulation exists to enforce the corrective steps outlined—and the subject of who will pay for them if and when they are taken has been totally ignored. The technocrats have given us a blueprint for correction. The challenge now rests with the politicians, the public, and the bureaucrats who serve them to turn it into reality.

If the San Joaquin plan is the prototype for the comprehensive Interior Department selenium search, as chief of that program Richard Engberg says it is, then the rest of the West is in for a very long wait for solutions. Which means that the waterfowl and other wildlife that frequent the nearly forty individual sites in twenty-six areas of seventeen states studied so far will go on suffering for many, many years.

The foregoing chapters have raised unsettling questions, but there are many others orbiting just around the periphery of the central wildlife, livestock, and human health issues I have addressed. No single agency or combination of them is moving on a coordinated front to tackle the increasing number of natural and man-made sources of selenium in our environment. Indeed, few of them are acting at all.

J. David Love, who knows as much about western geology as perhaps anyone alive, worries about the implications of inadvertently spreading selenium over the country's farmlands while coating them with phosphate fertilizers. Love and other geologists have uncovered widespread evidence of potentially harmful concentrations of the element in most of the phosphoria rock formations mined for fertilizer feedstock. There are places in America where supplements of selenium might be helpful, because they are deficient in the essential trace element. Ironically, one of those places is on the opposite side of the San Joaquin River, only a few dozen miles from Kesterson and the Tulare Basin. But there are many places where there is already enough or far too much for our own good health and the toxic burden there will be pushed needlessly and perhaps harmfully higher. And it won't stay just in the soil, either. Once oxidized into a water-soluble state, it is readily picked up by many crops.

Another example of regulatory disinterest involves the lack of air emission standards for selenium discharge from the nation's power plant, refinery, and petrochemical facilities. And the situation is little better for water pollution discharges. In early 1991, the San Francisco Bay Region Water Quality Control Board made its first regulatory assault on the element, an effort it considered reasonably aggressive. Even so, it allowed the continued discharge of at least 5,000 tons a year of selenium into San Francisco Bay with the requirement that by the end of 1993, ten years after Kesterson's painful experience, the rates would be cut in half by the major source of waterborne selenium in the bay: oil refineries.[1]

The Environmental Protection Agency, however, is growing increasingly concerned about the proliferation of selenium in the environment. In the San Joaquin Valley, it has rejected the state's proposed receiving water standard of 8 ppb selenium as too high and is promulgating a tougher standard of its own. It may do the same in San Francisco Bay, where the continuing industrial effluent is allowed to contain 50 ppb. EPA already has lowered its freshwater aquatic species protection standard from 35 ppb to 5 ppb. Too, federal biologists have presented compelling evidence that long-term discharges of even that much are a threat. In time, they could bioaccumulate to levels that could trigger death, deformity, and an unsettling suite of other adverse health effects to aquatic creatures.[2]

Abandoned tailings from uranium, vanadium, gold, silver, copper, and other mines that pockmark so much of the mineralized West are another major threat of harmful selenium discharges. Dangerously high levels of selenium have been found in such ore bodies by many researchers, and they are a major threat to contaminate streams and farmlands downslope in parts of Wyoming, Colorado, New Mexico, Utah, Montana, Idaho, and Oregon. But in this case, at least, the U.S. Office of Surface Mining in Denver is worried about the potential risks and is funding a new round of research into the problem.

Some of that money is going into the retrieval of historic and sometimes unpublished research of selenium searchers like Beath, Love, and others in order to locate obvious trouble spots. The information will be stored in a permanent selenium research center in the University of Wyoming Library's American Heritage Center. The collection is permanently endowed by Beath's daughter, Mary Elizabeth, who has bequeathed virtually her entire estate, at death, to the project in memory of her father. She, Love, and others are working to obtain the valuable selenium files of Dr. Arthur A. Kilness in a move that could make the collection the largest repository of historic selenium research work in the world.

But there are much bigger problems than the task of amassing archives. When the U.S. Food and Drug Administration first allowed selenium to be added, at a rate of only one-tenth of a part per million, to the feed of only a few animal species in the early 1970s, there was virtually no public review of the potential long-range public health implications. There was even less when the agency allowed that amount to be tripled in 1987 and fed to most of the nation's meat and poultry supplies. That same year, FDA abandoned its minimal inspections designed to ensure that anyone who mixes feeds for commercial livestock and poultry must perform tests to guard against overdosing the supplement mixes with selenium—even though there have been several prominent cases where animals died because of excessive doses. So far, FDA's Center for Veterinary Medicine has refused to perform environmental impact studies to assess the risk of selenium percolating beneath or running off feedlots and other areas where animal waste is piled. Nor has anyone studied the potential for long-term accumulation when such selenium-tainted fertilizing material is sold to farmers for use on their fields.

Whatever its initial hesitation to face the selenium issue, the Interior Department now has mounted—and funded—one of the most extensive studies of the adverse environmental impacts of agriculture ever undertaken. Two recent parts of that widening overview reveal how far the agency has come in dealing with the problem . . . but also how very much further it has to go.

Early in 1990, the staff of influential congressman George Miller (D–Calif.)—chairman of the House Interior and Insular Affairs Committee—signaled the government's first application of lessons learned from the Kesterson effect. Before any more western lands would be served with federally subsidized irrigation projects, they would first have to be studied for their potential to cause problems with selenium and other toxic trace elements. In the midst of one such hazards assessment, the Fish and Wildlife Service discovered dangerously high levels of selenium in the soil, water, and aquatic residents in, on, and around the service area of a proposed $180 million Lake Andes–Wagner Project, in the southeastern corner of South Dakota, including the Lake Andes National Wildlife Refuge.[3] The funding was denied.

Although the project's sponsors are scrambling to keep it alive with research grants to study ways to manage the tainted drainage, it's hard to imagine that researchers could find many more things to study. After all, California has already studied virtually every aspect of this quixotic element's geological history, present cycling patterns, and prospects for reducing or treating it. But, at least, the project will not be built without guarantees that it won't recreate more selenium nightmares. Score one for what the proponents of widespread selenium use call the "selenophobiacs."

But just how much more remains to be done—even in completing the registry of selenium hot spots in the West—was revealed in a Wildlife Service contaminant report of April 1990. The populations of piping plovers and the interior least tern are in such dire straits that both birds were placed on the federal list of threatened and endangered species in 1985. Approximately 22 percent of the Northern Great Plains piping plovers and 12 percent of the least terns nest on sparsely vegetated sandbars, islands, and shoreline of the Missouri River. Until then, most biologists involved in selenium study felt that wildlife risks would be confined mostly to terminal sinks, dead-end ponds, embayments, and deltas, in that order. Flowing streams, especially those as large as the Missouri River, with their great dilutional capabilities, were considered to have low-risk potential . . . except to fish and larger fish-eating birds.

Then researchers discovered an unusually high number of addled—fertile but undeveloped—least tern and plover eggs and had them analyzed for a wide range of toxic heavy metals and trace elements, including mercury, arsenic, and selenium. Only selenium was above background or safe levels—but so far above that the concentrations reached or exceeded levels associated with embryo deformity and mortality in several waterfowl and shorebird species. Researchers said the source of the contamination was high selenium in small fish upon which the terns feed and in tiny invertebrates that make up the plover's diet. "The selenium-caused mortality of a few eggs or chicks of an abundant species may be insignificant," stated the researchers. But, they continued, "With an endangered species, the selenium problem could be particularly acute because it may be additive to factors already inhibiting productivity and population growth that resulted in the species becoming endangered."[4]

Another sobering fact: Interior's West-wide inventory effort has found selenium in every place it has studied west of the 100th meridian. (West of this line, from the middle of North Dakota, south through Texas, and west to the Pacific coast, annual precipitation averages around 13 inches.) In twenty-four of twenty-six areas studied, several with eight or ten separate tainted sites, selenium levels are high enough to be toxic to a wide range of wildlife now or could well become a threat in the near future. The Missouri River site studied by biologists in the Pierre, South Dakota, field office of the Fish and Wildlife Service is not even on the list. Gradually, the Interior program has taken on the characteristics of the nation's Superfund effort to find, characterize, mitigate, and clean up industrial and military hazardous waste sites. But the program's funding is running out and Kesterson is the only place where cleanup and mitigation have even been attempted.

The reportage that went into this work was confined largely to the United States. But my most unsettling discovery was the account of horribly deformed human babies in a highly seleniferous zone of Colombia and subsequent historical accounts of sharply elevated levels of the trace element in so many other nations where little has been done to characterize adverse effects to humans, livestock, or wildlife.

So much for the exhilaration of riding the crest of discovery journalism.

Sources

It would be unreasonable to expect a complete reference list on the damaging effects of selenium in a book of this kind. In some of the published bibliographies I have seen, just the outstanding pieces of research alone number in the hundreds. The most definitive of these, "Selected Bibliography on Selenium," by the Geological Survey of Wyoming, authored by James C. Case and others (Bulletin 69 from the State Geologist's Office in Laramie), contains 811 references. Another detailed survey of literature on the agricultural problems of selenium has been compiled by Dr. Donald S. Heaney, extension director and agricultural agent for the Southern Ute Indian Reservation in Colorado. Many more of them are carried in outstanding research material like that in *Selenium in Agriculture,* Agricultural Handbook 200, by the USDA's Agricultural Research Service in 1961. A wonderfully varied, and authoritative, selection of technical research is combined in the three published proceedings of the annual series of symposia staged jointly by the Bay Institute of San Francisco and the Department of Conservation and Resource Studies at the University of California: *Selenium II* (March 1985), *Selenium III* (March 1986), and *Selenium IV* (March 1987). The Bay Institute is located at 10 Liberty Ship Way, No. 120, Sausalito, CA 94965.

For biologists and wildlife toxicologists, nothing compares to the insightful series of research papers prepared by U.S. Fish and Wildlife Service experts like Dr. Dennis Lemly, at the National Fisheries Research Center in Columbia,

Missouri, and by Harry Ohlendorf (since resigned) and Joseph Skorupa of the agency's Patuxent Wildlife Research Center's Pacific Coast field office in Davis, California. Unfortunately, these papers have not been pulled together in a single volume. There is similarly seminal work by geochemist Ivan Barnes and research chemist Theresa Presser and their several colleagues in the U.S. Geological Survey. The San Joaquin Valley Drainage Program, headquartered in the Federal Building on Cottage Way in Sacramento, has the written reports of research it funded, and its SJVDP Data Directory includes an extensive bibliography of both USGS and FWS work in connection with the program. But, without question, the principal work in the field is *Selenium: Geobotany, Biochemistry, Toxicity, and Nutrition* by Irene Rosenfeld and Orville A. Beath (New York: Academic Press, 1964).

What follows, chapter by chapter, are the notes cited in the text, some of the many general reference works used in preparing this book, and a listing of interviews with key figures in this long-running western tragedy.

CHAPTER 1

Notes

1. T. S. Presser and Harry M. Ohlendorf, "Biogeochemical Cycling of Selenium in the San Joaquin Valley, Calif.," *Environmental Management* 11(6) (1987):808.
2. Harry M. Ohlendorf, "Bioaccumulation and Effects of Selenium in Wildlife," in *Selenium in Agriculture and the Environment* (Madison, Wisc.: Soil Science Society of America, 1989), pp. 154 and 159.
3. Michael Saiki (research fishery biologist), U.S. Fish and Wildlife Service, personal communication.
4. W. E. Poly and A. L. Moxon, "The Effect of Selenized Grains on the Rate of Growth of Chicks," *Poultry Science* 17 (1941):72–74; and Irene Rosenfeld and Orville A. Beath, *Selenium: Geobotany, Biochemistry, Toxicology, and Nutrition* (New York: Academic Press, 1964), pp. 201–204.

General References

Bureau of Sports Fisheries and Wildlife. Memoranda on looming impacts to waterfowl habitat from development of "San Luis Unit, Central Valley Project, Calif. (River Basin Studies)," Sept. 13 and 29, 1961.

Gruenwald, P. "Effects of Selenium Compound on Chick Embryos." *American Journal of Pathology* 34 (1958):77–103.

Moore, S. B., and others. "Biological Residue Data for Evaporation Ponds in the San Joaquin Valley." Report prepared for the San Joaquin Valley Drainage Program, 1989.

Ohlendorf, Harry M., D. J. Hoffman, M. K. Saiki, and T. W. Aldrich. "Embryonic Deformities and Abnormalities of Aquatic Birds: Apparent Impacts by Selenium from Irrigation Drainwater." *Science of the Total Environment* 52 (1986):49–63.

Ohlendorf, Harry M., Arthur W. Kilness, M.D., and Jerry L. Simmons. "Selenium Toxicosis in Wild Aquatic Birds." *Journal of Toxicology and Environmental Health* 24 (1988):67–92.

USFWS. "Conceptual Plan for Waterfowl in the Central Valley, Calif." Sacramento: USFW Field Office, 1978.

USFWS. Memoranda to the Regional Director in 1961 from the Sacramento Field Supervisor and, in 1962, from the Regional FWS Director to the Bureau of Reclamation Regional Director regarding possible threats to wildlife from agricultural drainage.

Interviews

Felix Smith, environmental assessment specialist, USFWS, in Sacramento (several interviews); Harry M. Ohlendorf, research biologist, Patuxent Wildlife Research Center, Pacific Field Station, Davis, California (several interviews).

CHAPTER 2

Notes

1. Harry M. Ohlendorf, "Bioaccumulation and Effects of Selenium in Wild-life," in *Selenium in Agriculture and the Environment* (Madison, Wisc.: American Society of Agronomy, 1989).
2. Dr. Dennis Lemly, "Bioaccumulation of Selenium," in *Agricultural Irrigation Drainwater Studies in Support of San Joaquin Valley Drainage Program—Final Report* (Sacramento: Department of Interior, 1990); and personal communication.
3. T. S. Presser and Ivan Barnes, "Selenium Content in Water Tributary to and in the Vicinity of Kesterson NWR," USGS Water Resources Investigation Report 84-4122, p. 13.
4. T. S. Presser and Ivan Barnes, "Dissolved Constituents, Includes Waters in the Vicinity of Kesterson NWR and the West Grasslands, Fresno and Merced Counties, CA," USGS Water Resources Investigation Report 85-4220.
5. Ibid.
6. California Department of Fish and Game press release, October 19, 1984.

General References

Ohlendorf, Harry M., and Joseph P. Skorupa. "Selenium in Relation to Wildlife and Agricultural Drain Water." Paper presented at Fourth International Symposium on Uses of Selenium and Tellurium, Banff, Alberta, May 1989.
Ohlendorf, Harry M., and others. "Relationships Between Selenium Concentrations and Avian Reproduction." *Proceedings of 51st North American Wildlife and Natural Resources Conference*, pp. 330–342.
Presser, T. S., and Harry M. Ohlendorf. "Biogeochemical Cycling of Selenium." *Environmental Management* 11 (1987):805–821.

Interviews

Harry M. Ohlendorf (several interviews in 1984–1988); Felix Smith (several interviews); Ivan Barnes (several interviews and personal communications); T. S. Presser (interviews and personal communications); Rolf Wallenstrom, retired regional director, USFWS, Portland (interviews and personal communications).

CHAPTER 3

Notes
1. Sam F. Trelease and Orville A. Beath, *Selenium: Geological Occurrence and Biological Effects in Relation to Botany, Chemistry, Agriculture, Nutrition, and Medicine* (New York, 1949).
2. Wyoming State Board of Sheep Commissioners, 1908 Report; Trelease and Beath, *Selenium*, p. 2.
3. Hubert W. Lakin, "Selenium in Our Environment," paper presented to the Division of Water, Air, and Waste Chemistry Symposium, 162nd meeting of the American Chemical Society, Washington, D.C., September 15, 1971, pp. 96–111.
4. Steven Margolin, "Liability Under the Migratory Bird Treaty Act," *Ecology Law Quarterly* 7 (1979):989–1010; and USFWS memorandum from Drainwater Studies Coordinator to Regional Director, Portland, re: "Applicability of MBTA to Operation of Evaporation Ponds in the San Joaquin Valley," July 31, 1988.
5. "Selenium in Agricultural Drainage," in *Proceedings of Selenium II* (Berkeley: University of California Department of Conservation and Resource Studies and Bay Institute of San Francisco, 1985), pp. 83–84.
6. Ivan Barnes, "Sources of Selenium," in *Proceedings of Selenium II*, pp. 41–51.
7. William T. Davoren, "Selenium and San Francisco Bay," in *Proceedings of Selenium II*, pp. 150–160.

Interviews
Harry M. Ohlendorf; Felix Smith (interviews and personal communications); Marc Sylvester, USGS.

CHAPTER 4

Notes

1. USGS memorandum, "Water Quality of Applied Irrigation Water and Drainage Return Flows for U.S. Bureau of Reclamation Projects in Western U.S.: Work Plan," May 1, 1985.
2. *Sacramento Bee,* September 10, 1985.
3. Letter to California State Water Quality Control Board Chairman Carole Onorato in January 1985 from U.S. Fish and Wildlife Service Deputy Regional Director Joe Blum on "avian cholera"; Harry M. Ohlendorf, letter to Blum on February 15, 1985, citing diagnoses by National Wildlife Health Center in Madison, Wisconsin, of selenium toxicosis; memorandum from Charles Houghton, "Final Diagnoses of Dead Birds from Kesterson," December 12, 1987, on 103 more birds; and memorandum from Kathryn Converse, National Wildlife Health Center, to Regional USFWS Director, Portland, on selenium toxicosis as cause of bird deaths.
4. Prof. Arnold Schultz, College of Natural Resources, University of California, personal communication to David L. Trauger, director, Patuxent Wildlife Research Center, March 17, 1986.
5. Trelease and Beath, *Selenium,* p. 96; Rosenfeld and Beath, *Selenium,* p. 29.

General References

Beath, Orville A. "The Story of Selenium in Wyoming." Bulletin 774. Laramie: Agricultural Extension Station, University of Wyoming, 1963.

Bureau of Reclamation. *Project Data: A Water Resources Technical Bulletin* (Denver) (1981): 1, 405.

Cox, M. A., E. M. Bailey, and J. E. Thompson. "Salmonella and Other Enterobacteria Found in Commercial Poultry Feed." *Poultry Science* 62(11) (1983): 2169–2175.

Kilness, Dr. Arthur W. "Clinical Perspective: Selenium and Salmonella." *New England Journal of Medicine,* September 6, 1984.

Kilness, Dr. Arthur W. "Selenium and Public Health." *South Dakota Journal of Medicine,* April 1973.

Leifson, Dr. Einer. "New Selenite Enrichment Media for the Isolation of

Typhoid and Paratyphoid (Salmonella) Bacilli." *American Journal of Hygiene* 24 (1936):423–432.

Mann, E. D., and G. D. McNabb. "Prevalence of Salmonella Contamination in Market-Ready Geese in Manitoba." *Avian Disease* 28(4) (1984): 978–983.

Interviews

Ivan Barnes, USGS; Marc Sylvester, USGS (personal communication); Felix Smith, USFWS; Mitchell Snow, Department of Interior, public information officer; Lawrence Hancock, Bureau of Reclamation, regional director, Mid-Pacific Region; Morris Lefever, USFWS manager, Stillwater WMA; Steve Thompson, USFWS biologist, Stillwater WMA; Dr. Arthur W. Kilness; Mike Henry, rancher, Edgemont Valley, South Dakota; Samuel L. Bennett, rancher, Watauga, South Dakota; Gene Sipe, USFWS, refuge manager, Bowdoin NWR, Montana.

CHAPTER 5

Notes

1. Trelease and Beath, *Selenium,* pp. 13–52; Rosenfeld and Beath, *Selenium,* pp. 61–89.
2. Dr. Arthur W. Kilness, consultant, Department of Laboratory Medicine, University of South Dakota School of Medicine, Vermillion, S. D., "Selenium, Bacteria, and the Immune System," unpublished manuscript, 1987.
3. Dr. Raymond E. Lemley, "Observations on Selenium Poisoning in South and North America," *Lancet* 61(11) (1941):435–438.
4. Carlos Lopez Bustos, "Possible Biochemical Interpretations of Lathyrism," *Revista San Hig Publications* 20 (1946):1027–1045; "Toxic Principle of *Lathyrus Sativus,*" *Nature* 119 (July 1952):125.
5. Father Pedro Simon, "Noticias Historiales de las conquistas de tierre firme en las Indians occidentales," in *Biblioteca Autores Colombianos,* vol. 4 (Bogota: Kelly Publications, 1953), pp. 226–254.

General References

Presser, T. S., and Ivan Barnes. "Selenium Content in Water Tributary to and in the Vicinity of Kesterson NWR." USGS Water Resources Investigation Report 84-4122.
Sacramento Bee, March 16 and September 8–10, 1985.
USDA. *Selenium in Agriculture.* Agricultural Handbook 200. 1961.

Interviews

Dr. Arthur W. Kilness; Mike Henry, rancher, Edgemont Valley, South Dakota; Bruner Rhineholdt, rancher, Belle Fourche, South Dakota; Gene Sipe, manager, Bowdoin NWR, Montana.

CHAPTER 6

Notes

1. *Sacramento Bee,* September 8, 1985.
2. Ibid., September 9, 1985.
3. Ibid., September 10, 1985.
4. Ibid.
5. Ibid. See also letter to Interior Secretary Donald Hodel from Rep. George Miller (D–Calif.), chairman, and Rep. Dick Cheney (R–Wyo.), ranking Republican, Subcommittee on Water and Power Resources of the House Committee on Interior and Insular Affairs, September 17, 1985.
6. *Sacramento Bee,* December 3, 1985.

General References

Brogden, Robert E., and others. "Availability and Quality of Groundwater, Southern Ute Indian Reservation, Southwestern Colorado." USGS Water Supply Paper 1576-J, 1979.

Eisler, Ronald. "Selenium Hazards to Fish, Wildlife, and Invertebrates: A Synoptic Review." USFWS Biological Report 85 (1.5). Laurel, Md.: Patuxent Wildlife Research Center, 1985.

Resource Contaminant Assessment Program, South Dakota Field Office, Oahe Reservoir. USFWS Ecological Services, 1984.

Interviews

Dr. Arthur W. Kilness; Dennis Lemly, National Fisheries Research Center (interviews and personal communications); Harry M. Ohlendorf; Felix Smith; Dr. Jerry Simmons, pathologist, Sioux Falls, South Dakota.

CHAPTER 7

Notes
1. J. David Love, "Suggested Research Program on Geology and Related Studies of Poisonous Rocks," USGS report, Denver, February 25, 1949.
2. John McPhee, *Rising from the Plains* (New York: Farrar, Straus & Giroux, 1986).
3. H. W. Lakin, "Geochemistry of Selenium," in *Selenium in Agriculture,* USDA Agricultural Handbook 200, 1961, pp. 4–5.
4. Trelease and Beath, *Selenium,* pp. 62, 84, 99–100.
5. Trelease and Beath, *Selenium,* pp. 119–120; H. W. Lakin and H. G. Byers, "Selenium Occurrence in Certain Soils in the United States, with a Discussion of Related Topics, Seventh Report," USDA Technical Bulletin 950, p. 7.
6. Trelease and Beath, *Selenium,* p. 1.
7. K. W. Franke, A. G. Johnson, and others, "Report on a Preliminary Field Survey of the So-Called 'Alkali' Disease of Livestock," USDA Circular 320, 1934, pp. 1–10.
8. James C. Case and Cynthia Boyd, "Preliminary Report and Map on Potentially Seleniferous Areas of Wyoming," Wyoming Geological Survey Open File Report 85-14, 1985.
9. Trelease and Beath, *Selenium,* p. 2.

General References
Beeson, K. C. "Occurrence and Significance of Selenium in Plants." In *Selenium in Agriculture,* USDA Agricultural Handbook 200, 1961.
Byers, H. G., H. W. Lakin, and others. *Selenium in Agriculture,* USDA Agricultural Handbook 200, 1961.
Lakin, Hubert W. "Geochemistry of Selenium." In *Selenium in Agriculture,* USDA Agricultural Handbook 200, 1961.
Lakin, Hubert W. "Selenium in Our Environment." In *Trace Elements in the Environment: Division of Water, Air, and Waste Chemistry Symposium.* Washington, D.C.: American Chemical Society, 1971.
Rosenfeld, Irene, and Orville A. Beath. *Selenium: Geobotany, Biochemistry, Toxicology, and Nutrition.* New York: Academic Press, 1964.

Interviews

J. David Love; James C. Case; Mary Elizabeth Beath, daughter of Orville A. Beath; Stephen E. Williams, University of Wyoming plant physiologist; William Hepworth, biologist, Wyoming Game and Fish Department; Dr. Arthur W. Kilness; Ivan Barnes.

CHAPTER 8

Notes
1. "Selenium: The Poisoning of America," *Sacramento Bee,* December 4, 1988.
2. Dr. Arthur W. Kilness and Fred Hochberg, "Amyotrophic Lateral Sclerosis in a High Selenium Environment," *Journal of the American Medical Association* 237(26) (1977):2843–2844.
3. Dr. Donald S. Heaney, Southern Ute Extension Director and Agricultural Agent, "Selenium: Agricultural Problems on the Southern Ute Indian Reservation," February 1983; and "Selenium: The Poisoning of America," *Sacramento Bee,* December 4, 1988.
4. P. L. Brown and Marvin Miller, "Soils and Crop Management Practices to Control Saline Seeps in the U.S. Northern Plains," in *Proceedings of the Subcommission on Salt-Affected Soils* (Edmonton, Alberta: International Soil Science Society, 1978), pp. 7–9 and 15.
5. H. G. Byers, "Selenium Occurrence in Certain Soils," USDA Technical Bulletins 482 (1935):47; 530 (1936):78; and 601 (1938):74.
6. "Selenium: The Poisoning of America," *Sacramento Bee,* December 3, 1988.
7. Dr. Anna Fan and Dr. Kenneth Kizer, "Selenium: Nutritional, Toxicological, and Clinical Aspects," *Western Journal of Medicine* 153 (1990):160–167.

General References
California Department of Health Services. "Health Advisory on Selenium in Ducks and Fish in Western Merced and Stanislaus Counties and in Salton Sea Fish." DOHS Press Releases. July 20, 1985, and May 6, 1986.
Fan, Anna, and others. "Selenium and Human Health in California." *Journal of Toxicology and Environmental Health* 153 (1987):160–167.
Menkes, Marlin S., and others. "Serum Beta Carotene, Vitamins A and E, Selenium, and the Risk of Lung Cancer." *New England Journal of Medicine* 315(20) (1986):1250–1254.
Miller, Marvin R., P. L. Brown, and others. "Saline Seep Development and Control in North American Great Plains." In *Agricultural Water Management,* vol. 4. Amsterdam: Elsevier, 1981.
Robinson, Marion F., and others. "Blood Selenium and Glutathion Peroxidase

Activity in Normal Subjects and in Surgical Patients With and Without Cancer in New Zealand." *American Journal of Clinical Nutrition* 32 (July 1979):1477–1485.

Interviews

Marvin R. Miller, chief of Hydrology Division, Montana Bureau of Mines and Geology; Samuel L. Bennett, rancher, Sturgis, South Dakota; Dr. Arthur W. Kilness; Stanley Rye, rancher, Watauga, South Dakota; Gerald Jepson, farmer, Meckling, South Dakota; Alfred Haberman, Jr., stockyard manager, Yankton, South Dakota, and farmer, Fordyce, Nebraska; Walt and Yvonne Ehlers, ranchers, Presho, South Dakota; Irene Harmon, rancher, Ignacio, Colorado; Charles Muncy, rancher, Levitar, New Mexico; Ross and Pat Ligon, ranchers, Magdalena, New Mexico; Paul L. Brown, soil scientist, USDA, Billings, Montana; John K. Shanahan, rancher, Newark Valley, Nevada; William Robinson, geologist, Bureau of Land Management, Ely, Nevada; Dr. Burt Campbell, Burns, Oregon; Dr. Paul Burgner, Portland, Oregon; Dr. Bruce Furst, professor emeritus, University of San Francisco; Dr. Kenneth W. Kizer, director, California Department of Health Services.

CHAPTER 9

Notes

1. "A Management Plan for Agricultural Subsurface Drainage and Related Problems on the Westside San Joaquin Valley," San Joaquin Valley Drainage Program, Final Report, September 1990, p. 30.
2. T. S. Presser, Walter C. Swain, Ronald Tidball, and R. C. Severson, "Geologic Sources, Mobilization, and Transport of Selenium from California Coast Ranges to the Western San Joaquin Valley," USGS Water Resources Investigation Report 90-4070, 1990.
3. Ibid.

General References

Arkley, Rodney J. "Selenium in the Soils of the San Joaquin Valley." Paper presented at the Symposium on Contaminants in Agricultural Drainwater, University of California, Davis, December 3, 1983.

Blum, Deborah. "No Safe Harbor." *Defenders of Wildlife,* November–December 1984.

Fio, John L., Roger Fuji, and S. J. Deverel. "Evaluation of Selenium Mobility in Soil of Western San Joaquin Valley." USGS Open File Report 90-135, 1990.

Fuji, Roger, S. J. Deverel, and D. B. Hatfield. "Distribution of Selenium in Soils of Agricultural Fields of Western San Joaquin Valley." USGS Open File Report 87-467, 1987.

Hannah, George Jr., and others. "Agricultural Drainage Treatment Technology Review for the San Joaquin Valley Drainage Program." July 31, 1990.

Klasing, Susan A. "Selected Trace Elements in Biota of the San Joaquin Valley: A Screening Level Public Health Evaluation." Report prepared for San Joaquin Valley Drainage Program, Sacramento, California, September 1990.

Presser, T. S., and Harry M. Ohlendorf. "Biogeochemical Cycling of Selenium in the San Joaquin Valley." *Environmental Management* 11(6) (1987):805–821.

Tidball, R. R., R. C. Severson, C. A. Gent, and G. O. Riddle. "Element Association in Soils of the San Joaquin Valley." USGS Open File Report 86-583, 1986.

White, James R., and Paul S. Hoffman. "Selenium Verification Study: A Report to the State Water Resources Control Board by the California Department of Fish and Game." May 1987.

CHAPTER 10

Notes

1. "Kesterson Reservoir Biological Report and Monitoring Plan," Bureau of Reclamation, December 1990.
2. "Reconnaissance Investigation of Water Quality, Bottom Sediment, and Biota Associated with Irrigation Drainage": in the Kendrick Reclamation Project Area, Wyoming, 1986–1987, USGS Water Resources Investigation Report 87-4255; in the Sun River Area, West-Central Montana, 1986–1987, Water Resources Investigation Report 87-4244; in the Middle Green River Basin, Utah, 1986–1987, Water Resources Investigation Report 88-4011; in the Salton Sea Area, California, 1986–1987, Water Resources Investigation Report 89-4102; in the Stillwater Wildlife Management Area, Nevada, 1986–1987, Water Resources Investigation Report 89-4105; in the Lower Rio Grande Valley and Laguna Atascosa NWR, Texas, 1986–1987, Water Resources Investigation Report 87-4277; in the Tulare Lake Basin, San Joaquin Valley, California, 1986–1987, Water Resources Investigation Report 88-4001; in Bowdoin NWR, Milk River Basin, Montana, 1986–1987, Water Resources Investigation Report 87-4243; and in the Lower Colorado River in Arizona, California, and Nevada, 1986–1987, Water Resources Investigation Report 88-4002.

General References

Ohlendorf, Harry M., and Joseph P. Skorupa. "Selenium in Relation to Wildlife and Agricultural Drain Water." Paper presented at Fourth International Symposium on Uses of Selenium and Tellurium, Banff, Alberta, May 5–7, 1989.

Patuxent Wildlife Research Center, USFWS. "Effects of Irrigation Drain Water Contaminants on Wildlife." Summary Report. San Joaquin Valley Drainage Program. July 1990.

Skorupa, Joseph P., and Harry M. Ohlendorf. "Contaminants in Drainage Water and Avian Risk Thresholds." In *The Economy and Management of Water and Drainage in Agriculture.* Norwell, Mass.: Kluwer, 1981.

Interviews

Joseph P. Skorupa; Gary Zahm, manager, USFWS, San Luis NWR complex, California; Dr. Anna Fan (interview and personal communication); Marc Sylvester, USGS water contaminant specialist; Carroll Hammon, deputy director, San Joaquin Valley Drainage Program.

EPILOGUE

Notes

1. Jane Kay, "Oil Refineries Told to Cut Selenium," *San Francisco Examiner,* February 21, 1991, p. A-9.
2. Jane Kay, "Selenium in Bay Threatens Wildlife," *San Francisco Examiner,* February 17, 1991, pp. 1 and A-15.
3. "Survey of Trace Elements in Coot Eggs from National Wildlife Refuges in South Dakota"; "A Report on Trace Elements with Emphasis on Selenium in Coot Eggs from the Lake Andes NWR, South Dakota"; and "Survey of Trace Elements in Fish from Choteau Creek and Lake Andes, South Dakota," in *Contaminant Survey Report,* USFWS, Pierre, South Dakota.
4. "Selenium May Be Impacting Endangered Bird Populations on the Missouri River in South Dakota," in *Contaminant Survey Report,* USFWS, Pierre, South Dakota, 1990, pp. 1–5.

Interviews

Carroll Hammond, deputy director, San Joaquin Valley Drainage Program; Gary Zahm, manager, San Luis NWR Complex, Los Baños, California; Richard Engberg, coordinator, Department of Interior Irrigation Drainage Program; J. David Love; Stephen Williams; Mary Elizabeth Beath.

Acknowledgments

Where to begin? There are so many whose lives, courage, commitment, support, and integrity have made this book possible that an exhaustive listing of names is out of the question.

Eight years of tracking this elusive natural element through mountain and marsh, hallway and library, and, yes, even through Mr. Webster's good book, have given me a rich new perspective of the dedication to public service of so many rank-and-file bureaucrats and civil servants. While some use those terms as derogatory labels, to me they hold a very special meaning.

Let me work backwards, then, in the process of thanks-giving and homage-paying. (There are legions who think that is my normal bent, anyway.) To those at Island Press, who had the vision to see the merits of this story, my deep gratitude, especially Executive Editor Barbara Dean. She patiently walked me through the process and provided the most essential stylistic improvements. To the rest of the talented IP people whose various literary and marketing skills made such a difference, merci beaucoup. Individual recognition and deep professional respect and appreciation must be paid to Don Yoder, the gemologist of copy editors. None but I will know the artful cutting and polishing he did to bring grace, flow, and accuracy to this work and none but he (and maybe Barbara Dean) really know how big a job that was.

Professionally, and personally, few did more to shape and mold my selenium work, in this book and as a journalist, than Terry Hennessy. Whatever transitional obstacles or rocky verbal passages remain, they are in spite of, rather than because of, his editing. Moreover, he is every bit as decent a human being as he is a consummate pro.

Special appreciation is felt for the experts who devoted so many hours to checking the manuscript for technical errors of judgment and fact, though they should, in no way, be held accountable for its literary thrust or tone. The U.S. Geological Survey's research chemist, T. S. Presser, is foremost among those valued readers, but wildlife toxicologist Dr. Joseph Skorupa, and retired environmental assessment specialist Felix Smith, both of the U.S. Fish and Wildlife Service, and Harry Ohlendorf, just recently resigned from that agency, made invaluable contributions. University of Wyoming soil microbiologist Stephen E. Williams made many helpful suggestions. J. David Love, the Grand Old Man of Rocky Mountain Geology and geologist emeritus with the U.S. Geological Survey, provided rich perspective and technical understanding. Some of David's best suggestions, on structural organization, came too late in the process to be put to use but, David, we'll do it better in the sequel (just kidding, just kidding).

Perhaps none of this story would have come out if Marc Sylvester hadn't been so honest about the existence of the original work plan and so helpful, later, as the point man for the USGS role in the Interior Department's sweeping effort to look for other Kestersons elsewhere in the West. Bill Davoren and Alice Howard of the Bay Institute of San Francisco were more helpful than they know. Fish and Wildlife Service selenium expert Dr. Dennis Lemly was unstinting in his patient explanations.

The unrelentingly scrupulous science of Dr. Harry Ohlendorf was a fountain of revelation and an inspiration to keep digging for the truth. But more than any other person, Felix Smith was responsible for bringing the selenium story out of the closet into which some of his superiors at the Fish and Wildlife Service, and theirs in turn at the Department of Interior, initially tried to keep it locked up. While it was perhaps the finest moment in a distinguished career as dedicated public servant, Smith will be remembered more for his unswerving commitment to the true mission of his agency: the protection of this nation's wildlife heritage. He put his career on the line for the critters when it counted most.

To the pioneer selenium researcher of his time, Orville A. Beath, richly deserved, if posthumous, acknowledgment and appreciation. His achievement lives on, inspiring a whole new generation of researchers, thanks, largely, to the faith and works of a loyal, loving daughter, Mary Elizabeth Beath.

Finally, ultimately, to my two most dedicated teachers, Ivan and Doc. Ivan Barnes, superscientist, charismatic geochemist, and lover of good times, knew who paid his way and served them—the public—grandly and loyally. Fearless and insightful in his science, intensely straight-spoken in his opinions, he is sorely missed. And the crusty country-doctor-cum-surgeon, Dr. Arthur W. Kilness, riveted attention, and often controversy, wherever he went. Doc is gone now, too, one of the last of his profession devoted to the research and treatment of the toxic effects of selenium on people. It was his desire that his work would beget successors—that, finally, the real and potential human health costs of excessive selenium would be addressed by his profession. We shall see.

To Doc, who said he was only afraid of the dark, the secrets kept locked up, I dedicate this effort . . . to turn the light of public scrutiny on the dark corners of selenium. Rest in peace, Doc. You earned it.

About the Author

Tom Harris has been a full-time environment writer since 1969, first with the *San Jose Mercury* until 1984 and since with the *Sacramento Bee*. He was awarded an Energy Fellowship at Stanford University (1972–1973), has taught Environmental Journalism at San Jose State University, and has lectured on media and the environment at Stanford, at the University of California, Berkeley, at the University of California, Davis, at the University of Texas, and at the American Press Institute in Reston, Virginia.

Among his professional honors are the George Polk Award (Long Island University) in 1984 for a series on hazardous waste problems at military installations—"Uncle Sam's Hidden Poisons"—that also was a Pulitzer Prize finalist the same year; the Garretson Award (San Francisco Press Club) for "Selenium: Conspiracy of Silence" in 1986; the St. Francis Award (Catholic Press Association) in 1987 for a series on growth-driven environmental problems in California, "Trouble in Paradise"; the Clarion Award (Women in Communication) in 1989 for a series on the growing presence and threat of selenium in human foods, "Selenium: The Poisoning of America"; and numerous other state and regional awards.

He has written one previous book, *Down the Wild Rivers,* a guide to the streams of California (1972, revised edition 1973).

He and his wife Glenda live in the Sacramento, California, suburb of Rancho Cordova. They have three children.

Index

Also Available from Island Press

Ancient Forests of the Pacific Northwest
By Elliott A. Norse

Balancing on the Brink of Extinction: The Endangered Species Act and Lessons for the Future
Edited by Kathryn A. Kohm

Better Trout Habitat: A Guide to Stream Restoration and Management
By Christopher J. Hunter

Beyond 40 Percent: Record-Setting Recycling and Composting Programs
The Institute for Local Self-Reliance

The Challenge of Global Warming
Edited by Dean Edwin Abrahamson

Coastal Alert: Ecosystems, Energy, and Offshore Oil Drilling
By Dwight Holing

The Complete Guide to Environmental Careers
The CEIP Fund

Economics of Protected Areas
By John A. Dixon and Paul B. Sherman

Environmental Agenda for the Future
Edited by Robert Cahn

Environmental Disputes: Community Involvement in Conflict Resolution
By James E. Crowfoot and Julia M. Wondolleck

Forests and Forestry in China: Changing Patterns of Resource Development
By S. D. Richardson

The Global Citizen
By Donella Meadows

Hazardous Waste from Small Quantity Generators
By Seymour I. Schwartz and Wendy B. Pratt

Holistic Resource Management Workbook
By Allan Savory

In Praise of Nature
Edited and with essays by Stephanie Mills

Island Press Board of Directors